THE OUTSIDE STORY

THE OUTSIDE STORY

HOW DEMOCRATS AND REPUBLICANS RE-ELECTED REAGAN

Richard Brookhiser

DOUBLEDAY & COMPANY, INC.
GARDEN CITY, NEW YORK   1986

For my parents

Portions of this book have been adapted from articles which originally appeared in *National Review, The American Spectator,* and *Harper's.*

Library of Congress Cataloging-in-Publication Data
Brookhiser, Richard.
The outside story.
1. Presidents—United States—Election—1984.
2. United States—Politics and government—1981–
I. Title.
E879.B76   1986   324.973′0927   85–27552
ISBN: 0-385-19679-2

Contents

ACKNOWLEDGMENTS

I must thank William F. Buckley, Jr., for so much; Sam Vaughan, for his editing of this manuscript; Priscilla Buckley, for eight years of editing manuscripts; Henry Fasciani, Dorothy McCartney, Brian McDonald, and John Virtes for help with the stray fact; and Jeanne Safer, for everything else.

Foreword

Here we are little more than a year removed from the 1984 presidential elections; and, of the eight Democrats who exhausted themselves, dropping out or limping on through various laps in a race whose final reward would be its winner's crown as his party's appointed loser, the only one whose photographed presence can still manifest itself on the front page of the New York *Times* is the Reverend Jesse Jackson.

The others seem already entombed in time past, however recent; they are only the freshest of a host of victims of the law of politics that condemns all but a singular few of our candidates for President of the United States to those beginnings drawn from a box and ends dropped into the wastebasket that are the biographies of disposable tissues.

Will any of them return from the dustheap where he now lies crumpled? Perhaps Gary Hart will, although, as this author shrewdly observes, "nothing ages faster than yesterday's sensation"; especially, we might add in this particular case, when the sensation never advanced far enough beyond the tentative.

Comes now Richard Brookhiser with his log of his journeyings with these misfortuned voyagers on their way to each one's shipwreck; and his readers will be surprised at how much life can still be found on what has already become an archaeological excursion.

Brookhiser offers his narrative as "the outside story," and that it indisputably is, because no observer could be more the outsider than he. By the very nature of our politics, it is inevitable that aspirant losers are more active and accessible to the curious than incumbent winners. Brookhiser was on campaign as outrider for William F. Buckley's *National Review*, which venerates President Reagan's spirit while not invariably swearing by his letter; he was forced by circumstance to spend most of his time with Democrats, and, if his good nature protected his eye from hostility, we cannot demand that it be free of alienation.

Any such isolation has its uses, of course; and Brookhiser profited from their advantages. Philosophical distance separated him from the enticements and pitfalls offered by too many chances to cultivate sources of intimate misinformation; there was nothing for him to do except to look. And, granting his preconceptions, he has done that difficult chore keenly. The danger of ideological casts of mind—and Brookhiser's is unashamedly such—is that they are apt to tie us to what Henry James called the treadmill of abstraction.

Brookhiser cannot be asked to get all the way off that treadmill, but there are heartening moments when he departs far enough from it to suggest the only sort of mind we have any right to require, which is not the one that can be changed in its foundations, but the one that can be touched even against its will.

And Brookhiser reveals that cast of mind. Detached and even a shade derisive as his treatment of Walter Mondale the public figure remains, he is sensitive enough to recognize the gallantry of the private man carrying on after every hope has flown. He can deplore Jesse Jackson and at the same time keep his heart open to receive those moments when Jackson, alone among the candidates around him, sounded as though he were speaking not about but from the poor.

Such reactions and the thoughts they start are lessons that only the protracted experience of observation can teach the eye and ear. I must confess to wishing that, for all his merits, Mr. Brookhiser were more vulnerable to assaults on his notions of good sense than he has yet become. But then, when I was younger, I was a Democrat more bigoted than he is a Republican and certainly more than age now permits me to be. As a consequence, I was unable to conceive how much better the views expressed from the platform might work for the majority of others than they did for me; and it was a long time before I learned how reasonable, not to say delightful, it was to be irrationally caught in the beat of what truly did work and just to exult in a resistless ride on the tide of its nonsense. Brookhiser still holds himself withdrawn from the full indulgence of a sport that happens to be a vocational necessity for anyone who hopes to assess electoral trends with an approximation of accuracy; and those asides arguing and occasionally even carpings with this or that orator that now and then interrupt his narrative are reminders, stirred not without amusement, of my own younger self.

But no matter; experience has started him on a way that promises to bring him to even larger wisdoms; and meanwhile he has remorselessly but not unjustly called back to our attention personages we had too soon forgotten; and he has evoked them in a fashion at once lively and, given his by no means unuseful alienation, unexpectedly generous.

Murray Kempton

THE OUTSIDE STORY

1
The Outside Story

In the last days of the 1960 presidential election, a party of New York's finest, led by a deputy chief inspector of police —there were no Secret Service phalanxes then—boarded the upper deck of the old Brooklyn–Staten Island ferry, swept the lone passenger, a teenage kid, into a corner, and made way for the entourage of John Kennedy. The race was tight, the state was crucial, Kennedy looked exhausted. During the ferry ride, the Senator's aides readied him for the debarkation. One helped him into a fresh shirt. One passed a windup shaver over his face (where was *he* when Richard Nixon needed him?). One read through a sheaf of greetings, notes, messages, to which Kennedy responded with number-coded answers (as, give him a three, he gets a seven). A fourth aide, the most important, squatted in front of the candidate and flashed a series of photos, accompanied by biographical patter: *This is Mike O'Brien* [say], *Seventeenth Precinct, his son plays basketball for Villanova. Joe Antonelli, Twenty-third AD, his wife works with the deaf* . . . and so on, through the whole Brooklyn Democratic machine. By the time the boat touched Bay Ridge, the candidate was refreshed, rejuvenated, and rewired. When the gangway lowered, Kennedy didn't wait for it to fall completely into place, but gave a little hop ashore (so youthful was he). There to greet him were all the pols he had just been briefed on; back it all came. *Mike, hear good things about your son. Joe, it's great what your wife is doing . . .* They loved it; there were even damp eyes . . .

There was a lot in that glimpse: a shot of the Kennedy apparatus in action; a sense of the grinding routine we exact from all candidates; a sense of the even more grinding zeal with which they perform it. Only a glimpse, but a thousand make a picture. The only trouble with this small story is that no one ever reported it. The inside view never made it outside. Kennedy's ferry ride did not appear in *The Making of the President: 1960*, still less in the court histories. It doesn't even appear in the revisionist trashings. It reaches print here, twenty-six years later, only because the kid on the upper deck became a colleague of my wife's.

That is the trouble with inside stories generally. There is no omnipresence, and hence, no omniscience. You see one vignette, you miss fifty. The candidates themselves are not privy to everything worth seeing; how can observers be?

What is true of inside events is still more true of less concrete actions. Who is rising, and who supports him? Who is out, and who gave him the shove? What was the motive? What was the intention (not always the same thing)? Where will the next backstage maneuver come from? The answers to these questions can only come from the principals, which in the short run means they do not come at all. Either the parties don't talk, or they talk, self-servingly, all over the front page of tomorrow's Washington *Post*. When there is no consensus of testimony, there is only judgment. When there is consensus, there may be deception, and self-deception. Historians, with time and patience, can sift the conflicting accounts, and politicians must judge them by the seat of their pants every day. But the elusiveness of inside stories is an insurmountable problem of instant histories.

There is another way of looking at American presidential elections. That is to focus on what the candidates and their supporters say and do in public; to leave the green room and the wings and go out front, and attend, with respect, to the performance. In the course of the 1984 campaign, eight men sought the nomination of one of the major parties. The winner and his running mate then took on the incumbents, the nominees of the other major party. In the last year of the campaign alone, they spoke millions of words and made thousands of appearances. Surely they meant something by it? There were plenty of inside stories, too many; what of the outside story?

In looking at the outside story, several things emerge. Elections take on a deep calm. They are no longer brawls, marathons, endless aimless scrums. All the chaos and bawdry remains, enough for the most avid connoisseur, but it falls into simpler forms. Politicians, it turns out, are actually saying something; their antics have a purpose.

The voters, it seems, pay attention. There are good structural reasons why this should be so. Politics must be public wherever there are voters. In hermetic, totalitarian societies, where politics consists entirely of secret backstabbing, all stories are inside stories. The only source in Sofia is Deep Throat. In a democracy, however, where power is achieved only through presenting oneself to the public, politicians are obliged to be demonstrative. Since most politicians who aspire to be President have presented themselves repeatedly over a substantial career, they are also obliged to be moderately sincere. They cannot lie promiscuously, and mere razzle-dazzle wears thin. So it is that an outside story exists, and that voters do well to take note of it.

That is theory; the outside story can also be tested in practice. Jimmy Carter's 1976 rise from nowhere was the epitome of modern political technique. Four years later, George Bush (evidently assuming that technique had been decisive) alone of the Republican hopefuls studied the Carter game plan. He, like Carter, was rewarded with an Iowa Surprise. Suddenly Big Mo—the phrase Bush used to describe his momentum—was inevitable, unstoppable; Ronald Reagan was washed up, burned out. But only a month later, Bush perished like a bug on a windshield. Inside-story specialists came up with appropriate explanations for his collapse—Bush talked too much about his sudden prospects (but wasn't the image of snowballing success part of the plan?); Reagan's staff got its act together (why not before?); Reagan began showing spunk, particularly at a pre-primary debate in Nashua, New Hampshire, where Bush appeared stiff and indecisive. Yet would spunk have done Reagan any good if he hadn't also had forceful themes? Would dithering have done Bush any harm if he had had any? Isn't it possible that Reagan's 1980 campaign had a clear message while Bush's was murky?

The 1940 presidential race, though ancient history, figures in a clutch of recent biographies of some of the principals in a way that makes it even more suggestive. The Republican contest that year was honeycombed with inside stories. The campaign of Wendell Willkie had more cheerleaders than the Dallas Cowboys. *Time, Life, Look, The Saturday Evening Post* all puffed him shamelessly. The editor of *Fortune* became his campaign manager; the book review editor of the New York *Herald Tribune* ghosted his speeches (she was also his mistress—an early instance of user-friendliness). Willkie also profited from old-fashioned dirty tricks. The chairman of the Republican convention's committee on arrangements, a Willkie man, aborted a rival's speech by slipping in a dead mike. He also packed the galleries of the hall, so that the hapless delegates were battered by unceasing roars of "We Want Willkie"—the Big Mo of 1940. For the race against Franklin Roosevelt, Willkie was armed with copies of crackpot letters that FDR's running mate, Henry Wallace, had sent to a Russian theosophist.

> I have been thinking of you holding the casket [wrote the man who wanted to be a heartbeat away]—the sacred, most precious casket. And I have thought of the new country going forth, to meet the seven stars under the sign of the three stars. And I have thought of the admonition, "Await the stones."

The Wallace letters were never used, perhaps because Roosevelt had copies of letters from Willkie to his ghost writer.

But there was also an issue. Germany invaded Norway and Denmark in April and the Low Countries in May. France collapsed the week before the Republican convention opened. Of all the GOP hopefuls, Willkie was the only one forthrightly committed to helping embattled England. His rise in the esteem of Republicans tracked Europe's fall. The election offered a less clear-cut choice, partly because Willkie and Roosevelt both were internationalists at heart, partly because they both lied and waffled as the fall wore on. But the issue remained, and the electorate remained concerned. What did the majority finally place its trust in—Roosevelt's ability to steer through a period of international havoc, or his Teflon quality? Were the voters more affected by Hitler, or by the wheelings and dealings of *Fortune?*

This doesn't mean that politicians, or voters, choose wisely—that they always hit on the right remedies for the country's problems, or even the right ones for the problems they see. I do believe, though, that most presidential candidates are trying to offer something, and that most voters are trying to judge.

A few things the outside story is not. One approach to elections, which is superficially similar to it, in that it also seems to take into account public appeals, is the analysis of imagery. The cut of hair, the tone of voice, the subliminal cues—all these are indeed fashioned for public consumption. The most successful shapers of imagery—Ronald Reagan comes to mind—do not even exert their power consciously: the charm flows out of them, without thought or effort. Yet "How the Image Makers Do It" is in fact another inside story, reducing the relation between the candidates and the electorate to another set of inexplicit maneuvers and manipulations. The disposition to keep one's eye on imagery may derive from a larger social theory, that advertising controls markets. Fifties economists, brooding on tail fins, concluded that Detroit, allied with Madison Avenue, could get anything it wanted. Three decades later, Washington was bailing out Chrysler. The look-so-fine school of political science has had its own Chryslers, as mediagenic candidates falter and uncomely ones (Nixon, even shaven) endure.

The outside story is also more than a simple rundown of policy proposals. The kinds of promises that find their way into party platforms and political speeches are worth reading, and when they are broken, as they often are, the fact should be pondered for its political significance. But candidates are also judged on more than their promises—for a promise is always more than itself. Who makes a promise and how it is made materially affect the pledge. Candidates define their promises by the records they have fashioned, by the supporters they tolerate, by the rhetoric they use. Of the three, rhetoric can mean the most. What a politician would like to do, even if only in an ideal world, is important because it gives a clue to what he is likely to attempt in this world. "A man's arguments," wrote G. K. Chesterton, "show what he is up to."

The outside story, finally, never explains just one contest. We are always "up to" more than one election at a time. The only thing politicians care about as much as the next election is the one after that. They plan for it in all the "inside" ways—buying friends, buying off competitors, blocking enemies. But their most important preparation is their performance. Rhetoric opens all the little trails and wagon tracks which become the interstates of the future. A politician shows, by what he says and does, where he thinks the electorate is headed (and how only he can lead them there). The voters show, by their response, where at least they might be willing to go.

What follows is an account of the 1984 presidential election, giving pride of place to the outside story. It concentrates on appearances, pronouncements, rituals—on things that could have been seen or heard or read by any American with a few hours to while away. (As a political reporter, I had more hours at my disposal; and as a political addict, I had perhaps more disposition to use them. So although my picture is not grossly different from the average citizen's, it is more comprehensive.) The method is not followed dogmatically—memories, interviews, summary narrative fill in where required. There is even the occasional inside tidbit, like a pinup in a gym locker. But the outside story is the core —for it gives the best explanation of why Ronald Reagan was re-elected, and why the Democrats lost (two inseparable, but distinct questions), and it gives the best preview now available to us of what will face us in 1988.

You can learn a lot, Yogi Berra said, by observing. What did America observe as the 1984 campaign began in earnest?

2
Reagan in the White House: Background

When Ronald Reagan took office in January 1981, his administration bumped into a number of limitations, as do all new administrations. One of them was "The President." The President, of course, was Ronald Reagan. But in the parlance of his own administration, an odd thing happened; Reagan vanished with his taking of the oath and became, to those who worked for him—from the anterooms of the Oval Office out to the farthest reaches of commissions and semi-private corporations—simply "The President." Not "President Reagan," not "Mr. Reagan," not "Reagan," not "Ron." They said it, not just on the job, which might be understandable, but among themselves, after hours and over drinks. Ronald Reagan became, like YHWH, possessor of an Unnamable Name.

This ubiquitous locution, symbol of all that is stupid and stupefying about Washington, marked one sort of limit on the Reagan administration's record. "Power does not corrupt," a White House speechwriter told me. "First it deranges, then it corrupts." The best of the Reaganites crumbled only at the edges (even the speechwriter found himself saying, after hours and over drinks, "The President"). The worst schemed, backbit, seduced their secretaries, promoted their secretaries, went to the right parties, enjoyed the right parties, sought the right parties, were featured in the Washington *Post* "Style" section, grew in office. "The GSA regulations" on office perks, wrote a onetime Reagan staffer, "are quite detailed: Big shots get up to 750-square-foot offices, 50-square-foot kitchens with 300-square-foot dining areas, and 45-square-foot bathrooms. They are also entitled to wooden wastebaskets (rectangular metal ones go to mid-level people; round metal ones go to peons), 'executive' wood furniture (middies get 'unitized' wood, while the underlings get metal), water carafes, dictionary stands, rugs. . . . After all, the first decision a [NB: *the]* President has to make is not Do we go to war? but Who gets the corner office down from the Oval Office?"[1] Isn't this the behavior of every large organization, more or less? Yes, but in Washington, unlike Los Angeles, or Houston, or New York, or other places, there is only one, vast, all-permeating organization. Washington is the last and largest company town, except that instead of sweated Slovak miners, it is filled with junior and senior executives. All they like sheep have gone astray.

So the Reagan administration did not repeal human nature. It was also unable to undo previous actions, whose consequences it suffered from. It could not, for instance, change the map of Central Europe. The Solidarity labor union began, in the fall of 1980, as a strike in a Baltic shipyard and became a renaissance. For the first time, a workers' paradise heeded workers; a state that had promised to wither away actually drooped a little. The Poles told desperate, gallant jokes: A Polish soldier is simultaneously attacked by a Russian and an East German; which one does he shoot first? The German; business before pleasure. (Polack jokes in this country meanwhile—did anyone notice?—virtually disappeared.) Solidarity was thrilling, astonishing, and doomed; at least, doomed to get no help from the United States. There is nothing in the order of nature that gives

Moscow fiat over Warsaw. But there is also no way in nature to restore the conditions of 1944 or 1956, when something practical might have been done about it. So the most anti-Communist President of the postwar period was reduced, after the crunch, to expressions of sympathy that, under the circumstances, sounded little different from petulance.

But between the inescapable and the untouchable lies the margin of will called politics. Many of the political "actions" of the Reagan administration were acts of omission; some good from his point of view, some bad. There was no Law of the Sea treaty. The White House was not used as a bully pulpit to plug the flagging ERA. No blue-ribbon panel convened to study the grievances of striking air-traffic controllers; they were simply fired. Reagan was not wakened when American fighters shot down Libyan planes that had jumped them in the Gulf of Sidra. "When a horse flicks off a fly," noted columnist George Will, "it's a crisis for the fly, not the horse."

The Reagan administration made no concerted push on the so-called social issues—busing, racial quotas, abortion. Reagan published an article in the *Human Life Review*, a right-to-life journal, attacking the abortion laws. But two efforts to remove the issue from the reach of the courts— one a proposed constitutional amendment, one a simple bill —killed each other off in the Senate. There was no attempt to pursue the environmentalist agenda. James Watt, Reagan's Secretary of the Interior, was a conservative true believer with a knack for the unbuttoned statement. Some of these were shrewd—"Ansel Adams never took a picture with a human being in it"—others silly, as when Watt ruled that the Beach Boys were too sinister to play at a Fourth of July concert (the Beach Boys are about as all-American as pink Thunderbirds). A crack finally did him in; Watt remarked of a commission on coal production which he had appointed that it had "everything . . . a black, a woman, two Jews, and a cripple." The joke, strictly speaking, was about minority quotas, not minorities. But etiquette had been affronted, and Reagan bowed to it (though not to environmentalism).

All these were negative actions, things the administration refused or failed to do. But after four years as "The President," Ronald Reagan could look back on three large positive achievements. One was an honorable extension of old policies; one a reorientation of American politics; one an application of the epitaph of George Washington Plunkitt— "He seen his opportunities and he took 'em."

The decision to deploy American intermediate-range missiles in Europe was not Ronald Reagan's. It had been requested by Helmut Schmidt and made by Jimmy Carter.

The cause of Schmidt's and Carter's concern was the new Soviet intermediate-range missile, the SS-20, and their fear was simple: Would America continue to threaten overwhelming retaliation for a swift and strictly local assault? If Hamburg went—or might go—would Americans still be willing to pitch in Chicago? And if the Euros feared the Yanks would waver, what deals would they be tempted to cut on the side? Installing the Pershings and the cruises, so the thinking went, would give America a more flexible and credible response, and everyone that much less reason to pull apart.

The Soviets accordingly put on a full-court press against the missiles. They cheered on the American freeze movement, and more than cheered on the more bellicose European anti-nukes. Reagan was widely shushed for suggesting as much (and for citing *Reader's Digest* as his source). But the Soviets engaged in unquiet diplomacy as well. On the eve of the 1982 West German elections, Andrei Gromyko traveled to Bonn and scolded the parliament for its contumacity. Schmidt's successor as leader of the now-soft Social Democrats was invited to Moscow for extended dalliance. But Reagan and the German electorate held firm, and NATO survived.

For another season. The tactical success was encompassed in a larger strategic stagnation. The nations of the

NATO alliance are straining apart, or so their actions would seem to indicate. Everyone has designed his own pattern of détente, and none of them match; the day Solidarity was crushed found Helmut Schmidt hobnobbing with East Germans, a pastime he refused to curtail even to express condolences. There is an obvious way out of the diplomatic impasse: for America to leave NATO altogether and for the West to stop feigning a unity it does not feel. True unity of purpose, it is argued, would then emerge. It is an idea so seductive there must be something wrong with it. It is hard to imagine the NATO countries all letting go without some of them sliding into the Finland position. Forty-year-old structures should probably be junked only after some thought.

The problem of NATO was enfolded in the larger problem of Soviet policy. Ronald Reagan was widely accused of lacking one, an accusation that may have been both accurate and irrelevant—for what kind of a Soviet policy, in the sense of a definite goal to be reached by achievable steps, can there be? Richard Nixon's *Real Peace*, published the year after Reagan's election, made a strong argument that hardheaded détente—carrots plus big sticks—was the best way of managing Soviet aggressions: a thesis that would probably win the assent of most policy gamesters. The consensus breaks down where the policy does, in political implementation. Americans believe in the brotherhood of man or in the war of the worlds, not in balance of power. The Machiavellians themselves, when in office or seeking it, lurch from one mood to the other (as Mr. Nixon, who toasted the Long March twelve years after expressing his willingness to die for Quemoy and Matsu, could attest).

Reagan made one new contribution to the situation. In March 1983, he proposed that the United States make a major investigation of defensive anti-nuclear weapons. There had been advocates of various anti-missile programs, most of which involved satellites—whence the nickname Star Wars—but the military establishment had pooh-poohed them, understandably. The idea was revolutionary;

it meant abandoning an entire strategic doctrine—that the best way to keep the peace is to balance mutual threats of annihilation. Also, as a consequence, it meant abandoning the ABM treaty—a lesser problem, since the Soviets had been violating it for years. From listening to administration spokesmen, it was not clear whether Space Defense or Star Wars was regarded as a hope, a plan, or a bargaining feint (give up A or we'll build B). There remained work here, not only for the next President but for the next generation of thinkers and officeholders. Meanwhile, giving the NATO engine another tune-up had been accomplishment enough.

The Reagan term ended in a clamor for new ideas. Politicians touted them, questioned them, demanded them; mostly they produced them, like fifteen-year-olds writing love poems. How many were new, and how many of these were actually good, was another question. During the term itself and the six or so years beforehand, there had been one truly new idea. Its godfather had been Congressman Jack Kemp.

I first heard of Kemp-Roth in 1978, from a Kemp disciple who was then working on the New Jersey Senate campaign of Jeffrey Bell. He drew the Laffer Curve (on a napkin, no less) and gave me to understand that this was nothing other than the salvation of America—as well as Jack Kemp's ticket to the White House. "Phil Crane's notion of a conservative revolution," he explained loftily of Kemp's curveless competition, "is to elect as many of his siblings as possible to Congress; Reagan's is to co-opt liberal Republicans by picking them as running mates."

Reagan's notions, it turned out, also included recognizing a fresh idea when he saw one; and he clasped Kemp-Roth like news from Sinai. As with all simple economic notions, the supply-side idea embodied in the Kemp-Roth bill sought to appeal beyond economics to common sense. If you tax a thing, you will have less of it. Tax effort, tax production, tax imagination, they wither. High tax rates hurt their supposed beneficiary, the government, as well as their victims. Taxes are the price of government; when tax rates rise, people will buy less of it, putting their money instead into shelters, collectibles, underground transactions—anything to evade the IRS. (Supply-siders liked to cite the price of gold under Carter, which hit $800 an ounce.) The Laffer Curve was a hypothetical line connecting two extreme points: no taxation and zero revenue; and 100 percent taxation, which (after the first shock of confiscation) would also yield zero revenue. Supply-siders bickered among themselves about a dozen things: fine points of doctrine; degrees of fidelity; order of precedence (Arthur Laffer, a USC economist, first sketched the curve on a cocktail napkin over drinks with a skeptical White House aide in 1974; but who first glimpsed its Form?). On one thing they agreed: America in the late seventies was on the wrong slope of the curve.

In the event, the curve had kinks in it. The Kemp-Roth bill had called for three successive income-tax-rate cuts of 10 percent; it was hoped that the first cut would be made retroactive to January 1981. What Congress finally delivered was an initial cut of 5 percent, effective six months later. In 1982, at the peak of a recession, the Republican Senate lost heart and pushed for a $95 billion tax increase. This, plus Social Security payroll tax increases, which had been mandated in 1977, virtually wiped out the relief the income-tax-rate cuts had afforded. There was one clear tax cut, unaffected by subsequent retreats: the top income tax rate was dropped, from 70 to 50 percent—a long way from a flat rate, but at least down off the Andes of progressivity. Here there was also a clear supply-side effect, as the upper income brackets paid a larger share of the total tax take than they had previously. Thus both Democrats and supply-siders were right: Reagan did help the rich, and the rich in gratitude paid more. For the middle classes, however, as far as taxes were concerned, the Reagan term was a period of treading water.

The major effect of Kemp-Roth was political. The terms of the debate were entirely transformed. The Republicans changed themselves from a party of gimlet-eyed accoun-

tants to boosters and go-getters. As the recession gave way
to a roaring recovery, the rhetoric seemed amply justified.
The only thing the Democrats meanwhile could think to
interpose before the torrent was—the balanced budget.
There, suddenly, was *The New Republic*'s TRB (the old
TRB, the one who'd been around since Teapot Dome), explaining to his astonished readers that deficits require the
federal government to *print money,* or borrow; if government *borrows,* then interest rates *go up.* . . . "America is
living on a credit card. Has the crunch come?" It read like a
press release from Scrooge and Marley. Politicians who had
never counted a dime in their lives took up the same prudent psalm.

The deficit indeed grew to alarming proportions, rising
throughout the term (the 1982 tax hike, designed to shrink
it, did no such thing). Rhetorically, the situation favored the
Republicans, who were at least in the position of having
betrayed a principle they had once held, and presumably
still understood, whereas Democrats were forced to use a
language they had never known, and which, in their
mouths, sounded necessarily false. Neither party addressed
the cause of the problem, which was spending. Middle-class
entitlements—Social Security and Medicare—were repeatedly declared sacrosanct (with some justice—if the middle
class's tax burden is not in fact lowered, why should they be
asked to give up their goodies?). A commission of businessmen, appointed by Reagan and chaired by Peter Grace,
came up with a list of $424 billion of miscellaneous fat in the
federal budget, from overpriced military gadgets to Medicare payments sent to dead people—too late in the term for
action to be taken.

On many fronts, the situation was fluid. Kemp and Senator Robert Kasten of Wisconsin put their names to a Republican flat-tax proposal; Senator Bill Bradley (the victor, in
1978, over Jeffrey Bell; maybe he'd learned something) and
Representative Richard Gephardt of Missouri fathered a
flat-tax bill on the Democratic side. Out in the state capitals,
the balanced-budget amendment—the reform proposal

most detested in the company town—crept closer to the number necessary to require Congress to summon a constitutional convention. Practically, the revolution in taxing and spending was still unconsummated.

I saw Maurice Bishop in the summer of 1983, a few months before he died. He came to New York to address the Council on Foreign Relations. He wore his revolutionary's gear, a kind of stylized safari outfit, and brought with him a crew of bodyguards, similarly dressed. Before lunch, at the head of the Harold Pratt House's swooping staircase, he mingled with the dark-suited businessmen and foreign-policy types, who sipped tea out of the council's pink-and-green china cups, while Bishop's roughs—kids, no older than seventeen, by the look of them—eyed everyone nervously. "Don't reach for your pen too fast," I warned a companion, "or we'll all go down in a hail of lead."

The council's rules require that all meetings be off the record. Bishop didn't say anything worth quoting. He frankly acknowledged that he was the leader of a revolution, which necessarily involved cutting some human-rights corners. He had come to America to try to meet with the administration, and he must have felt events closing in on him.

The night of the American landings, an enterprising New York television station thought to get the reactions of the local Grenadian community. There was a group of the usual suspects, assembling a manifesto. But all the Grenadians the cameramen found in stores or on the streets were well pleased. The most vehement was a bearded, middle-aged cabdriver. "It's *about time*," he said, in that lilt that makes English a calypso. "I'm sick and tired of all these *Com*mies running a*round* the *world.*"

In the end, Bishop went down in a hail of Grenadian lead, from the guns of fellow corner cutters. (Did the bodyguards, I wondered, die with him? or shoot him?) Reagan justified the intervention on the grounds that the ensuing upheaval would have imperiled the safety of the American medical students on the island; that, certainly, was their opinion when they arrived in the States and gratefully kissed the tarmac. At the same time, the administration had not been caught dreaming. Grenada had been a watched trouble spot for years; in October 1981, the armed forces held a Caribbean exercise involving the imaginary islands "Amber and the Amberdines" (anyone who imagined Grenada and the Grenadines would not have been far off).

It was simple attentiveness. In the years since the 1979 revolution, Grenada had been thoroughly satellitized. Bishop and his friends had swallowed Leninism bottle, cap, and label. They were raising up the young to be soldiers and building up the island into an arms dump. Grenada sits astride major tanker routes and offers a foothold in the English-speaking Caribbean. It was a minor problem that could only have gotten worse.

While the 82nd Airborne was landing in Grenada, the Marines were digging out their dead at the Beirut airport. The Lebanese venture was the great positive blunder of the term: trouble actively sought, and found. It is hard to remember why the Marines were there. That was the problem. Were they defending Israel? Restraining Israel? Supporting Gemayel? Evacuating Arafat? Warning Syria? Or (obliquely) Khomeini? Or the Soviets? Could the Marines have accomplished any of these missions? Which of them were worth accomplishing?

Like most disasters, it seemed like a good idea at the time. The PLO buccaneer state in southern Lebanon had been smashed by an Israeli invasion in the summer of 1982; the Phalangists proposed to reconstruct the country; Britain, France, and Italy agreed to go into Beirut with us; securing the airport did not seem like a major commitment. An impossible one, nonetheless. The Marines were like pins in a bowling alley. Nothing was learned from one terrorist attack to the next, and counterattack was ruled out by the nature of the mission. It was military statesmanship, and State Department generalship. Where Grenada was clear, close, and doable, Lebanon was murky, distant, and difficult. After sixteen months, the Marines went home; not a life too soon.

There was one more event of the term that should be included in the background of the election. Ronald Reagan's shooting recalled Robert Kennedy's—not so much the incident as the way it was reported. All that morning, those eighteen years ago, the radio played the commentary of the distraught newsman who was there in the hallway of the Los Angeles hotel—played it and replayed it until you had memorized every panicky inflection. The shooting of Reagan gave, on the evening news, the video equivalent—the pained look, the prone bodies, the shaking, shouting Secret Service men, over and over. One announcer on a public radio station expressed the wish that John Hinckley had had a .45. He was an aberration. The nation—the normal nation —was shocked; prepared once again for anger and disgust.

It is ironic that masochistic anxieties over the sickness of American society should have come, through assassination, to be associated with the Kennedys, for whining was not one of the family vices. Reagan was luckier than the Kennedy brothers, for he survived. But he survived in a way that, on a purely psychological plane, redeemed their deaths. Reagan's characteristic tone of voice—all those self-deprecating one-liners, as comfortable as old sofas—did not waver. The jokes he told—the same jokes in an emergency room as at a rubber-chicken lunch: "On the whole, I'd rather be in Philadelphia"—lanced the boil. The tone transformed the event. That, too, was an accomplishment.

The Reagan record, as it accumulated, became the Democrats' background, part of their own set of unchangeable givens. They could reinterpret it, or distort it; they could even (like bats squeaking around trees in the dark) ignore it. What they had to do, in their caucuses and primaries as 1984 approached, was settle on an alternative. Four achievements, one flop, a million draws: what could the Democrats offer instead?

3
All of Those Politicians

... Finally he nudged me.
"Farrell, do you see all of those politicians up there?"
He pointed.
"Every one of them thinks he can be President of the United States."
—James T. Farrell, introduction to
H. L. Mencken, *Prejudices: A Selection*

The roads of Iowa are laid out by ruler. Driving them is like driving on graph paper. A turn is a major event; it rotates the whole state ninety degrees. Road signs, when they appear, give a little shock like marquees: BUMP. Every so often, there is a dark fur tuft, whipped in half; or trucks going the other way suck you over. The only other sights in midwinter are fields trimmed with gray sheets of water.

Iowa has joined New Hampshire as an all-season resort for politicians. The Iowa caucuses entered the political process suddenly, and not all that long ago. As recently as 1968, Norman Mailer (in *Miami and the Siege of Chicago*) could step back from his main canvas to take note of Hubert

Humphrey's quiet accumulation of delegates, mostly in caucus states, as if it were a secret process, a rite of 32nd Order Masons. Four years later, it was open to everyone. George McGovern used a surprise showing in the Iowa caucuses to get himself a crucial early leg up for New Hampshire; next time around, Jimmy Carter, who had much less in the way of experience in office or a red-hot booster issue than McGovern, did the same. Now it is on everybody's schedule. There have been complaints, mostly from Democrats, that Iowa, like New Hampshire, is too unlike the nation as a whole to bear such weight: odd, crabbed, uncharacteristic. The complaints are probably overdone, for the truth is, the country is at a point where everything is everywhere, even Iowa. The Des Moines phone books list one and a half columns of psychologists, three synagogues, two mosques, ten massage services (the raciest being Garter Belt Girls), one Abortion Advisory, one Catholic Social Service (Free Counseling Around Pregnancy Issues), four dealers of Fender guitars and amps, and one store advertising Nikes, Pumas, and Adidas. Even places in the more barren quadrants of the graph—Collins, Colo, Zearing—can get the same papers, watch the same TV. If it isn't in town, they can drive to it. There are no more Shangri-las or Sleepy Hollows. Everything is everywhere.

But not everyone is anyone. People don't take it all in uncritically. They choose, which means they choose differently; because they are, in fact, different. If a politician finds the right difference—like a geologist scanning the strata for wrinkles—he can hit a gusher that may take him all the way to New Hampshire, or further. Which was why Reubin Askew had come to Eldora.

Askew came to Yale during my senior year there, while he was still governor of Florida, to get some sort of fellowship. The singing group I belonged to was asked to entertain at a cocktail party in his honor. We sang *(When I see all the lovin' that they waste on babies / Why did I grow up at a-a-all?)* and mingled. I shook Askew's hand and spoke to him for no longer than it takes to exchange introductions. The next day I was strolling down York Street when I heard my name. It was Askew, hand outstretched. I was profoundly impressed.

It didn't look as if Askew would have much trouble recalling the crowd in Eldora. The Iowa road, as it runs through town, passes a brick courthouse and a cast-iron Civil War monument. The Askew rally was in a pizza and steak house on the square. The first to arrive was a young woman with a lovely blond daughter. She said she was a homemaker, and that this was the first election she'd taken part in; she couldn't remember the Carter caucuses of 1976 (I felt like the Ancient Mariner). Askew was the next to arrive. The owner, a Greek, introduced himself and made tea. A middle-aged woman showed up, a Republican. Everyone else was an observer from some other candidate's campaign. Askew waited till it was certain that this was all the audience that would show up, and started in.

Askew had good political looks—nicely graying hair—and a soft-edged, soothing voice. He also had a record. He had spent twenty years in Florida politics, standing up for integration and clean government, neither of which had ever been in much demand in the Sunshine State. In his first gubernatorial race in 1970, he had beaten a vehement opponent of busing; two years later, he keynoted the Democratic convention, and he tended to make the medium-sized lists of possible Vice-Presidents. No longer.

You have to be "captured by no one," Askew was saying, "so you're willing to challenge anyone for the good of all Americans." This is typically the talk of people who don't have many friends, and one of Askew's non-friends was organized labor. He had done a stint as Special Trade Representative for Carter, after leaving the statehouse, and he took a cold view of labor's attempts to institute protection by means of domestic-content laws. Protecting the automobile industry, he explained, would eliminate three jobs for every one it saved in Detroit, and raise the price of cars a thousand bucks. Askew had also come out against the nuclear freeze. He had, it is true, a kindred proposal which he called a "frost," and which, as he explained it, would limit the quantities of nuclear weapons. He opposed a freeze, however, because it would forbid modernizing the systems already in place. So much for the freeze vote. "My ambition," Askew explained, making a virtue of no support, "is to get elected President in such a way that I'll be free to govern."

Askew's greatest drawback as a campaigner, though, was that his presentation was chaotic. Every statement came preceded by nine qualifications. The gathering in the pizza and steak house would lose track around number five, and so sometimes did he. After one compact explanation—of domestic content—he went on to inflation, to the 1981 tax bill, to defense, to depreciation, to the tax bill again, to indexing (against), to cost-of-living adjustments. "It all boils down"—he caught a breath—"to fiscal solvency."

The lone Republican asked him about the flat tax, and he bubbled up again like a pot. He explained Bradley-Gephardt, the Democratic proposal, then wondered whether there couldn't be "broad national goals . . . on the basis of patriotism." The bicentennial of the Constitution might inspirit us. He turned to education and quoted Jefferson. We needed a tax code, he concluded, "that allows the greatest investment in people."

There being nothing more to say, the meeting adjourned. The Republican called him "one of the greatest living Americans," and the spies returned to headquarters with their reports.

In 1975, Patrick Caddell had approached Governor Askew with a memo on how a Southerner could win the presidency. Askew decided he wasn't ready for it, and Caddell took his memo to Georgia. Eight years later, when the former governor finally moved, he endorsed a number of positions which justified his old reputation. He proposed repealing the third year of Reagan's tax-rate cuts and raising corporate taxes. He supported the ERA and gun control and opposed the MX missile and the B-1 bomber. (If the

Pentagon may be said to support every weapon, Democratic presidential candidates tend to support every weapon except those which are ready to be built.)

But Askew also opposed protection and the freeze, as we have seen. He approved of the invasion of Grenada, and had been hissed for it at a candidates' forum in New Hampshire. He backed right-to-work laws and the death penalty and had supported Anita Bryant's 1977 campaign in Dade County against homosexual teachers. He wanted Congress to set a national standard on abortion; the standard he favored would have allowed it only in cases of rape, incest, and abnormal fetuses and would have offered federal funding of such abortions. (The right-to-lifers of Iowa were well mobilized; in 1976, in the days when the declaration that a politician was "personally opposed" to abortion appeared to mean something, they had helped put Carter over. Askew, whose position, though scarcely hard-line, made him look in the Democratic context like Mother Teresa, hoped to tap their votes again.) Askew, be it further noted, was a born-again Presbyterian elder who did not drink or smoke.

He was that rare thing, the genuinely heterogeneous man —not consistently conservative or liberal on the issues, or on any cluster of issues. The fact that he stood, in the field of Democratic candidates, on the right sideline said something about the changing shape of the Democratic party. For sixteen years, the Democrats had been extruding a certain kind of voter. George Wallace's third-party campaign of 1968 failed to achieve the bedtime dream of every third party, to throw the election to the House (there hasn't been an election thrown there since 1824). It succeeded in the only way that meaningful third-party movements do succeed—in identifying and energizing a bloc of voters. The Wallace constituency was not just Confederates. It included non-Southerners who were bellicose on foreign policy, resistant to social upheaval, potentially open (but for the limitations of Wallace's own soak-the-rich political background) to the tax revolt. Most of these voters were Democrats. Conservative Republican strategists had been eyeing them for years, but they were not easily pried from their home party. In 1972, the day after he was shot, Wallace, back in the party fold, won the Michigan and Maryland primaries and had the lead in primary delegates. Four years later, Henry Jackson, with the personality of overcooked rice, managed to win Massachusetts and New York. (Jackson's constituency overlapped with Wallace's chiefly on defense and foreign policy.) The best explanation of Jimmy Carter's success—no zip, no record, a good game plan; that and a dollar gets you a subway token—was that he bridged the party's rifts, mollifying all factions, including the disgruntled right: he was a white Southerner with black friends, a compassionate efficiency expert, a Washington outsider, and a born-again Christian (why not the blest?) who nevertheless knew to wipe his feet. He would also be the only Democrat in three straight elections to pull more than 43 percent of the vote. (After four years in office, he couldn't turn the trick again.) Askew was going to give the trick one more try.

Outside the john of the Eldora pizza and steak house, we passed. He remembered my name.

Askew's only company on the Democratic pseudo-right was the only other Southerner in the race, Ernest "Fritz" Hollings of South Carolina. Where Askew's evasions were due in part to bad forensic habits, in part to accommodations with an idiom that was uncongenial—his attempt to borrow the meteorology of the freeze, for example—Hollings's evasions were deliberately calculated.

As the official opening of the pre-election season gets pushed back earlier and earlier, the logic of the quick start pushes the unofficial opening back still further. To get a jump on New Hampshire in Iowa means getting a jump on Iowa. One of the best methods devised for this has been the straw poll, a pre-election year ballot of any handy group of party regulars. In 1983 there were straw polls of state party conventions in California (January), Massachusetts (April), Wisconsin (June), and New Jersey (September). The New

Jersey Democrats, gathering in an Atlantic City hotel, were locked up for John Glenn long in advance, but Fritz Hollings came anyway. The beach and boardwalk, under a lowering sky, were empty save for a few huddled, mewing gulls. The hotel glowed and throbbed, on the first floor with blackjack, on the sixth with politics.

"I'm a professional politician," Hollings began, with pride. He looked like one, southern senator division: a sweep of white hair; angular, aquiline features. He sounded like nothing else on earth. The cream of Charleston society are called SOBs, not because of their character, but because they live South of Broad Street, in the sugary houses on the peninsula's quaint tip. Hollings was an NOB, branded on the tongue. It is an accent that defies transliteration, to say nothing of comprehension. Lars-Erik Nelson of the New York *Daily News,* in a heroic effort to get it in type, produced this: "Ah spint foteen yahs own a skewel bode." What Nelson could not capture was the ever-shifting tempi. In his brief casino talk, Hollings waltzed about six syllables out of "realize," then jerked a phrase like "we are winners" down to two, all in a rich booming baritone.

It's probably just as well some of his words got lost, for Hollings was the Democratic party's Robert Dole—a zesty incendiary, who could not resist a squib, even if it exploded in his own face. At various times, he had said: of Grenada, an "attack on a golf course"; of Walter Mondale, he "was not born; he was appointed." Mondale on educational research: "What is he going to find—another *McGuffey's Reader?*" John Glenn: "Sky King." Howard Metzenbaum: "The senator from B'nai B'rith."

But there were positions in the rumble. He touched on a few for the New Jersey Democracy. "Everybody says, 'Free trade! Free trade! Ooey! Ooey!'" (he tossed his hands in a pantomime of jubilation). But Hollings was not jubilant. A senator from a textile-industry state, he was a proud protectionist. "It's our government that's forgotten how to compete." He also had an offer for the teachers' unions—a $14 billion program to raise salaries, charged to savings from the canceled MX and B-1. "Don't you think the skewelchildren of America are worth at least one weapon system?"

But Hollings's main message to the regulars was that the party should clean up its act. We must "sober up from our binge and become realistic. The people in November 1984 will not be looking around to give the fairness award, or the good government award. They'll want results."

Hollings blamed Democratic losses since the late sixties on economics: programs that were cockeyed and a record that was woeful. "Richard Nixon didn't elect himself," he liked to say, "we Democrats reincarnated him. George [McGovern; Hollings believed in first-naming mere peers] wanted to cut the defense budget in half and mail everybody a thousand dollars. In 1980 the question was, could the economy survive four more years of Carter-Mondale?" Hollings's recipe for results was a "shared sacrifice"—a freeze on all federal spending (a few welfare programs, such as food stamps and Aid to Families with Dependent Children, would be exempt). Meanwhile, he would repeal indexing and raise other taxes directly, chiefly on corporations.

It was a strategy for preserving big government, by keeping it temporarily from getting bigger. Reagan's intention, in Hollings's view, was to dismantle it. Deficits were a deliberate instrument of this policy: "He likes deficits. That's a good handicap on Democrats."

Hollings also said he supported the nuclear freeze, though here it was possible to suspect him of guile. Hollings and James Buckley, the Republican-Conservative from New York, had been the only senators to vote against the SALT I treaty. Cognoscenti credited Hollings, rather than Georgia senator Sam Nunn, with being the real Democratic brain in the fight against SALT II. The man who offered fiscal restraint as collateral for future spending might not be above preaching the freeze as a cover for strength. At the level of conventional arms, he favored bringing back the draft (the volunteer army: "an armed Job Corps").

Hollings's rise in politics had been swift: the South Carolina House at age twenty-six, governor at thirty-six, senator at forty-four. His slide to the center was slower. He had reconciled himself to desegregation during his time as governor; and he announced his conversion to a paternalist position on welfare after going to Washington.

He closed his address to the New Jerseyans in good form, with a double shot at Reagan and Sky King. "If it's waving, he can outwave John Glenn, I can tell you that. If they bring in a movie star, let's bring in an astronaut."

John Glenn had already come in, an hour or so before Hollings spoke, to savor his forthcoming victory. Hollings stood before a half-empty hall, noisy with Democrats coming in and out to register for the polls. For Glenn, the room was full and attentive.

On the dining-room hutch in the house where I grew up sits a plate commemorating Glenn's orbit of the earth. His face is stenciled on it in gilt. How many Americans have such a knickknack? Thousands? Millions? The face had not changed much in twenty-one years. Glenn was bald as a peach. His pale eyes glinted. He looked like Opie Taylor grown up, and he had the pugnacious cadences and gestures of Hubert Humphrey. His introducer hailed him as a "genuine American hero" who, when the automatic controls of *Friendship 7* failed, manually "brought the ship home," and "into the mainstream of American politics."

"Mainstream" was the key word. That was where Glenn wanted to put himself, with Ronald Reagan off in the boondocks. (His Democratic opponents could also be placed there as need required.)

"Reaganomics," Glenn began, "means mortgaging the future of this country" (in 1981, Glenn had voted for the watered-down Kemp-Roth tax-rate cut, a fact which would become important later in the campaign). Specifically, Reaganomics meant "passing $200 billion deficits to our children." Hadn't some of that deficit gestated under Democratic administrations and Congresses? Glenn acknowledged that it had. "We overdid some of those programs. But [since the thirties] we moved millions of people out of poverty" and into "a house, [with] kids in good schools, maybe a camper in the back. We didn't do it with socialism. We didn't do it with Communism. We didn't do it with fascism. We did it with good Democratic programs."

Glenn sketched programs suitable for the present crisis. "We can't revive the economy overnight." He wanted to step up federal support of education and of basic research. "New technologies are changing our world as fast as the Industrial Revolution. Jobs for today are not enough. We need tools for the future."

He bustled on to other matters, in no particular order. Glenn yoked two subjects, the environment and civil rights, by asserting that the necessary laws were for the most part already on the books; all we needed was vigorous enforcement, which Reagan was not giving. One law, the Equal Rights Amendment, needed to be on the books—"at the federal level, the state level, and, if we could, the county level. Making one woman a justice doesn't bring justice to women." Claps.

The speech congealed again when it came to defense. Glenn had a five-point program for arms control: accept a freeze; dispatch a crack team to the arms talks in Geneva ("the *fin*est diplomats, the *best* negotiators"); halt proliferation; include all nuclear states in the bargaining process; and, finally, negotiate lower levels of conventional forces. There were questionable items here. The second proposal was pure suds (who did Glenn think Reagan had sent over, the swabs?). The fourth would count the missiles of the French and British *forces de frappe* as part of our deterrent, and force us to scale down accordingly—a result the Soviets devoutly desired. Glenn dwelt, not on the program, but on his convictions and his experiences. "There is no substitute for keeping our defenses the strongest on earth. As a twenty-three-year veteran of the Marine Corps, I reject the President's contention that his is the only party that stands for America's defense. . . . I do not need to stay up and watch late-night TV to know what combat is like. It is horrible, hideous stuff. I've written next-of-kin letters. You go back to the States, and knock on the door, and you hope it won't be answered."

Glenn finished with the Pledge of Allegiance. "Too often we let the words of that pledge roll off too easily. *One nation.* Think about that. It doesn't say north or south, east or west, black or white, Catholic, Protestant, Jew . . ." He ran over the final phrases one by one, through *liberty and justice for all.* "Have we reached that yet? No, we haven't. But we can, if we just work, if we just keep on the track: *one nation, under God, indivisible, with liberty and justice for all.*"

"To think," mused Senator Joseph Biden of Delaware, who was the next speaker, "that I used to sit next to John Glenn on the Senate Foreign Relations Committee—and that he used to talk to me."

Glenn's biography has been made famous twice—in the early sixties, by the ballyhooing of the Mercury program, and again, in 1979, by Tom Wolfe. It can stand another rehearsal. John Herschel Glenn, Jr., was born on July 18, 1921, in Cambridge, Ohio. His father was a plumber, his mother a teacher. The Glenns moved to New Concord, another small western Ohio town, when John was two.

Wolfe wrote of "the awesome voltage of live Presbyterianism" still lingering on from the nineteenth century in New Concord when Glenn was growing up. And indeed, at his first press conference, astronaut Glenn would testify, "I am a Presbyterian, and I take my religion seriously." His youth was otherwise unremarkable. He did what one does, what fades in a year and sticks in the deepest dreams: lettered in sports; dated (he married Anna Castor, his high school sweetheart, when he was twenty-two); built model airplanes. In 1939, he enrolled in Muskingum College, the local Presbyterian school.

Pearl Harbor came junior year, and Glenn left for the Marines. In the American push through Micronesia, he flew over the Marshall Islands, winning two Distinguished Flying Crosses. John, Sr., wanted his son to come home after the war and take up the plumbing business. But the Marines had other ideas. Korea brought him two more Distinguished Flying Crosses. In the last nine days of the war he shot down three MiGs; his comrades painted the motto MIG-MAD MARINE on his fuselage. Ted Williams, who flew at his wingtip, called him "crazy."

Out of combat, Glenn volunteered for test flying. He was good, and ambitious. In 1957 he conceived and executed the first cross-country supersonic flight. That same year, the Soviets launched Sputnik. Five years later, my parents bought the plate.

There is an impression, based on careless readings of *The Right Stuff,* and reinforced by the movie, that the astronauts were lesser beings, inferior in every way to the righteous pilots who tested the X-15s. Certainly Charlie Yeager is the hero of Wolfe's account; the book ends with what can only be called an epic plane crash, with Yeager surviving by guts and skill. But *The Right Stuff* begins with an equally powerful passage, an almost Gothic description of Pete Conrad, later one of the Mercury seven, slogging through a Florida swamp in search of the shattered corpse of one of his fellow test pilots. The implication is clear, whether Wolfe intended it or not: whatever PR indignities the astronauts later underwent, and however limited their mission, they had all, as former pilots, passed certain tests. They all partook of the right stuff. (Poor Glenn, who had to have his image, however transiently, at the mercy of Hollywood. At least Reagan's movies were thirty years old, and not about him.)

The Kennedys encouraged Glenn to go into politics (he was in Los Angeles working for Robert when Sirhan struck). His first tries were inglorious. Glenn pulled out of the 1964 Ohio senatorial primary after hurting his inner ear in a bathroom fall. Six years later, he took on Howard Metzenbaum, a liberal millionaire businessman. (Glenn hadn't been doing so poorly himself; he had by this time become a vice-president of Royal Crown Cola and an investor in several successful Holiday Inns.) Glenn's campaign was an organizational disaster. Metzenbaum beat him in the primary, and lost the election.

Metzenbaum got into the Senate in 1974 by appointment, and Glenn had another shot at him. This time around, the gears in the Glenn machinery meshed. Metzenbaum also made a notable blunder, accusing his opponent of never having held a job. "You go to a veterans hospital," Glenn answered, "see their mangled bodies, and tell them they didn't hold a job. . . . You should go down on your knees every day of your life thanking God that there are some men who had a job." Metzenbaum went down, and Glenn got a new job.

In 1976 Senator Glenn was on Carter's short list of possible running mates—until his keynote speech to the Democratic convention, an address of unrelieved somnolence (critics called it Glenn without mission control). Seven years later, Glenn had a new target; in April 1983, he returned to New Concord to announce his presidential candidacy formally and greet well-wishers at John Glenn High School and Muskingum's John Glenn Gym.

"You can't serve the national interest," Glenn told the pols in Atlantic City, "by catering to the special interests." Did Glenn's record match his professions? "John's problem," a long-time supporter confessed, "is that he's a 90 percenter." By which he meant that Glenn refused to go all the way for the groups with what might be called season tickets to the Democratic Party. Still, 90 percent was an awful long way.

Glenn went furthest on the social issues—the issues that, for the most part, became issues in the wake of liberal innovation. Glenn backed busing, affirmative action, gun control; he supported Medicaid payments for abortions and, of course, abortion itself. He opposed tuition tax credits and school prayer. Some of the nuances stumped him. In July, Glenn went to San Antonio to woo the National Women's Political Caucus, where he let slip the asymmetrical words "man and wife," then foundered like a swamped canoe. "I am usually very careful to make certain I say men and women. When you talk about a married couple, though, maybe we should say male and female. I don't know. What's the preferred term these days?"

Glenn did cast a lone vote (lone in terms of his career) for Reaganomics and for the FY 1982 Republican budget. He quickly came to his senses, voting to limit the tax-rate cut to one year and, later, to repeal the third year. He identified "massive tax cuts for individuals" as "the real cause of enormous deficits and resultant high interest rates." He had voted against indexing and the balanced-budget amendment. Early in his career, he opposed common-situs picketing, whereby a single striking union could shut down an entire construction site. But he backed the Chrysler loan and domestic-content legislation.

Defense and foreign policy, not surprisingly, seemed to engage the former colonel's best thinking. Glenn was credited with helping to talk Carter out of withdrawing American troops from South Korea. He supported the B-1 bomber and voted, in a Senate tie broken by Vice-President Bush, to produce a new nerve-gas bomb. Glenn's proposed defense budget hike—5.5 percent—was greater than that offered by other Democrats, though less than Reagan's. Among his suggested savings were the Rapid Deployment Force and the MX ("a 192,000-pound monster"). There were also surprises. Glenn urged Reagan, on the eve of the mammoth European anti-missile demonstrations, to delay deploying the cruise as an earnest of "good faith." A month before Atlantic City, he brought his Middle East policy into the shop for an overhaul; having once or twice suggested that we might have to negotiate with the PLO, he now announced they were "thugs" and proposed moving our embassy in Israel to Jerusalem. Glenn also had second thoughts on SALT II. He had fought stubbornly against the treaty, but explained during the campaign that his opposition had been due to anxiety over the loss of Iranian monitoring sites. Satellites having since taken up the slack, he declared himself well satisfied (though several years too late to save SALT II).

Glenn was plagued with staff problems throughout his campaign. There was one major shake-up in October 1983 and a second three months later. Headlines and takeouts spoke of "the wrong staff." But there was a deeper confusion than how to run him: What was he running for? Glenn stood forthrightly for one thing, the national interest; by implication and, later, accusation, the other candidates were selling it out. Yet Glenn's positions, when examined, were virtually identical to those of his leftward opponents.

They were virtually identical because there was no reason for them to be different. The cry of "special interests" came oddly from Glenn. In the rhetoric of old populism, the special interests—banks, railroads, whatever—were malign forces that should have had no power at all. The goal of good citizens was to throw them out. For Glenn, the special interests represented worthy causes that had in some undefined (and undefinable) way gone too far. The remedy for the excesses of feminists, labor unions, black leaders, and all the rest was not to reject their claims, but to exhort them to moderate their demands.

Some liberal Democrats, calculating that they could accomplish more by prudence, supported Glenn quite frankly as effective cover. In the opinion of Senator Paul Tsongas, as reported by *The Wall Street Journal,* a President Glenn— ace, astronaut, self-styled moderate—"could more easily win congressional acceptance of an arms-control treaty, tax increases, or major social legislation." Or 90 percent thereof.

The month after New Jersey brought more state straw polls. But the most important party event was the New York Presidential Forum. Each of the candidates appeared, on a different night in a different city in New York State, before a convocation of party members, to speak, to be questioned, and to answer. There was to be a poll at the end of these performances too, with two straws, belonging to Governor Cuomo and Senator Moynihan.

Glenn spoke in Syracuse, and in the final grand chorus of all the candidates at Town Hall in New York City, October

6. Some thirty Glenn supporters, mostly kids, awaited him on the corner of Forty-third Street and Sixth Avenue. All wasted. What was a crowd in midtown Manhattan at seven o'clock in the evening? Moonies? A Manet show? Three-card monte? New Yorkers shrugged, and went back to cursing cabs. Inside, the candidates lined up onstage in virtually identical dark suits and red neckties. And, although Mario Cuomo didn't put it quite this way in his introduction, identical opinions. They differed, Cuomo said, "on how much we should cut defense, on how much more we should give to education, on the exact components of an industrial policy." Yet they all agreed to "help the homeless, the unemployed, the disabled." Cuomo complimented their "intellectual vitality," then stepped back to let them slug.

Glenn worried that the Democrats would "offer a party that can't say no to anyone with a mailing list." He asked his opponents, "How would you balance special-interest groups?" No one asked him.

He got to speak trenchantly only once, in reply to a panelist. James Barber, a political science professor at Duke, intended a serious question on his qualifications—what on earth, John Glenn, have you done?—but it came out snottily, comparing the astronaut to Evel Knievel or a Niagara Falls barrel rider. It was Metzenbaum all over again; the house burst into angry applause as soon as Glenn opened his mouth. When it subsided, Glenn ticked off his careers in the military, business, the Senate; his most recent victory had been the biggest in Ohio history, and he had run ahead of Ronald Reagan. "I wasn't doing *Hellcats of the Navy* on a movie lot when I was doing 149 missions. When I was on that booster getting ready to go, it wasn't *Star Trek* or *Star Wars*, it was the real thing."

Well said. Glenn's problem was to demonstrate what that kind of heroism, and the concepts of service it reflected, had to do with politics.

Ninety percent might work for Glenn; 100 percent is all the world gives. But in every election there have to be a few

110 percenters—more-Catholic-than-the-Pope hard-liners
who will call in St. Petersburg for ending Social Security, or
in Seattle for slashing military spending. The dominant faction of a party can always afford to sustain at least one.
Indeed, it prefers to, as a regulator and keeper of its conscience.

For much of 1983, Alan Cranston served in that role. The
success of his inherently improbable candidacy—he held
third place on many tip sheets for some time—was a tribute
to his shrewdness and to the appetite for purity of the
party's left wing. This, despite a set of campaign themes
that were pitched at about the level of ten-year-olds.

Cranston's early successes were due almost entirely to
the nuclear-freeze issue. Every Democrat, except Askew,
supported the freeze. Cranston supported nothing else. He
would initiate a freeze, he said, the day of his inauguration.
The freeze became his call letters, his watchword; the thing
that accompanied him wherever he went, like "Lara's
Theme." To even mention other issues in the same breath,
he implied, was to invite Armageddon; only he clearly saw
the danger. But since other issues would intrude on a Cranston presidency, he perforce addressed them. He went to
Central America and came to New York to talk about it a
few weeks before the Town Hall Forum.

Bald, beaked, gaunt, Alan Cranston looked like some prehistoric proto-bird. He was three years younger than Ronald Reagan, but could have been his uncle. "I traveled to
Africa to cover the aftermath of the fascist invasion of Ethiopia," he began, recalling a youthful journalistic assignment.* "There is nothing like firsthand experience."

Unfortunately, Cranston had experienced nothing in
Central America he could not have read on the editorial
pages back home. He put his faith where most American
foreign-policy types put theirs—in a negotiating process.
The relevant process in Central America was the Con-

---

* And an expensive one. In 1938, Cranston, working for Hearst, reported
an Italian tale that Haile Selassie had sawed in half the nephew of an
enemy. The exiled emperor sued for libel, and collected 15,000 pounds.

tadora process, a framework sponsored by Mexico, Panama, Colombia, and Venezuela. Cranston had concluded from his trip that we should follow the Contadora lead. (This may be the real lure of processes—not to get anything we want, but to get us off the hook.)

He recited a list of our misdeeds in Latin America, back to the building of the Panama Canal. Now the United States was encouraging Costa Rica to have an army—the "only country on the face of the earth" without one, he noted. He admitted it was "not clear what would happen" in El Salvador if Contadora policy prevailed; he "assume[d]" no Soviet arms would be sent there.

Cranston ended with a theory of the presidency and a refinement of his basic campaign message. Presidents, he had observed, really only have a chance to carry out one or two policies. If they divide their attention among more, effectiveness dissipates. Therefore, the Cranston White House would devote itself to two goals—ending the arms race and—this was a new one—full employment.

Behind the Tinkerbell talk, Alan Cranston was actually a keen politician. He attended the founding meeting of the United World Federalists and served as its second president (another member: Ronald Reagan). He moved on to boost the Democratic party in California, a thankless task which he performed well enough to win the state controllership and, in 1968, a Senate seat. Senator Cranston's subsequent re-election margins ranged from large to vast. He accomplished this by seasoning his prime-cut liberalism with a sedulous attention to the needs of local interests. Agribusiness, independent oilmen, Lockheed have all benefited from his efforts. Cranston the freezenik even supported the B-1 bomber (Democrats do support actual weapons, if they are built by their constituents).

He was not seeking the presidential nomination as a nuts-and-bolts man. He told feminists he would "consider withholding federal funds for bridge repairs" from anti-ERA states (infrastructure with a vengeance). He branded the Grenada invasion "illegal and outrageous." He called Ron-

ald Reagan "a trigger-happy President" with a "simplistic
and paranoid world view."

Cranston won the California straw poll, in part by urging
his fellow Californians not to humiliate him in his own state.
He finished a surprise third in Massachusetts, and won, even
more surprisingly, a poll of Alabama Young Democrats in
May (which allowed him to claim strength in the South). His
greatest coup was the Wisconsin straw poll. With the support of deep-freezers and a fleet of buses to bring in his
troops, he managed to upset Walter Mondale (Cranston
blandly explained the buses as a way of aiding the poor and
the halt). It was a remarkable technical operation, a
splendid feat of life support. But why should the faithful
stay with Cranston once someone even more pure in heart
became available?

"You have to do what you have to do, and I have to do
this." So George McGovern announced his candidacy in
September 1983, almost the last Democrat to do so. "I believe I am ready now as at no previous time in my life to
lead this country." If Cranston's candidacy seemed unlikely, McGovern's was at first incredible. He not only bore
the onus of the worst defeat ever received by a Democrat in
a two-man race; he had been hauled out of his Senate seat
by the posses of the New Right eight years later. There were
comparisons to Harold Stassen, forever snatching at the lost
last chance; there was talk, more cynical, that McGovern's
lecture circuit fees had sagged and that the adventure
would give them a boost. McGovern insisted that he was in
it for real, and that he was properly compared, not to Stassen, but to Barry Goldwater—the man of principle, once
thought extreme, who remade his party in his own image.

Election years are boons to Iowa social studies classes.
The candidate-student ratio at a centrally located school in
midwinter must get close to the teacher-student ratio. To
the students in the auditorium of Dowling High School in
West Des Moines on the afternoon McGovern came there,
1972 was distant history—"I don't even know what McGov-

ern looks like." "That's McGovern, right there." McGovern, a former history teacher, was in his element. Age had bared his brow and pinched the nasal, Plains state voice into yet more creaky registers. It had also mellowed him. "No presidential candidate in modern history," wrote Stewart Alsop of the first McGovern campaign, "has imputed to his rival such foul and evil motives." That stridor was mostly gone now. McGovern's nickname among the cameramen shooting him this time around was McGoo. He had started to look a little like Mr. McGoo, but he had also acquired the character's bumbling avuncular benignity.

He outlined his program to the students slowly and carefully and clearly, as if it were the Articles of Confederation or Manifest Destiny. Of its ten points, the first three were give-peace-a-chance. We had to end military operations in Central America. "Hundreds of thousands of people in those little countries to the south of us are unhappy with the governments that are exploiting them." We should also pull out of Lebanon—"not a partisan recommendation," he pointed out, for it had also been made by Senator Goldwater ("the former Republican presidential candidate," he explained). "Two hundred and sixty-four marvelous young men who are now dead would have been removed. . . . Is there anyone in this auditorium today who has a quarrel with the Druses?" McGovern added to this basically isolationist argument two Vietnam-era corollaries: we are bad— for shelling rebel Lebanese strongholds—and so are our allies—"do not [Lebanese Moslems] have the right to protest against a government which does not represent them?" Finally, Freeze Now—unilaterally if necessary. "If the Soviets want to continue this nonsense to their own economic disadvantage, they do not weaken us."

He also had thoughts on other matters (not that Alan Cranston didn't, but McGovern was willing to make something of them). He wanted to rebuild America's railroads and, interestingly, put in place the Bradley-Gephardt flat-tax plan. He was big on federal loans—one-time mortgage loans up to 10 percent, and student loans, to be paid back to the IRS. "You young folks are not old enough to know much about the Internal Revenue Service, but let me tell you—they'll do the job." He recalled that he had run the Food for Peace program under the Kennedy administration. ("Do you know what that was?") We can "feed the hungry in our country" and "dry up the swamplands of hunger in which Communism breeds. . . . We're under a biblical command to do that. The whole Judeo-Christian tradition commands us to do that." Farm state politics also commands us to do that, but presumably everyone there already knew what that was. One figure of the Bronze Age did not require explanation. "It's true I lost very heavily to Richard Nixon. But how many people are happy about that?" Applause from the kids. Nixon has become a Demon, like Darth Vader, known to everyone. But the New McGovern had a good word even for him. "I thought détente was one of the best things my old nemesis Richard Nixon did. That's why I went to see him a few weeks ago." Nixon and McGovern had met earlier in the year, and uttered admiring remarks about each other afterwards. The press speculated whether McGovern might thereby pick up a rock-ribbed farmer or two. As for Nixon, it was only one more careful tack in his long upstream sail to elder statesmanship. America and Russia "have two different systems," McGovern went on. But we ought to compete peacefully, because "the alternative is death."

McGovern's next lecture that day was thirty miles north, in Ames, at Iowa State. The students at the university had about the same experience of the 1972 campaign as the high school kids. But this event flushed out some of the original faithful and they set the tone. It was like a rally of Jacobite clans.

The students filing in were greeted by a pair of folk guitarists. On the cutting edge of the East Village avant-garde, there is supposed to be a group of punks who have washed the dye out of their hair, put on berets, and learned the twenty-year-old songs of Peter, Paul and Mary. Everything is everywhere, but it doesn't travel that fast. The guitarists sang Buffalo Springfield—*Thousands of people in the streets*—and the students listened to the strange sounds gravely, as to music from Bali.

They were followed by a rotund banjo player, in a cloth cap, round glasses, and a beard like a koala's hair. He said, as he tuned up, that he had heard McGovern's acceptance speech to the 1972 convention on television. "I swore allegiance to him ever since." He was a good picker, and he tried to take his audience even further back in time with "This Land Is Your Land." There was a little uncertain clapping-along, but he wanted singing on the choruses too. He waved the crowd in with a hammy hand; only a few tried.

He was not fazed. He did a little patter—"I keep thinking how much money we're paying the War Department. It's not a Defense Department, you know"—and performed a lyric of his own, to the Chiquita Banana jingle.

But understand we must—if we want to survive,
We must stop this insane spending while we're still alive.

Hot from the lights of the TV news crews, he removed his cap, revealing a bald pate, which made him look like a Victorian banker, and did another song, about farm foreclosures, "billions" rhyming with "more guns" (what Congress spends billions on). He managed by the end to get an ovation.

After the music appreciation course, Iowa State's student body president took over. She spoke fluently, and had a handsome hard little face. "A class that I'm taking in foreign policy has solidified my commitment to getting Ronald Reagan out of the White House." This could be taken as an instance of the baleful influence of liberal educators. I took it with a grain of salt; I could not imagine a student politician who didn't know, months in advance, precisely how many on-campus votes there were on an issue, what their phone numbers were, and when they could be reached. She did say, accurately, "It used to be, it was in vogue to be liberal. Now it's in vogue to be conservative." The key word

was "vogue"—which explained (and discounted) the sixties
as well as the eighties. The last warm-up speaker was a
chemistry professor who had also remembered the 1972
acceptance speech. He read passages from it, with emotion.

McGovern, still the history teacher, urged everyone to
vote. "Stay with your convictions. Don't throw those precious gifts away." His first campaign had been "a campaign
of candor and compassion and common sense." Now the
issues had become "much graver. All men, women, and
children must face the most terrible choice God has put
before them since the creation." Reagan was "undoubtedly
the most dangerous man ever to hold that office." Loud
claps. McGovern recalled an incident not usually mentioned at peace rallies, the Soviet shooting down of Korean
Airlines Flight 7, but managed to wring from it an acceptable moral: the Russians had debated two hours before firing, but our Pershing missiles in Europe had a flight time of
only six minutes. He invoked Dwight Eisenhower. At Eisenhower's last National Security Council meeting, during a
debate on nuclear weapons, Ike had exclaimed, "Why don't
we just go completely crazy and build another ten thousand
of those nutty things?" Today, McGovern said, we have ten
times as many. "Why don't we have the common sense,
right now, not to construct one more nuclear weapon? . . .

"The age of successful big power intervention in the affairs of little countries is over. . . . We came to greatness
not in whimpering about what we were against, but what
we were for." America could have good relations with revolutionary regimes; McGovern offered as examples China
and Yugoslavia.

Finally, he plugged the ERA. American prosperity and
power "rest on a commitment to our founding ideals," of
which equal rights was one. Women were, if anything, more
equal. The "gender gap is a fancy term for saying that
women have Reagan's number better than men do. Women
do not like this macho, shoot-'em-up, John Wayne approach
to the world." Applause.

There was a question about South Africa. If they didn't

clean up their act, we should "break . . . completely any kind of contact." Just like Yugoslavia. He worried about the deficit, which could be lessened by cutting the defense budget (the banjo player let the term pass) by 25 percent. "Just think how terrified you'd be if you went to work tomorrow morning at eight-thirty and had to spend a billion dollars before five. That's a considerable burden on these people."

He ended with a theme he would take up again and again. He wanted to win; indeed, he was the best candidate. But it was a worthy field—"the best field of Democratic contenders since 1960." *Since 1960* was just a grace note. What affinity did George McGovern have with Hubert Humphrey or Lyndon Johnson, two 1960 contenders he later execrated, or with John Kennedy, the winner, who accused Eisenhower of having permitted a missile gap? (Nuclear weapons weren't "nutty things" to JFK, at least during the election.) But the message of unity and satisfaction was sincere. Aside from Askew's confusions and Hollings's deceptions, he could in conscience support all his opponents, and they could support him.

McGovern was the son of a Methodist minister. After serving in World War II as a bomber pilot, he studied divinity for a time, but ultimately got his Ph.D. from Northwestern in history. While in school, he and his wife served as delegates to the Progressive party convention of 1948; his most vivid memory, according to his autobiography, *Grassroots,* was the group singing led by Pete Seeger (so he came by his accompanists legit).

McGovern got into mainstream politics by becoming executive director of South Dakota's Democratic party—like Cranston's Democrats in California, a forlorn organization. Like Cranston, he managed to win a Senate seat. He worked assiduously for farm interests (he and Robert Dole became point men for the food-stamp program), which pleased the home folks. But his national reputation came from the Vietnam War. He voted in 1964 for the Tonkin Gulf resolution—"the worst vote I ever cast." It was a lone deviation. He made a quixotic, last-minute bid for the presi-

dential nomination in 1968. Four years later, his first-min-
ute bid was masterminded by one Gary Hart. James Cox
and John Davis, buried by Harding and Coolidge, received
smaller percentages of the popular vote than McGovern did
against Nixon, but they took the still-solid South in the Electoral College. The only major-party candidate in a two-man
race to do worse was Alf Landon. McGovern held on to his
Senate seat in the Watergate election. But six years and a sea
change later, Congressman James Abdnor buried him, 61
percent to 39 percent.

The most interesting detail in this biography was undoubtedly McGovern's political debut, in the 1948 Progressive party of Henry Wallace (he of the guru letters). The
Wallace campaign, covertly at first, then more and more
openly, was run by the American Communist party, which
is to say, by Stalin. Among McGovern's recollections of the
convention, besides the singing, were "a few hard-line
Communists whose rigidity and fanaticism I found obnox-
ious. But most of the delegates were idealistic middle-class
Americans who wanted a foreign policy based on restraint
and reason." McGovern later on in his memoirs describes
Wallace as "an old-fashioned free-enterprise capitalist and a
practical internationalist." These judgments were honest
enough. The "few hard-line Communists" ran the show, but
many of the Progressives, even at the end, were in the
campaign, not because they obeyed Stalin, but because they
trusted him, and thought a world of peace could be based
on working with him. They were attracted to the Wallace
campaign by its professions, not by the realities. The success
of George McGovern in the Democratic party was the success of those professions. As well as the accompanying na-
ïveté.

Not every McGovern rally was nice. Though he had for-
sworn dirty work himself this time around, he was willing to
let other people do it. One of his last appearances in Des
Moines before the Iowa caucuses was at a meeting at St.
Ambrose Cathedral featuring Dr. Helen Caldicott. Dr.
Caldicott had been the leading light of Physicians for Social

Responsibility, an anti-nuclear medical group. Her purpose
was to scare the daylights out of people. She was brisk,
attractive, competent, and clean-cut, and she performed
her task well. After a folk singer (another one!) and a reading of Matthew 5:9 (blessed are the peacemakers), Dr.
Caldicott got down to work.

Nuclear war, she told the congregation, was "the issue
that will bring us together and make us grow as Jesus
wanted us to. Jesus was the greatest psychiatrist ever. . . .
The Soviet leaders are old paranoid men." After all, the
Soviet Union "is the only country in the world surrounded
by hostile Communist countries. . . .

"I know, as a physician, when a patient that is clinically
paranoid comes into a hospital you don't frighten them."
Instead "you enter into a therapeutic relationship. It is
medically contraindicated to threaten the Russians." She
had also met Reagan, on an introduction from his daughter
Patti. She said he had taken out the *Reader's Digest* article
on the Communist associations of freeze backers. Laughter.
"I staggered out, really clinically shocked, I guess. . . . The
next eight and a half months are going to decide the history
of this planet. . . .

"I'm going to drop a bomb on this beautiful cathedral and
I want you to think of your children, everyone you know
and everyone you love, turned into fallout by the heat of the
sun. . . . At six miles, everything is destroyed. Out to a
radius of twenty miles—think where ya live [Caldicott is an
Australian and has the clipped accent]—there will be winds
of five hundred miles per hour. . . . Glass fragments" will
travel at "one hundred miles per hour. People sucked out of
buildings become missiles traveling at one hundred miles
per hour. . . . If you look at the flash, your eyes will melt.
People turn into charcoal statues. . . . The firestorm will
suck the air out of fallout shelters and you'll be asphyxiated
and the shelters will become crematoriums. . . ." Carl
Sagan had predicted a nuclear winter of "snowstorms rag-
ing across the planet. . . . People will die and they will be

thirsty when they die. . . . We have plans to destroy this country and God's creation. . . .

"There's a paper being done by a mathematician to prove that nuclear war is a mathematical certainty" if cruise missiles stay in place. The "opportunity is now. . . . Patriotic fervor" is "pre-nuclear thinking. . . . How many people here think it's a true democracy" in America? Two hands went up, one mine. "How did you allow this to happen in this wonderful country of yours? You've abdicated. . . . We practice psychic numbing. It's too scary, so we don't think about it." Dr. Caldicott had advice. She outlined the "stages of grief: shock and disbelief . . . profound depression" (including "loss of appetite" and "loss of sexual drive") ". . . anger—you can channel that . . . acceptance. I accept the facts. I'm going to use everything in me to save my children and all the children of the world, because I took the Hippocratic Oath."

After Grand Guignol and group therapy, she lost the thread a bit. Men, she said, "are inadequate in a sexual way." The "appropriate men for a nuclear age" cry. Women's "bodies are built to mature life. . . . Look at babies, stars, gardenias. . . ." Archbishop Hunthausen of Seattle, who had called the Trident submarine the "Auschwitz of Puget Sound," got her back on track. She quoted him: "Anyone who seeks to save his life through nuclear weapons will lose it, but anyone who gives them up for Jesus' sake will save it." The congregation stood and applauded. "I honor and admire the [Catholic] bishops," she added, "for their pastoral letter" on nuclear war. McGovern, who had been sitting in the front row, gave her his "personal thanks." She returned it: "Here sits a statesman."

McGovern's diehards, the professors and banjo pickers, always thought so. His campaign was a test to determine whether the party at large thought so too.

Iowa students aren't the only ones to profit from the democratic system. On a bright, breathless June day, the members of the Dover (N.H.) High School class of '83 as-

sembled on the infield of their newly chalked track to receive their diplomas, and to hear the mayor of Dover and
Walter Mondale. (If any of them were going on to Iowa State
in the fall, they could count on catching Mondale again, if
not the mayor.) The mayor, a blunt-spoken man with a
granite accent, told them they were crossing a divide; before, they had been the responsibility of others, chiefly their
parents; but from that day on, they would be strictly on
their own. "And heaven forbid," the mayor warned, "you'll
ever have to ask your government to take care of you."
Mondale did not bat a brooding eye.

The graduates were less interested in speechifying than
in skimming mortarboards and hailing friends and family in
the bleachers; probably friends and family were less interested as well. It would be seven and a half months before
anyone in New Hampshire would have to vote on Mondale,
up or down. But this was a latish stop for him, for he had
been running for two and a half years.

There was a dread word shadowing the Mondale campaign throughout its earliest phases; at the first serious loss
or stumble, it would be invoked to doom him. That word
was Muskie. Edmund Muskie had been senator from Maine,
Hubert Humphrey's running mate, and Secretary of State
for Jimmy Carter. But the implied comparison would have
been to Muskie's own run for the nomination in 1972. Muskie had been catapulted to front-runner status by television.
In the closing days of the 1970 off-year elections, the national parties took to the airwaves back to back. The Republicans went with a gritty, *cinéma vérité* clip of a slashing
Nixon speech. It was a little more *vérité* than they bargained
for; the sound crackled, Nixon waved his arms; it looked like
a home movie of the Beer Hall Putsch. Cut to the senator
from Maine: calm, soothing, "Lincolnesque"; for trailers,
there were shots of wildflowers, like the jackets of those
Robert Frost anthologies sold in drugstores. The contrast
was electric. For eighteen months, Muskie was number one
—until it came time to count some votes. Muskie, it tran-
spired, had no message, no organization, no constituency.

The end was swift and ignominious. After six primaries, Muskie pulled out. Thus perish front-runners.

But that was in the days before the permanent campaign (George McGovern, who beat Muskie, was one of the first permanent campaigners). Mondale would not, at least, make the mistake of inactivity. He had made the decision to run while the confetti from the Reagan inauguration was being swept up. Mondale set up a political action committee, Citizens for the Future of America, fourteen days after leaving office. He did radio broadcasts, raised money, and fed it to deserving congressional candidates (he also, of course, used it for his own purposes). He made his first tour of New Hampshire in March 1982 and visited Iowa that April. Not all of these early efforts were dashing successes. In November 1981, Mondale appeared in *The New York Times Magazine* in the role of a hermit just crawled down from his desert pillar with a new credo. Mondale's afflatus was pompous and dull—so much so that when an editor hit the wrong computer button, causing a rough draft to be printed instead of the final version, no one at the *Times* seemed to notice. (There was one interesting touch—the abandonment of the word "liberal" for "pragmatic progressive"). But it put Mondale's face on a lot of brunch tables. Whatever else might befall, he would not be caught napping.

The most important victory of the early, pre-dawn stages of the campaign was not of Mondale's doing. On December 1, 1982, Teddy Kennedy announced that he would be sitting this one out. He cited the strains campaigning puts on a family. There may well have been other motives. With the double aura of invulnerability and inevitability dispelled by his 1980 loss, he could afford for the first time to pick and choose. Running against an incumbent Reagan may not have looked like a good choice. Perhaps also he had finally admitted to himself that he did not want to be President (his first serious try had been so inept and dispirited, at least at the start, as to suggest self-destruction). Whatever the reason for it, his bowing out left Mondale in the position of front-runner. Which, all things considered, is still better than back-runner.

For Dover, Mondale had chosen a light text, a send-up of commencement speeches, ending with a poem by Dr. Seuss. There have been better stand-up comics. Mondale had a dry wit and a deadpan delivery. When the 1980 Carter-Mondale campaign picture—which was to show Mondale behind Carter's shoulder, looking over—was shot, the photographers put Carter in place, then told Mondale to step up, closer, closer, and closer. If he got any closer, Mondale finally quipped, they would carry California. (Carter didn't get it.) But the humor was all lost on sit-down audiences. Fortune gave Mondale baleful, fishy eyes; fortune and high school football (at which he excelled), a nose that looked like a failed design for a can opener. The nose was also the place from which his voice emerged, about a quarter of the way down the bridge by the sound of it, where the bone ends and the cartilage begins. Mondale made it up on his hair—brown gone gray, smooth and handsome as a badger-tail shaving brush. On his hair and on his grin, which could light up his face—except when he was trying to be funny. Mondale recited his speech solemnly, like someone explaining the facts of life.

In back of the bleachers, after the ceremony, Mondale granted a brief press conference. That day, his lack of oomph was not only a forensic problem. He had come to New Hampshire from Milwaukee and an upset loss in the Wisconsin straw poll. While Cranston had been moving hearts and renting buses, too many of Mondale's voters stayed home, soaking up the June sun. There was a rustle of Muskie in the air.

Mondale's opening remarks touched on an issue and a theme. The issue, education, was new; it had blown up with squall-like suddenness in the wake of what is usually a guarantee of halcyon obscurity, the report of a presidential commission. A "rising tide of mediocrity" has engulfed American schooling, a commission appointed by Reagan announced in March. Mondale responded in May, with a

program and a price tag: modernized laboratories; more
student aid; scholarships for student-teachers; grants to
communities, funneled through local education commissions (a Fund for Excellence)—all to the tune of $11 billion.
"This country," he said at Dover, "cannot afford ignorance."

Mondale's theme concerned the man he hoped to oppose
two autumns from then, and it underlay all his issues. Education, he explained, had been brought to its parlous state
"by what I now think is a radical President in Washington,
D.C." Now, and months ago. "Ronald Reagan is not a conservative," Mondale had said the previous September.
"He's a radical. He's like Mao Tse-tung." Reagan, Mondale
argued, had broken with the mainstream consensus on a
host of issues—education, employment, the environment,
arms control. Mondale, it followed, was not a partisan, but a
defender of the consensus.

After a few questions from reporters, all, like racetrack
announcers, interested in who was ahead, Mondale's three
cars took to the road. In fifteen minutes, they were winding
through Farmington (no graph paper here; in New England, roads go anyhow). Mondale stopped at the brick city
hall, where some fifty people had gathered in the community center, down in the basement. He circled the tables,
shaking every adult hand and smiling at every child's face,
then stood in front of the buffet his audience would eat
when he had gone.

"We've had a bad spring. So today I wanted to show you
what a Mondale presidency would bring. The clouds
parted; children are playing . . ." There, where he could
look his crowd in the eye, his humor worked better, his grim
visage making an effective backdrop. Education reap-
peared. "This administration has been the most anti-educa-
tion in American history. If we're going to defend ourselves" with sophisticated weapons, "if we're going to
compete" in world trade, "the federal government has to
do its role." Reagan the Great Helmsman followed close
behind. Mondale quoted Will Rogers on Herbert Hoover:

"It isn't what he doesn't know that worries me; it's what he knows for sure that ain't so." Reagan, he said, preaches the "survival of the fittest." He had raised payroll, cigarette, and telephone taxes while giving tax breaks to the wealthy ("to his wealthy friends" was a favorite way of putting it).

The audience pitched a few questions, all, in the manner of these events, waist high and slow. On school prayer, Mondale, a Methodist minister's son, gave a good statement of the best argument against it. "Some people say, 'Our children are prohibited from praying.' But *our* kids pray. I don't want the politicians to write your prayers." The possibility of a tax on Social Security benefits was the home-run ball. "Social Security is a matter of right. It's a deal. I don't want to see that bargain broken." The inning ended with the Chrysler loan, a matter of direct interest since a local rubber company had Chrysler contracts. "The Republicans were willing to let Chrysler go down the drain. We saved it. That," Mondale concluded, "is what government is for—to help people when problems overwhelm them."

He pressed more flesh, and posed, on the blazing steps, with twin baby boys in matching T-shirts, one reading MON/19, the other DALE/84. They wriggled. The former Vice-President buzzed his lips ("That always works"), then returned to his car, back down the twisting road.

Theodore Sigvaard Mondale, one of the two men most responsible for Walter's thoughts on government and people, was a stern, determined man who lived and preached in rural Minnesota. The life required all his determination. Two of his farms were foreclosed; one of his churches burned; his first wife, Jesse, died of encephalitis. He himself got lockjaw after a home tonsillectomy, and devised a home cure: he would shove a top-shaped instrument between his teeth and screw his mouth open, after a year of which his jaws worked normally again. In 1925, on the verge of his fifties, he married Claribel Cowan. On January 5, 1928, in Ceylon, Minnesota, Walter Frederick (whence Fritz) was born. The family moved to Heron Lake and, finally, Elmore.

Mondale grew up the way half of America did at the turn of the century, and only a fraction of it does in the suburban now. He sold vegetables door to door; he collected corncobs to burn in the stove, for lack of wood. He worked at one point as a pea-lice inspector. The motto beneath his senior yearbook picture read: "A little nonsense now and then is relished by the best of men." He also absorbed politics. The Reverend Mondale stood at the cusp of rural religion and social uplift; he was a fervent supporter of the Farmer-Labor party, which later merged with the Minnesota Democrats, and he voted for Norman Thomas in 1932 (in part because FDR was a "wet"). When Fritz was ten, the elder Mondale drove the family to Washington in a flatbed truck. They called on one of their senators, who took them to lunch in the Senate dining room; the future senator came in bare feet.

Walter's second mentor was Hubert Humphrey. Humphrey was in his first term as mayor of Minneapolis when Mondale entered Macalester College across the river in St. Paul. Mondale worked on his re-election campaign; he also carried spears in the fight to subdue the supporters of Henry Wallace. "We're not going to let the political philosophy of the Democratic Farmer-Labor party be dictated from the Kremlin," Humphrey declared (he saw through the "foreign policy of restraint and reason," even if George McGovern didn't). Only six weeks after Humphrey's first Senate victory, in one of those transitions too pat for fiction, Theodore Mondale died. Walter took a year off to work in Washington. Back home, in law school, he worked for Humphrey's former campaign manager, Orville Freeman. Mondale became Freeman's campaign manager in a 1958 race for the statehouse. When the state attorney general resigned in 1960, Governor Freeman appointed the young lawyer to fill the vacancy.

Mondale had taken time out in 1955 to meet Joan Adams, a Presbyterian minister's daughter. (The Reverend Adams's parishes were a lot tonier than Theodore Mondale's had

ever been, though he too had voted for Norman Thomas.)
After eight dates, Mondale proposed.

Attorney General Mondale inherited a ripe investigation
—malfeasance in a charity for the handicapped—the kind
on which reputations are built. He built his, and at the next
election won handily in his own right. A second vacancy
occurred in 1964, with Humphrey's elevation to the vice-
presidency, and again Mondale was appointed to higher
office. He won his Senate seat on his own in 1966 and 1972.

Looking ahead to the post-Watergate election, he enter-
tained presidential ambitions, but after trailing "Don't
Know" in early polls, he dropped out. "I was impressed," he
recalled, "with how the American people adjusted to my
announcement." He was thus free to receive his last, and
loftiest, appointment, at Madison Square Garden in 1976.

Mondale's service as Carter's Vice-President was an am-
biguous credit. When Mondale said he had worked more
intimately with the Oval Office than any previous Vice-
President, it was simple truth. Spiro Agnew, whose offices
were in the Old Executive Office Building, would look
across the parking lot to the White House and say he might
as well have been in Baltimore. Mondale asked for, and got,
a central role in all Carter's decision making. On the other
hand, most of Carter's decisions were inept and unpopular.
Mondale's strategy, in later years, when confronted with
real turkeys, was to point out that he had opposed them in
private.

Humphrey once remarked of his protégé that he was the
only man in America who could get appointed President.
When Mondale made his formal announcement in February 1983, he chose for the site the political incubator that
had served him so well, the state capitol in St. Paul.

One of the benefits Carter wanted from a running mate
was the good opinion of the Democratic party's dominant
liberal wing. Walter Mondale supplied the need. Mondale
could have filled a whole Sunday *Times* with the words
"pragmatic progressive," but the ideas that animated him
had always been liberal. He began his career when twenti-

eth-century liberalism was in full, confident flood; he followed exactly its subsequent course.

Liberal economic thinking at the beginning of the eighties tended to take two forms: stimulating "traditional"
industries, through public works and various forms of
government-business cooperation; or encouraging new
technologies, according to the gospel of Jerry Brown. They
were not necessarily exclusive. Mondale edged into the second with his calls for more research. But over the years he
concentrated on the first. The Chrysler loan was one paradigm. Protection was another. For a while there in the fall
of 1982, Mondale was sounding like John Connally: "What
do we want our kids to do? Sweep up around Japanese
computers?" He came to say, as do most protectionists, that
we should erect tariffs against the Yellow Peril only as a
bargaining tool. At the height of the recession, Mondale
wanted the second tax-rate cut delayed six months and the
third repealed altogether. By the summer of 1983, he was
calling for repeal of the third for anyone making over
$60,000 (a warped-rate tax). He opposed indexing, and
wanted the Federal Reserve to reflate the currency, so as to
boost exports.

Mondale, like all Democrats, expressed shock at the Reagan deficits. He issued periodic plans for cutting them, of
which one constant element was "scal[ing] the defense budget back to reality." He opposed the B-1 and the MX, and
dismissed space laser planning as "Star Wars fantasies."
President Mondale planned to rely on the Stealth bomber,
the Trident submarine, and the cruise missile, though Senator Mondale had voted against the last two programs
throughout the seventies. He wanted to give SALT II another run in the Senate. Mondale did oppose the suggestion
that America forswear first use of nuclear weapons in a
European war—one point of agreement with Ronald Reagan. He had also opposed, as Vice-President, the post-Af-
ghanistan grain embargo—another point of agreement.

During the Carter administration, Mondale had pushed
for a Department of Education. When the Bakke case

reached the Supreme Court (Alan Bakke was a white med school applicant who claimed that the University of California's admissions policies discriminated against him), Mondale argued for a liberal stance—that is, one in favor of reverse discrimination. He supported ERA and abortion, which his handouts called "a private question of reproduction."

Behind almost every one of these issues stood some mobilized Democratic group. Mondale's economics was labor union economics. His Bakke position was the Urban League's and the NAACP's. His education policy was the NEA's; his stands on ERA and abortion were NOW's. When homosexual activists entered the lists, he keynoted a fundraiser for the Human Rights Campaign Fund, a homosexual PAC.

Mondale reaped the institutional rewards of his fealty. On September 30, 1983, the directors of the 1.7-million-member NEA gave him the organization's endorsement. Six days later, the AFL-CIO, convening in Hollywood, Florida, joined the Mondale column. On December 10, the governing board of NOW backed him, with the first presidential endorsement in its seventeen-year history. That same day, the Alabama Democratic Conference, the state's most important black political organization, gave Mondale the nod in Mobile.

From time to time throughout the campaign, Mondale's (unendorsed) rivals would depict these votes of confidence as venal transactions, as if Mondale had sold himself to get them. "He's a good lapdog," Ernest Hollings said of him, "he'll lick every hand." They got it backwards. Mondale was able to go to these groups, dog dish in hand, because he had been with them all along, fighting their fights. He had done it according to his temper—carefully, thoroughly, with sure, steady feet. He lacked any trace of the kamikaze, which some activists found uninspiring (when Mondale had an appendectomy in 1967, one Minnesota Democrat said, "I hope they stuffed him with some guts before sewing him up"). Still, he had fought. "I know you," he told the Alabama

Democratic Conference on the eve of its vote, "and you know me." Liberalism had endorsed the efforts of Mondale's groups, and they endorsed liberalism in the person of Mondale.

On the only cluster of issues which lacked a strong interest constituency, Mondale had also moved with the liberal pack ice. In September 1968, Senator Mondale called for an unconditional halt to the bombing of North Vietnam. That same month Hubert Humphrey, in the midst of his campaign, proposed a bombing halt as an "acceptable risk for peace." Thus the former harriers of Henry Wallace reached a position with regard to the world situation similar to George McGovern's. Not identical—McGovern in 1984 called, as we have seen, for a hefty defense budget cut. The Carter administration had increased the defense budget, and Mondale pledged as President to do the same—though by an increment about half that of Ronald Reagan's. But who had moved closer to whom? "Right now," Mondale declared at the California Democratic convention in January, "[if I were President], I'd get on that hot line and I'd say this: 'Dear Mr. Andropov, please meet me in Geneva this afternoon, and let's sit down and do some work to bring some easing of tensions.'"

He had brought the Reverend Mondale's message a long way from Ceylon, Minnesota.

In a backyard in Rochester, New Hampshire, thirty-odd people had congregated, a mixture of supporters and the curious. The daughter of the house asked Mondale to autograph her yearbook. She is the "pride of the high school," her mother informed him. The daughter could die. "She is, she is," Mom insisted, "President of her class."

(Signing) "I'm trying to be President myself. How did you do it?"

(Shyly) "I worked hard and I smiled a lot."

"That's just what I'm doing."

Poor Hoover was dragged from the grave once more. James Watt also had sparks of immortality in him. "I want

James Watt to stay on an extra day, because I want to fire him." Claps.

Nuclear arms control is "our single most important priority." On this, as on the environment, "this administration has been radical. Can we reach across this chasm of disagreement? I'd like to eliminate those dreadful weapons before they destroy us all.

"We need a President who knows what he's doing. I've spent my life learning it."

The sun sank, a cardinal descanted. Questions. Central America for the first time that day. "Two years ago, Central America was a problem, not a crisis. Now it's a crisis. We were beginning to make some progress. This crowd took over," and a political task "is now a military task. We should have learned in Vietnam." On the economy, he acknowledged that the recession was abating some, but he warned that the minute a real recovery began, "these interest rates'll go right through the roof."

Darkness had risen when Mondale reached Somersworth. Forty people had assembled in a house, new when Grover Cleveland had been a campaigner, that was an explosion of wood—dentils, fish scales, moldings, spindles, fanlights, beads, spokes, bouquets, blossoms, tendrils, bull's-eyes. The Watt line made another hit. "I also want to get rid of the person who appointed James Watt."

This crowd was composed entirely of supporters; by the time Mondale finished, they were revved up. One asked, incredulously, why he had lost in Wisconsin. Deadpan. "We were short of votes." He shook the last hands of the night, and left them to party, while he went out among the weeping crickets to catch a flight to Maine.

He did not believe that America had turned away from liberalism. He was probably right. Most Americans would have no objection in principle to the role of government he enunciated in the Farmington city hall. His problem was that liberalism, inevitably, had turned away from liberalism; that the role of helper and satisfier, so baldly asserted, has no logical end, but stretches to infinity; that, since the infinite desires of all would conflict, the desires of some must be chosen; so the common good envisioned by the old preacher, the new mayor, and the green student had become a collection of very particular goods—particular, and insatiable.

A terminal moraine is the hill of debris—pebbles, rocks, boulders—which a glacier pushes into place as it advances, then leaves behind when it melts. Walter Mondale was the terminal moraine of liberalism. Two last candidates, every bit as solidly left of center as he, claimed to have a view of something different beyond it.

Gary Hart's main political credential, and claim to Democratic attention, besides the fact that he was a two-term senator from Colorado, was that he had been George McGovern's campaign manager. Yet Hart downplayed that experience; he was no longer interested in how the party had got where it was, only in where it could go.

Hart came to the New York Hilton in the fall of 1983 to address a breakfast meeting of the Association for a Better New York, a group of boosters and businessmen. I drowsed over coffee while the master of ceremonies, a distinguished, white-haired executive, made the usual chitchat—a joke, a greeting, a thumbnail-clipping biography—until, after five minutes, I realized with a start that the man I was listening to was John Lindsay. *Young John Lindsay.* He had become a *memento mori* for all beautiful politicians.

Gary Hart in fact was neither all that young nor all that beautiful. The picture on the jacket of his first book, *Right from the Start,* a 1973 postmortem on the McGovern campaign, showed a wavy-haired would-be movie star; if you looked at it quickly, in dim light, you might see Warren Beatty. Ten years later, the sideburns were shorter and grayer, and the nose, lean and rugged straight on, had a beefy, Roman profile—late Roman. The face may have changed, but the mind had not. Many a trait that would characterize his 1984 campaign was prefigured in that memoir. The year 1972 had been Hart's introduction to

"special interests." When it became clear that McGovern
had won the nomination, all the Democratic party's pressure groups swarmed around him, and his campaign manager, with their requests and demands. Hart's account of
dealing with them at the Miami convention had the tone of
an Ayn Rand hero indignantly facing down the expropria-
tors. They wanted "to possess the campaign. There seemed
to be an unwillingness to accept the fact . . . that we were
not the creation or creature of any group." The McGovern
campaign had also prompted thoughts on the changing of
political generations. "The old must give way to the new.
The ineluctable tide of new generations" was "our most
certain protection against stagnation." But (here Rand gave
way to Freud) the old "relinquishes [its] power only under
duress, because the loss of power is a blunt reminder of
mortality."

The subject of his talk that morning was not the mortality
of his party's leaders, but "industrial strategy." America was
in need of one, he said; a technological revolution and a
burgeoning world market had so far been met only by a
"jumble of tax breaks and bailouts." Hart's non-jumble
would begin by toning up "keystone industries," on the
basis of "compacts worked out in the Oval Office" between
business and labor. "Infrastructure" would be another
pressing item. Hart hoped to institute a non-partisan inven-
tory of crumbling roads and bridges, to avoid pork-barreling. Workers meanwhile would be retrained for the future,
courtesy of a fund built up through deductions from their
paychecks.

Hart's latest book, *A New Democracy*, assembled for this
campaign, added other particulars: encouraging pension
funds to invest in deserving industries ("A 'made in America' answer to the Bank of Japan"); a Council on Emerging
Issues, analogous to the Council of Economic Advisers, for
peering ahead.

During the question period, Ned Regan, New York's Republican comptroller, threw a small rotten vegetable by
asking what the keystone industries were and who would

pick them. "We can all agree" what they are, Hart asserted, and went on to name some industries and the possible pickers. But then, we might *not* all agree, which is how logrolling and pork-barreling arise.

This new idea, at least, had a familiar ring to it—as familiar as the American cult of the manager. It appeals to corporate minds whenever they go to work in Washington. It appealed, most strongly, to the two Presidents who had engineering training, Hoover and Carter. In a fight with politics—exchanging real favors among real people—it always loses. Hart believed in his vision of orderliness (he voted against the Chrysler bailout), but one could, along with Ned Regan, all too easily foresee it rent into Carteresque tatters.

Hart had had better success with his other main interest, the military. He was a charter member of the military reform movement, a collection of theorists and politicians (Congressman Newt Gingrich [R., Ga.] was another leading light) pushing a variety of proposals designed to make the military more efficient and flexible. Hart wanted a return to the teaching of military theory in the service academies, and a turn to a regimental system on the British model ("Soldiers," he wrote in *A New Democracy,* "fight for their buddies"). He also wanted to replace the present strategic doctrine of attrition and firepower with one of maneuver and surprise: to replace, as it were, Ulysses S. Grant with Robert E. Lee. Maneuver warfare had the advantage that it could be accomplished with cheaper weapons—small carriers, to take a favorite Hart example, rather than the current behemoths. It had the possible disadvantage that most of history's great maneuverers (Lee, for instance) ultimately succumbed to attrition.

Gary Warren Hartpence was born, according to his campaign literature, November 28, 1937, in Ottawa, Kansas. His father sold farm equipment and his mother taught Sunday school; both belonged to the Church of the Nazarene, a breakaway sect that considered the Methodists too easygoing. Hartpence went to Bethany Nazarene College in Bethany, Oklahoma, where he met Lee (née Oletha) Ludwig; their marriage had survived two separations. He also met Prescott Johnson, a philosophy teacher who encouraged him to aim for bigger things. In 1958, Hartpence aimed for Yale Divinity School.

The midwestern boy (he had never before been east of Indiana) completed his bachelor's degree in divinity. But he had also begun swotting up literature and politics. He shortened his surname and went through Yale Law School.

Hart worked in Washington for four years, under Bobby Kennedy at Justice and Stewart Udall at Interior. After Nixon's election, he moved back West, to a private practice in Denver. In 1970, he sent a memo to Senator George McGovern offering political advice on carrying western states.

Hart wrote later that McGovern lost the election on the issues. His own maiden campaign, for Colorado senator in the banner Democratic year of 1974, hit the issues skillfully. The New Deal, he said, had become dogmatized; it was time for new ideas ("new ideas," in the context of Hart's career, was an old idea). He beat the incumbent, Peter Dominick, soundly. Six years later, he had to struggle: Mary Estill Buchanan, a liberal Republican, held him to just over 50 percent.

Hart got off to an early start in his presidential campaign, but for the longest time he ran in place. Mondale and Glenn had the headlines; Cranston was showing long-shot political finesse. On the stump, Hart frequently gave signs of having a higher opinion of himself than anyone else was ever likely to have. Making a pitch in front of the National Women's Political Caucus, Hart ran fifteen minutes over his time limit, and ignored repeated warnings that his time was up. The women judged him excessively patriarchal.

Hart had one insight, or at least a necessary prelude to an insight. He believed that the Democratic party had lost the 1980 elections for a reason. Its ideas had failed, and it needed new ones. This had been his most important lesson from 1972. McGovern had "brought to the surface a whole new generation of political organizers . . . But he did not bring out a new generation of thinkers. He did not because it [wasn't] there. . . . American liberalism was near bankruptcy." Walter Mondale did not believe any such thing. He couldn't; if he represented the national consensus now, and had represented it in 1980, then Reagan's election was a freak, an aberrant conjunction of variables: Carter's manner, Soviet restlessness, stagflation, the hostage crisis. The trouble with Hart's new ideas was that they vanished at the first hard look. Most of the new thoughts weren't new, and the rest weren't thoughtful. His call for a generation of new leaders (led by himself) also eluded sense. What new generation was he talking about? Hart was closer to Mondale's age than Mondale was to Reagan's. He was born before World War II. He was in grad school when Kennedy was shot, in grade school when Roosevelt died. He remembered Packards. When such things were pointed out to him, he would explain that the new generation was defined by its mind-set, not by its birth date. Which went right back to new ideas . . .

The Hart campaign was interesting; but it looked to be a dilettante's interest, of short duration.

The Reverend Jesse Jackson, the last Democrat to announce his candidacy, flew to Damascus on December 29. On January 3, he left with Lieutenant Robert Goodman, who had been shot down in a sortie over Lebanon, and returned to Andrews Air Force Base the next day. The second-guessing and the instant-replaying began almost immediately: Since the Syrians gave Goodman up, it could only have been because they had nothing to gain by keeping him, and nothing to lose by letting him go, particularly to a black, pro-Arab Democratic presidential candidate *(take that, Reagan)* playing off his own bat. But Wednesday the fourth was Jackson's day. He spoke at an evening rally in the Shiloh Baptist Church in one of Washington's run-down black neighorhoods.

Rally or service? The pillars that supported the gallery were festooned with red-and-silver foil. A red-and-green banner, "Tithe for God," hung over the pulpit. There was a standing-room-only congregation, maybe six hundred people, all but a dozen of them black, and all dressed to the nines. The older women and Queen Elizabeth use the same hatmaker (Quentin Crisp thought such hats sit on the top shelves of closets, waiting to leap out onto unsuspecting heads below). With a bounce, a grand piano cued the green-robed choir, which strode swayingly down the side aisles, singing, *"He has done great things for me, I'm gonna be a witness for Him."* (Jesus or Jesse?)

"A family," the pastor began, "is grateful. A community is grateful. A nation is grateful. A world that has known many wars is grateful—because a soldier and a son has returned home. Lieutenant Goodman has returned to this land of the free and home of the brave. Speaking of land of the free, an outstanding citizen went to a distant land and returned a captive. Speaking of home of the brave, this man had the courage to go and bring home a captive. It is said: All that is necessary for evil to prevail is that good men do nothing. We are glad this man did something." ("When," a four-year-old who had squeezed with his mother into the press section asked, "is Jesse Jackson coming?") "Most of all, we are grateful to God." *Yes*, cried a voice, voices. "We are grateful to Him because in the words of the New Testament, Blessed are the peacemakers." *Yes*. "For they shall be called the children of God." *Yes*.

But the four-year-old and this twenty-eight-year-old had to sit through a veritable Chinese fire drill of introducers and introducers of introducers, ministers and pols (Walter Fauntroy, District of Columbia delegate-at-large; Marion Barry, mayor of Washington), all saying their piece and grabbing a piece of the spotlight. The worst was first, a stout white minister whose name slipped past, who had forecast the coming election, he explained, from Second Samuel, thus: David had been one of eight sons, just as Jackson was one of eight candidates; David and Jackson were each the youngest; and David's father was named Jesse, which bent the parallel a little, but the congregation treated him with indulgence. The best was second to last, Dr. Franklin Richardson, general secretary of the National Baptist Convention. "We've come here tonight," he said, heavy and sweating, "to affirm and celebrate that God does work in human history. God interrupted the affairs of men, and caused the pilot to fall from the sky. If we have a personality on which we can hang our hopes and our dreams, O what a blessing it is. O what a blessing it is to believe that justice can flow like a mighty stream. O what a blessing it is that we are on the threshold of a new day.

"Testimonies are more important than titles. Pharaoh had a title, but Moses had a testimony." *Teach.* "Nebuchadnezzar had a title, but Daniel had a testimony." *Preach.* "Agrippa had a title, but Paul had a testimony." *Teach, preach.* "Pilate had a title, but Jesus had a testimony." Bedlam. "Ronald Reagan has a title . . ." Two-minute standing ovation. "Ronald Reagan has a title" (did the sly old shouter repeat himself because he sensed the continuity had been interrupted for the TV cameras?), "Jesse Jackson has a testimony." Pandemonium.

He was the best, that is, until the last introducer, Louis Farrakhan, leader of the Nation of Islam. Farrakhan, who had been part of Jackson's Syrian expedition, was not yet generally famous. He wore a high-collared shirt and a natty off-yellow bow tie with a matching handkerchief.

"In the name of Allah the Merciful . . ." he began in a soft voice, his gestures small, precise, almost effeminate. Every rule book of speechmaking tells you to build to your climaxes. Farrakhan didn't build; he went, without warning, to warp speed. "Give God the glory. Men's shoulders are too weak to accept praise." But there was praise coming. "He used our brother as an instrument of His peace. As long as we remain humble, He exalts us because He has the power to raise us higher and higher and greater and greater." *Teach, teach.* "America, you have not been good. You have not been just. You have not been kind. You enslaved an innocent nation that did you no wrong." He bounced on the balls of his feet, brandished a green-cov-

ered Koran. "Those who claim to have the light have it no
more." Those like, in the seventh century, Byzantium and
Persia (Mohammed's first enemies); in the twentieth, America and Russia. Fauntroy, at the end of the dais, listened
rapt, grinned like the Cheshire Cat. "The Christian world is
in darkness, the Moslem world is in darkness, the Jewish
world is in darkness. In the United States is spiritual darkness. Here sits a man—" Jackson, sitting behind Farrakhan,
shook his head, as if to demur. "From the son of slaves,
comes one saying, 'I have a vision.' He was more than presidential, he was God-like." Downshift, *subito.* "Listen: the
spirit of God is moooving in the world. It's bigger—than
guns. It's bigger—than bullets." Fans flicked in the hot
building. Farrakhan wound it up, Jackson embraced him,
the piano kicked in. Thirty signs waved: GOD BLESS YOU/
JESSE JACKSON.

At last, we got what we were waiting for. A white photog-
rapher, ponytailed and mustached, looking as if he'd missed
a connection and come there from 1969 by mistake, forgot
his camera and clapped and beamed. Jackson, forty-two,
actually looked more boyish than he did ten years ago.
Cover up the British infantry sergeant's mustache, and
those big, wide eyes would have looked about eight. His
voice was ragged and cracked. (Farrakhan sat at his side,
mopping his brow, drinking water.) He was tired from traveling, he said, and Brother Farrakhan had preached sufficiently unto the hour. He read out the telephone numbers
of campaign operatives in a flat, administrative voice, and I
thought, *They've topped their main act.* Foolish me.

"Mr. Reagan has been President now for—" *Too long.* "—
three years. . . . There are more people on welfare. There
are more people in poverty than since 1965." More infant
mortality, malnutrition, and tuberculosis. "Our mission is
not to fight fire with fire. If the Democratic candidates
embrace the invasion of Grenada; if they embrace the military budget; if they do not support sanctions for South Africa; if they do not enforce the Voting Rights Act—they're
trying to fight fire with fire.

"Throughout the history of this nation, there has been a struggle between the restrictionists and the expansionists." History prompted a digression. "America started with a military dictatorship, overthrowing a repressive regime. These militarists ran the country for a decade. Then they called on the best minds of that day" to write a constitution. "They looked at black people, and calculated us as three-fifths of a person. With all their brilliance, they didn't have the brilliance to count to one. Women couldn't vote—restrictions. Blacks couldn't vote—restrictions. Common workers couldn't vote—restrictions. It was an aristocracy, by any practical definition, called a democracy. One hundred years later, there was a Civil War. Brothers and sisters, mothers and fathers, destroyed each other in a fit of greed. One hundred years later still, blacks could vote. So there was this struggle between expansionists for freedom and those trying to shut them up. If you don't know where restriction is, you will watch ball games. You will choose entertainment over education. If you don't know any better, you will put dope in your veins instead of hope in your brains.

"You are not," Jackson said, "midgets. You are not grass-hoppers. You are not the bottom of the nation—you are the foundation. The bottom is where you end up when you fall. The foundation is where you *begin with*. You can do without a bottom, not a foundation. If you live in a twenty-three-story building in the penthouse, if the roof *falls*, no one cares, except those who live in the penthouse. If the foundation shakes, everybody must make adjustments. We must shake the foundation. Our time has come."

He shifted from strictures to the potential they bind. "The deep-sea diver knows the dive is worth it, because there are pearls. . . . If you ever get them, if you ever polish them, the dive was worth it. . . . Who knows but what in some child's mind—born out of wedlock—" *Yes.* (Jackson was.) "—locked into welfare, might be the cure for cancer? Who knows but what in the mind of some child in the slums, might be the equation for world peace? . . .

Boards of education distribute money. *God* distributes genius.

"Reach out! Make room for the locked out!" From time to
time, Jackson stepped back, with a ballet dancer's lift, or a
bullfighter's. "Whenever we feel restrictions, we react.
When the Democratic National Committee says you must
have 20 percent to have your vote count . . ." An issue; the
party's rules, revised in 1981, required candidates in primaries to win 20 percent of the vote in a congressional district
before they could be awarded delegates; Jackson claimed it
discriminated against blacks. ". . . You mean one person
gets 19.9 and gets zero, another gets 20.1 and gets forty?
That isn't New Math, it's *bad* math." Laughter. "No winner
take all, winner take what you *get.* Ain't no statute of limitations on stealing . . .

"I don't want America"—back to the general—"to with-
draw the invitation that made America great. When the
television stations go off at night, they don't show bombs
bursting on people, they show bombs bursting in air. When
the television stations go off at night, they don't show you
Indians drowning in their tears, marching west. When the
television stations go off at night, they don't show blacks
coming bound and shackled and chained. They show you
the Statue of Liberty, inscribed, 'Give me your tired, your
poor, your huddled masses yearning to breathe free.' . . .
Stretch out! Reach out! When you give life, you gain. When
you help somebody there's a divine law of reciprocity—you
can't help but be helped." Farrakhan, revived, riveted,
blurted, *You are amazing!*

"Saul of Tarsus"—it was inevitable—"was saved through
grace, knocked from his horse, traveling to Damasscuss"—
hissed sibilants—"Syria. Greats things seem to happen on
the road to Damascus. Early one December morning, not
far from the birthday of Christ, not far from the birth*place*
of Christ, another young man was knocked from his place.
. . . The spirit moved in us, we took the wings of morning
. . . a chance for the giants to talk *to* each other, not *at* each
other."

Jackson's standard peroration concerned America's special duties—to "the children in the dawn of life, the poor people in the pit of life, the old people in the sunset of life." That night, he elaborated on each element, taking as his symbol of old people his grandmother. Words outran my flagging wrist, and I could only reconstruct.

"My grandmother. She's old now; she's eighty. She can't read or write. She's a genius—you can't live to be eighty in this country and not read or write unless you're a genius." Laughter. "Her sight's bad now, but she has *in*sight. I remember when I was a little boy, she took me by the hand and whispered in my ear, 'If you put your head in God's hand, you can *be something* someday.' My grandmother." *Grandmother.* "And she can't walk like she used to. Her legs are all arthritic. But when she was younger and she missed her bus to go to work, she *walked.* My grandmother." *Grandmother.* "And she can't lift what she used to. Her arms are weak. But when she saw the children of the people she worked for reading and writing, she thought, Why can't my children do that? And she'd lift—heavy books she couldn't understand—so I could read. My grandmother!" *Grandmother!*

At evening's end, he asked everyone who was not registered to vote to come forward and do so. He had spoken for forty-five minutes without a note. How can you argue, as Reagan said in the Rose Garden celebration of Goodman's return later that week, with success?

Jesse Louis Jackson was not dealt the sort of hand usually associated with success. He was born October 8, 1941, in Greenville, South Carolina, son of Noah Robinson and Helen Burns, a high school student. Robinson was married —to someone else. When Jesse was two, his mother married his namesake, Charles Jackson, a post office janitor. Thirteen years later, Jackson formally adopted him. All that time, however, the Robinsons continued to live next door. "When Jesse was nine," according to biographer Barbara Reynolds, "Robinson would see him standing in the backyard, gazing into [his] window."

"As soon as I would go to the window and wave," Robinson remembered, "he would wave back and run away."

Jackson ran hard in high school: honor roll, French club,
quarterback of a championship football team. He went to
the University of Illinois on a football scholarship, and trans-
ferred after a year to North Carolina Agricultural and Technical State University in Greensboro. In 1964, he married
Jacqueline Brown. He headed back North to attend the
Chicago Theological Seminary, but left in 1965 to work for
Martin Luther King in Selma.

The Southern Christian Leadership Conference (SCLC)
gave the bright go-getter his start. It was also the occasion
for one of the more controversial episodes in his career.
After King was shot in Memphis, Jackson claimed to have
been at his side to hear his dying words—an account of the
pietà universally disputed by the old King cadre. "I would
never support Jesse Jackson to be president of Martin Luther King's organization," said Ralph Abernathy. "That's a
moral thing." (Abernathy later supported him—immorally?
—for President.)

But Jackson was striking out on his own. Ordained in
1968, he became, in a phrase of Edmund Burke's not
quoted at Shiloh Baptist, a political theologian and a theological politician. He announced for mayor of Chicago
against Richard Daley in 1971, abortively; challenged the
Illinois delegation at the 1972 Democratic convention, successfully; turned out the vote for Republican Senator
Charles Percy against conservative Democrat Alex Seith in
1978, and for mayoral candidate Harold Washington in
1983.

Jackson's main effort was Operation PUSH (People
United to Save—later, Serve—Humanity). The theme of all
its projects was black self-help; the pattern of many of them
was a bright idea—proclaimed by Jackson—and faltering
follow-through. PUSH threatened black boycotts of firms—
Coca-Cola, 7-Up, Heublein (Kentucky Fried Chicken)—unless they agreed to put more blacks in better jobs and do
more business with black firms and banks. In 1982, PUSH

took on Anheuser-Busch, which called its bluff. The ensuing boycott fell flat, and Jackson made an agreement with the brewers that was not significantly different from their previous practice. In the course of the struggle, a black newspaper, the East St. Louis *Sentinel,* accused a PUSH subsidiary, the International Trade Bureau, of, in effect, taking kickbacks. (The bureau registered black businessmen—with whom cowed corporations could deal— for a $5,000 fee: "If you want to play," Jackson was quoted as saying, "you've got to pay.") PUSH sued for libel, but settled out of court after being ordered to produce its records. Sloppy accounting also hurt PUSH-EXCEL, an educational crusade begun in 1976 to encourage children to study ("What does it matter if we have a new book or an old book if we open neither?"). By 1981, PUSH-EXCEL had rounded up thirty-five participating high schools and $4.5 million in federal grants. The Reagan Department of Education stopped the grants, and discovered more than $2 million of undocumented or unjustified spending.

Jackson ventured into foreign policy. He flayed America's dealings with South Africa. In 1979, he went to the Middle East, where he bussed Yasir Arafat ("a true hero"). He picked for director of PUSH's International Department one Jack O'Dell, an old Communist booted out of the SCLC in 1963.

In the grim Reagan years, Jackson turned to voter registration. His stem-winder to the twentieth-anniversary March on Washington was a state-by-state incantation of totals of unregistered blacks—"rocks lying around" to smite the Reaganite Goliath. All through the summer of 1983, he swung through the South, signing up voters. Many of them, it seemed, wanted to vote for him. Jackson announced his candidacy on November 3.

Since Jesse Jackson's chances of becoming President were to say the least slight, speculation focused, as with McGovern, on what he was really up to. Jackson's campaign was framed as a Rainbow Coalition of all hues and creeds; yet Jackson's best opportunity in the whole exercise was to become black spokesman. Once he achieved that goal, King could have died in George Wallace's arms, for all it would matter. This was one function of Jackson's vendetta over the delegate rules—to make himself an image and incarnation of black disadvantagement. It was also a reason for the coolness of other black leaders toward his candidacy. Julian Bond, Andrew Young, Benjamin Hooks, were being eclipsed, and they knew it. Some preferred to be brokers with Mondale rather than acolytes for Jackson.

The position of Number One Black could have increased political clout, largely because of Jackson's efforts. He had visions of unregistered black landslides, which were fantasies. But if black turnout were to increase by only 5 percent over 1980 (assuming also, not unreasonably, that blacks would vote 93 percent Democratic), seven states—Alabama, Arkansas, Massachusetts, Mississippi, North Carolina, South Carolina, Tennessee—would show a Democratic increase larger than Reagan's 1980 plurality. Of course, there would be no benefit if Reagan's vote increased.

Ideologically, Jackson was poised at the beginning of 1984 to go any number of ways. What had always distinguished his public performance from previous black phenomena was a healthy disengagement from whites, whether as objects of hatred or purveyors of handouts. "While I know that the victimizer is responsible for the victim being down," he once told an interviewer, "the victim must be responsible for getting up." (Perhaps Jackson's childhood influenced him here; the first, worst thing that was ever done to him was done by people with black faces, and he knew it.) Preaching or politicking, Jackson had been primarily concerned with the advancement of blacks, and by their own efforts. Hence his calls to replace dope in veins with hope in brains; to rally blacks to the polling place, or away from Budweiser. Hence even (in part) his desire for a black foreign-policy icon, such as South Africa, and his unwillingness to nod to the Jewish icon, Israel.

What Jackson lacked was judgment. Any advance was as good, to him, as any other, however accomplished—

whether by joining the mainstream economy or seceding from it, whether by work and study or by welfare and rhetoric. Since blackness was not enough to fuel a presidential campaign, even a symbolic one, Jackson was obliged to speak to other issues, where his indiscriminateness showed even more strongly. He trimmed his sails on abortion: Jackson, pre-campaign, called it "murder" (his mother had considered aborting him, until her minister talked her out of it); Jackson the candidate, while refusing to "encourage" it, said women had a God-given freedom to choose. When Jackson was in Syria, his wife went, with Bella Abzug and others, to Nicaragua, seeking "to raise the consciousness of the American people and to make them recognize the struggle here for peace and free self-determination." Jackson's white supporters looked like scrap from left-wing body shops: Ramsey Clark, Randall Forsberg, Barry Commoner.

Jackson was not in the liberal impasse, for he was not a traditional liberal. Over the years white liberals had defended blacks, stood up for them, spoken for them; now a black wanted to speak. Liberalism offered blacks a place at the table. Jackson wanted the head, or a new seating. It would be interesting—it would be a vital interest to whoever got the nomination—to see where he would go.

4
The Search for Mondale

The Magnificent Eight were all respectful of each other. It was, among other things, in each one's interest to be so. There was a definite sense, in almost all of their 1983 joint appearances, that the quality of the group reflected on the quality of the individual: What a good person I am, they seemed to be saying, to belong to such a good party, that has so many good people . . . But since nominations don't go to committees, the candidates were obliged, as the first for-real voting approached, to demonstrate each other's deficiencies.

The innovation of this election, designed to help the candidates for the Democratic nomination mix it up, was the televised debate. Strictly speaking, they were not debates at all. There was almost no opportunity for candidates to interact; the formats, which varied, permitted them to ask questions of each other, with questioner and questionee chosen by lot beforehand. (Cranston and Hollings rehearsed an exchange before the New York City debate in October. "Fritz," Cranston asked, "why do you think the press keeps calling this a two-man race?"—whereafter the candidates were sternly warned not to cheat.) There was little time for extended presentation, the three-minute summation being the longest they were allowed to run at a stretch. Essentially, the debates were competitive press conferences. Since the press conference itself is an effort by a candidate to slip in as many paragraphs of his stump speech as he can, the debates were discontinuous, mixed orations—Cuisinart stump speeches. With a field of eight candidates, at least five of whom were generally unknown, this was not a bad thing. There would have been no point trying to plumb the depths of Ernest Hollings's soul when people in San Diego and Pittsburgh didn't know his face.

The debates performed one other function, though; they offered opportunities for the dramatic moment—the phrase that would linger, the good new line that would stick. Ronald Reagan had improvised such a moment in his Nashua, New Hampshire, debate with George Bush in 1980,* and sprung a prepared line on Jimmy Carter during the election: "There you go again." Occasionally in 1984 the press interlocutors asked tough questions (the strength of the press is not cleverness, but persistence). But the most memorable moments would come from the candidates themselves. The successful candidates were those who fashioned the most resonant events. They were also, frequently, the candidates who were willing to ignore the rules. The politicians who sat back and waited to speak until spoken to did not get heard.

The eight came together for the first time in 1984 at Dartmouth College on January 15, one month before the Iowa caucuses, five weeks before the New Hampshire pri-

---

* Reagan and Bush were scheduled for a two-man debate under the auspices of the Nashua *Telegraph*. There arose a problem about the cost, and the Reagan campaign agreed to foot the bill. The Reagan camp then decided to invite the other candidates to join in. When Bush and the *Telegraph* editor insisted on sticking with the original format, Reagan bellowed, "I paid for this microphone"—an echo, probably unconscious, of Reagan's slogan on the Panama Canal four years earlier: "We bought it, we paid for it, it's ours, and we're going to keep it." Then, as before, Republicans went wild.

mary. The snowy nowhere of Hanover was overrun with green-badged reporters and clean-cut young men with wires running out of their ears. Quilts of snow wrapped every tree branch and cornice. Two lunatics paraded in front of the Hanover Inn, offering to boost the field to ten. Pro-lifers rallied on the subfreezing green across from the auditorium where the debate took place, carrying hand-done signs with scrunched-up letters along the right-hand margin: BE A GIVER, NOT A TAKER—CHOOSE LIFE; ARE WHALES BETTER THAN BABIES? Their speakers were equally unpolished. "It's only a few steps," warned one, "before we degenerate into mass murder, and other things." They would be coming, snow or shine, to every major Democratic event for the next ten months.

Glenn was the man carrying the hidden hardball that afternoon, though he did not pitch it for nearly two hours. The eight took their places by drawing numbers out of the dun-colored top hat of Daniel Webster (Dartmouth, Class of 1801). "When Glenn starts talking," said someone in the audience, "that's when you need the sleeper seats." There were two moderators, splitting the event between them. Phil Donahue, white-haired now but forever fifteen, paced among his followers, telling them they were okay. It was "an opportunity to become more familiar with the men who wish to serve you from the White House." Ted Koppel took the first inning. "I will only be here ninety minutes. You gentlemen will be here three hours. Don't drink a lot of water."

Koppel showed some initial asperity. His first question asked if there might be a woman running mate; after Glenn, Jackson, Hart, and Mondale gave their speechlets on equal rights, Koppel urged "anyone else [who] would like to say something nice about women" to speak up. But the candidates settled down, or Koppel became resigned, and the event continued with the proper decorum.

The conventional wisdom on Askew and Hollings was that they were running for Vice-President (so it was thought of all southern politicians, from the Civil War until

Jimmy Carter, and he was probably as damaging to the hopes of future Southerners as Appomattox). They didn't look like very attractive Veeps. Askew had brought along a wrench which he had bought in a hardware store but which the Pentagon was purchasing for hundreds of dollars more. Even this visual aid, however, did not penetrate the ramble. Hollings managed to hijack a discussion of the nuclear freeze. "I want to talk about the budget freeze, something I *can* do in four years." It became clear, however, that his budget freeze had holes sawed in the ice. He proposed a coast-to-coast day-care-center system, which received the scorn of Phil Donahue: "Here come the spending Democrats!"

Cranston hastened to stake out the nuclear freeze first thing. "I have the best chance" of achieving one "because I'm the only one" who would make it "the central purpose of my presidency." He asserted that he had been opposing nuclear weapons since 1945. "I met Albert Einstein; he warned me of the danger." Later, he called Ronald Reagan "a trigger-happy President." McGovern was the more attractive McGovernite. He got off the cleverest line of the afternoon. "I don't know who my running mate will be," he told Koppel. "I want to make one pledge. This time, I'll be careful." His remedy for military spending was to "get hold of somebody like Lee Iacocca and make him Secretary of Defense."

Hart got to mention his characteristic themes—new ideas, and, where defense spending was concerned, that "better is better." "What does that mean?" Koppel asked, reasonably. Hart explained it meant higher pay and less complex, more effective weapons. Most of what he said, though, was standard Democratic foreign policy, even slightly to the left of standard. He noted that Carter "and Mondale" had reintroduced draft registration, and that "the problem in Central America is poverty. . . . [We should] challenge Castro to elevate the standard of living" there. For South Africa, five minutes later, he prescribed a "deadline" for the end of apartheid, to be followed if missed by "all-out economic sanctions."

No one had gotten a fix on Jackson yet. He had come back with Lieutenant Goodman only twelve days earlier. He looked like a tropical fish in a tank full of carp; he also had the noisiest claque, which clapped and whooped at every pointed line that fell from his lips, as if such cleverness had never been heard before. His exotic position did, in fact, allow him to say some genuinely novel things. Three times, he noted that Western Europe and Japan had matured and ought to pay for more of their own defense. Taking a leaf from PUSH-EXCEL, he said that one reason for declining educational performance was that kids watched too much TV. Donahue whiffed a crazier notion than Hollings's day-care centers—"the federal government can't control how much *TV* children watch"—but Jackson responded, to general applause, that "it's got to be a common effort."

And Glenn—poor Glenn—he sounded as if he had taken elocution lessons from Askew. To a simple, early question from Koppel—wouldn't shifting from nuclear to conventional weapons cost money?—he gave a dizzy spin of the globe: Africa, Syria, Iraq, Ethiopia, South Yemen, Angola, Kampuchea (the "old Cambodia," he explained helpfully), the northern islands of Japan. And what about all these places? We had to "look at what the Soviets are doing" there. End of (non)answer. His solution to the deficit was a "pay-as-you-go plan"—more of an engineer's fantasy than anything Hart ever dreamed up. Since Congress always wants more than it can pay for, the question would become —as it has always been—what would you *not* pay for as you went? That, in turn, would require choices, which people would be entitled to some preview of. But that would require Glenn to make some in his own mind—a more difficult project than paying as you go. He also envisioned a 10 percent surtax. "We have to be honest enough to ask for sacrifices from the American people."

So he limped, until halfway through the Donahue segment. Mondale was taking a turn at the deficit. Mondale had sat self-contained and a little hunched throughout, as if it was a function he should not have had to attend. His answers were distant, but also crisp and clear. He had come up with some numbers for closing the budget gap. He would produce others throughout the year. They were, like everyone's numbers, fantasies—attempts to measure the tide by grabbing a handful of water. He gave, however, a very precise notion of how he would proceed in office. "Corporations," he began, "have gotten away with murder . . ."

Glenn interrupted. "That's the same vague gobbledygook of nothing we've heard throughout this campaign. . . . Is this going to be a Democratic party that promises everything to everybody and then not even bothering to go through the checkout counter? I wish the former Vice-President would make specific proposals that can be compared."

Mondale rose out of his seat like a Roman candle. "There's just been about a six-minute speech, all of it baloney." Askew got a word in. "They're both right about each other." "We must approach this," Jackson admonished, "in a vein of seriousness."

It was fun. For Glenn, fun and futile. He had chosen to attack Mondale on the point—gobbledygook—on which he himself was most vulnerable. What else could he do? (It all went back to Glenn's fundamental problem: how do you shoulder aside someone with whom you basically agree? By reciting the Pledge of Allegiance?) Donahue switched to Hart, who said, "you cannot lead this country if you've promised everybody everything." Mondale broke back in. "I haven't promised everything. I have promised to put people back to work . . . to protect the environment . . . to pass the ERA . . . to seek a safer world . . . to give old people a friend in the White House. What's America about, if not promises?" There was a rhetorical U-turn—from no promises to all promises, in seven phrases. They could have smelled the burning rubber in Boston.

Finally, they could drink all the water they wanted. The

crisp blue sky was black. Each candidate held a post-debate reception in some college building on the green. Jackson's was full. "Let's go see Glenn," said a disappointed student. "He looks like Jackson."

There were no overt clashes at the second confrontation, three and a half weeks later in Des Moines. But Mondale received a quiet question far more damaging than Glenn's assault.

The debate was delayed by fog. The state was blanketed; Hart had been forced to land in Omaha and drive. Except for two minutes of the afternoon, he needn't have rushed. His notions of revitalizing the economy seemed older and older. He defended his vote against the Chrysler loan by explaining that he had opposed it only because it was a one-shot deal. "I don't believe government ought to go around bailing out individual companies." The Chrysler loan might, however, serve as a paradigm for whole industries. Hart also remarked that he couldn't "remember anyone saying in three years that Ronald Reagan has read a book." Hart had done a thesis on Faulkner at Yale Divinity School; he had managed, in taking two graduate degrees, to read the books every studious English major reads, which certainly made him a prodigy among politicians. Still, he might better have left the line to Hollings. Most of the fire that night was directed at Reagan. Mondale thought the international situation was "as dangerous now as it has been in the history of the world." Cranston declared that "fear and hatred are the legacy of Ronald Reagan," and that "America's vision of peace and freedom" was being "blasted by the guns of the U.S. Navy in Lebanon, the guns of U.S. paratroopers in Grenada, and the guns of U.S. helicopters in Honduras and El Salvador." Reagan, Glenn said, with disapproval, had never looked Yuri Andropov in the eye or shaken his hand (the former KGB leader had died two days before). It was a "modern tragedy," McGovern agreed, that Reagan had never met him. One of a panel of five Iowans who questioned the candidates—a peculiarity of this debate —suggested that the eight of them make up for it by going together to the funeral. Lebanon accounted for a large number of condemnations, even though the Marines were being withdrawn to offshore ships even as the candidates spoke. They redeployed their criticisms, from the incompetence of the operation to the immorality of the policy (Glenn called it a "moral outrage"). Reagan was flayed on other subjects. "Do not let Mr. Reagan get his hands" on the Supreme Court, Mondale warned. "It could well be the end of the rest of justice in America." The best way to ensure equal opportunity for blacks, said Jackson, was to "retire this repressive regime."

In ten days, it would be the moment of truth for Askew. "Join the Askew Ambush," his leaflets invited; he made a desperate appeal for right-to-life highwaymen. "I speak for those who value the potential of life both before and after birth." Wrong audience, wrong party. "Wouldn't you make a greater contribution to the right to life," asked the man whose convention Askew had keynoted, "if you came out for a nuclear freeze?" Big hand. McGovern was in excellent form generally. "What lessons," Cranston asked him, "did you learn" from 1972 "to help us beat Ronald Reagan?" "There are some things," McGovern replied with dignity, "worse than losing an election. I wouldn't change places with the man who won." Another big hand. He did offer advice. Most mistakes came from fatigue; "so don't try to work too hard to catch up to me." His closing pitch was masterly. "If you agree with me, you owe me a vote, for this reason: . . . that's the only way you can send a message to the eventual winner. Don't throw away your conscience." A huge hand. In their hearts, they knew he was right.

No one would be throwing their conscience away on Glenn; perhaps he sensed it. He flailed at "special-interest leaders, kingmakers, bosses" who had told the party "we have spoken, you don't need to think anymore." For the rest, he seemed harried and lost, and made the mistake of trying to embarass Hollings by suggesting that he had opposed equal opportunity hiring quotas on Capitol Hill. Hollings ticked off his hiring record, and stuffed the shot back in

Glenn's face. "It's not what you say, it's what you do. You just all confused in that *cap*sewel of yours."

But the big score went to Hart. Have you ever, he asked Mondale about ten minutes before the Glenn-Hollings dustup, disagreed with organized labor? "They came to me," Mondale answered. "They trust me." He berated Reagan, then returned to the main point. "I'm my own person —a candidate they can trust, not one they can run." In the context of the debate, it was a forceful answer. It was even partly true. It also completely evaded the question. Mondale had reacted like a fundamentalist asked to enumerate his disagreements with Holy Scripture. In fact, he had disagreed with labor—on the Clinch River breeder reactor, which environmentalists opposed and labor (the work force) supported; also on the Simpson-Mazzoli bill, an attempt to deal with illegal aliens—labor had supported it (protection of the work force), while the Hispanic lobby in Congress, to which Mondale deferred as the relevant interest, opposed it. But it took him two days to think of these examples. The delay was noted.

Not in Iowa. The big loser of the Des Moines debate had been Glenn. He had done indifferently, and he had needed a miracle. He had begun to talk, in the final pre-caucus days, not only of the forces of darkness, bosses and kingmakers, but of the "sensible center," the forces of light who would rally to his crashing campaign. A poll in the Des Moines *Register* outlined part of his problem. Even supposing Glenn had something definite to offer the "center," there would be little of it to draw on on caucus night. Sixty-four percent of all Iowans, according to the *Register*, called themselves "conservative," as opposed to 33 percent "liberal." Among registered Democrats, the percentages were more nearly equal, but "conservatives" still held the lead, 50 to 44. Among those who "definitely" intended to attend the caucuses, the percentage was reversed—30 percent conservative to 66 percent liberal. The process was circular —there was no gung-ho core of centrists, because Glenn had done nothing, in his rhetoric or in his proposals, to

energize them. The cavalry can't make a rescue in the last
reel unless some cavalry exists.

Glenn had budgeted February 18, the last Saturday before the Monday caucuses, for a swing through the western
end of the state. It was also the twenty-second anniversary
of his flight. The weather was a demonstration of why space
shots are not launched from Iowa. The Glenn campaign
flew a load of reporters from Des Moines to await Glenn's
arrival in Sioux City. The snow arrived first.

Glenn supporters trickled into the private airline out-
building where he was due to arrive, with snow dusting
their shoulders and the bouquets they had brought. Beyond
the plate-glass windows the warm, wet flakes whirled down.
Half a hundred reporters slumped in front of a television
set, watching "The Best of Billiards." From time to time, a
radio receiver crackled out bingo cancellations and road
reports: ". . . completely covered with pack snow and ice
. . . visibility is poor, travel is difficult . . . flood warnings
. . ." "We'll know in fifteen minutes," the hopeful Glenn
staff announced, "if Senator Glenn's plane is going to land."

The snow fell faster. Plows roared over the runways, to no
effect. People who stepped out to check the sky returned
after a minute with their entire windward flanks white and
mottled. A full hour and a half later, there was the faint
buzz of a plane making a pass. Glenn had probably been
safer on *Friendship 7*. The visibility at ground level was no
more than a hundred feet. On the second pass, somehow,
they landed. Out in the gray waste, figures struggled in like
stricken French soldiers on the retreat from Moscow.

Glenn retired to consider what to do. There were a hundred people awaiting him at a factory in Onawa, thirty
miles away, but Glenn's luck was not a thing to push. He
decided to do it all for the cameras at the Sioux City airport.

"There are those who say"—a trope, in this circumstance,
for everybody—"that the sensible center I've been talking
about won't come out. You in the sensible center can make
the Democrats the majority party again." Glenn had an
idea how this might be done—each supporter would bring

out ten more people, making "Ten for Glenn." Right, and if *they* all brought out ten, there'd be a hundred when you blundered. "Big money, big influence, big power brokers" had been "deciding this thing thousands of miles away, six months ago." Also "activists . . . people on the fringes of their party" who "devote a couple of hours whatever the weather."

At this stage, the only newsmen with substantive questions were foreigners: a Japanese reporter asked him about domestic content, a Swiss asked about arms control. He hit Mondale on the union spending that was going into his campaign—"a charade and a mockery of the election laws" —an issue he would not be able to make use of, though others would. Then everyone mushed out to Glenn's plane —the blizzard had lightened marginally—to fly back to Des Moines.

Sunday morning, Glenn had an interview in the banquet room of the Hotel Savery in Des Moines with WHO (Ronald Reagan's old station). The room was already being set up with tally boards and other news-headquarters paraphernalia for the next night. Telephones rang, workmen hammered and shouted. Before the anchorman started in Glenn waved to his wife, who was sitting on a nearby riser, and smiled. "I saw you in New Hampshire," he called. They had a private gesture—a flat palm, a jaunty swoop of the hand. *We're taking off!* it said. They did it together. The racket and the thick carpet muffled most of the inquisition when it began. ". . . power brokers anointed . . . sensible center . . . fringe elements . . ."

"Will you support Walter Mondale?"

(Dogged) "I'll support the nominee."

There was a Glenn rally afterwards at Capitol Square, a not-quite-rented space with a high central atrium. It swept up thirty stories or so; the lines were clean and white; it looked like a Piranesi, only nice. One Glenn supporter explained her reasons for preferring him. "A humanist believes everything starts with man. Where does that put God? You talk to the Mondale people about that, and they don't give you an answer." Glenn came forty minutes late. There were a hundred fifty people, ten signs.

"Who," he asked, "has the experience and background to deal with those unknowns that lie ahead of us in this world? Education and research [are] going to lead us into the future." There would have to be "new taxes. It's a tough one.

"Just to see things cut back means we will regress. I believe this country can out-invent, out-produce, out-research, out-educate, out-do everyone on the face of this earth. Who controls their own future? Who has the best standard of living; the best guarantee of jobs and new industry; the best progress in refurbishing smokestack industries? That's what being number one means. Those are the goals we want to set.

"Along with that we can have compassion. We quite often open public events with the pledge to the flag. I wonder how many times we think about what we're saying. . . . *Under God.* Our goals do not come from some politburo or monarch. Whether we're Jews, Catholics, Protestants, whatever our approach to that supreme being, that shapes our goals. *Indivisible.*" John Glenn was overcome. "These are magic words. They should be sacred to us. . . . Education is not just for kids in the castle. Every single person in this country is a king or queen. . . .

"If we come before the people of this country again overspending and weak on defense, we've just dug ourselves into a hole."

He gave a thumbs-up sign. A line formed to greet him; a Glenn operative in a navy wool coat and a foulard tie directed Iowans to the line's end.

The sensible center did not hold. Three thousand Iowans came out for Glenn, 3.5 percent of the total, which put him in sixth place, with no delegates. Cranston finished fifth, also below expectations with 7 percent. "Undecided" was fourth, at 9 percent. McGovern came in a surprise third, with 10 percent and 2 delegates. The kingmakers pulled out the vote for Mondale: 49 percent of the vote, 50 delegates. Only a nose ahead of McGovern and thirty lengths behind Mondale, like the number-two horse in Secretariat's Belmont, but still in second place, was Gary Hart.

Between Iowa and New Hampshire, the press made a moment of drama, one of only two it would fashion during the election year. Jesse Jackson, accustomed to dithyrambs on peace and do-it-yourself diplomacy, found himself trying to explain "Hymie."

The word first appeared in the Washington *Post*, February 13, in a story headlined "Peace with American Jews Eludes Jackson." "In private conversations with reporters, Jackson has referred to Jews as 'Hymie' and to New York as 'Hymietown.' " The next paragraph, equally brief and blank, carried a denial. " 'I'm not familiar with that,' Jackson said Thursday. 'That's not accurate.' " The ensuing controversy, which smoldered for months with several subsidiary flare-ups, was marked on every side by overstatements, evasion, and bad faith.

For starters, the press's handling of it was unusual. Jackson had been getting a media free ride since he announced his candidacy. His wispy qualifications, his wilder statements (viz., the Founding Fathers were "militarists"), his administrative record at PUSH—all were ignored or given a few stories with no follow-up. It almost seemed as if "Hymie" would be ignored too. The *Post* saved it for the thirty-seventh paragraph, on the third page of its article. It took a week for anyone else to pick the item up. No one brought it up at the Des Moines debate; the New York *Times* did not touch the story until February 23. It might have been argued that the whole practice of executing public figures for ethnic slurs had gotten out of hand. But the press had always upheld the etiquette of ethnic politeness in the past (Watt's dumb joke was next-day headline news). Whether they were reluctant to damage a colorful politician who was a source of good copy; whether a black candidate was deemed to have too much social importance to be allowed to damage himself; whether there was some uneasiness about making a sensation of remarks that were originally off the record (in which case, why print them?)—the press handled the story like a hot brick.

Jackson made the matter worse by his own handling. For almost a fortnight, he couldn't decide whether he had said anything or not. (In one morning, campaigning in New Bedford, New Hampshire, he refused to "deny" or "admit" the *Post* report, then said he had "no recollection." "From my point of view, it's a denial.") February 26, at a candidates' forum in a temple in Manchester, Jackson admitted that his choice of words was "insensitive" and "wrong." He added that one of his daughters, during an interview to get into Harvard, had been asked "by a Jewish attorney" what she thought of her father's Middle East positions. "And then he cursed." Jackson ended by urging Jews to join the Rainbow Coalition.

Louis Farrakhan, Jackson's warm-up speaker at Shiloh Baptist, made matters still worse. On March 11, after the first tremors had subsided somewhat, Farrakhan gave a radio speech that went off the Richter scale. The Muslim cleric called Milton Coleman, the *Post* reporter who had originally heard the "Hymie" remark, a "Judas" and an "Uncle Tom" (Coleman was black). "One day soon," Farrakhan warned, "we will punish you with death." He advised Mrs. Coleman to "go to hell with your husband," and observed, in passing, that Hitler had been "a very great man," albeit "wicked." After much outcry, Jackson announced that Farrakhan would no longer work his rallies, though he refused to repudiate the Muslim's support.

Until that point, Farrakhan had had an even easier time of it in the press than Jackson: he had been ignored. It wasn't as if his opinions were secret. Farrakhan had been a calypso singer named Louis Wolcott (stage name: "The Charmer") before converting to the Nation of Islam in the 1950s. The Black Muslims were a black triumphalist sect that had grown up in the twenties (the same decade that produced the Rastafarians in Jamaica). Muslims believed in hard work, strong families, and clean living. They also believed that whites were devils, spawned from a prehistoric

breeding experiment by an evil doctor on the island of
Patmos. When the founder and chief theorist, Elijah
Muhammad, died in 1975, his son Wallace (later Warith)
began nudging the sect in the direction of Moslem orthodoxy. That meant, among other things, abandoning race
hatred. That was too much for Farrakhan, who put himself
at the head of a group of schismatics who remained true to
the old dispensation. For eight years, he had been preaching on Chicago's South Side. He did not meet Jackson until
the fall of 1983. Then came the trip to Syria. Farrakhan
broke with strict Muslim tradition by urging his followers to
register and vote. If Jackson lost, Farrakhan believed, blacks
would finally have to carve their own nation out of American territory, perhaps before the next election. "We can't
go on like this another five years."

It was possible to feel a pang of sympathy for Farrakhan.
There he had been, in his Chicago Zion, as remote from the
main currents of American life as a Hutterite, when suddenly he was being quoted in the *Times,* and called on to
defend every utterance—for an audience of devils, no less.
It was less possible to sympathize with the man who had
hauled him into national prominence.

Behind the Hymie controversy was a much broader issue
—the stress of black-Jewish rivalry. Many Jewish leaders,
who had defended and encouraged black interests and demands for decades, broke with black leaders in the late
sixties on the issue of racial quotas; they were also dismayed
by the anti-Semitism of the Black Panthers and other fe-
vered groups. Jackson's candidacy represented a challenge
that went far beyond quotas, however, and it aimed to stake
out a place in the political mainstream. "The traditional
alliance between blacks and Jews," Jackson was quoted in
the "Hymie" article, "has to be redefined. Many things have
happened to both of us in the last 15 years. [Blacks] have a
far greater sense of self-reliance now." The leading issue
was the Middle East. Jackson's effort at redefinition proceeded at two levels—he wanted Israel and the Arab nations to share the same relationship with the United States;

and he wanted Jews and Arabs to be equal in their relations with blacks. In part, this was traditional State Department politics, a policy of being friends with all the kids on the block.* "There are twenty-two nations in the Middle East," Jackson said at Dartmouth, "and 110 million people. . . . Our relationship with Israel can't protect the Strait of Hormuz." In part, it was a frank attempt by Jackson to bid up his price (a successful attempt—the Arab League contributed $200,000 to PUSH-EXCEL and PUSH). In part, it was an expression of resentment. Jackson's 1979 trip to the Middle East had been prompted by Andrew Young's forced resignation as UN ambassador after it emerged that he had been winging negotiations with the PLO. In large part, Jackson was feeling the tug of the Third World. "I'm a Third World person," he told the *Post*. "I grew up in an occupied zone" —by which he meant Greenville, South Carolina—"and had to negotiate with the superpower, really the colonial power, for the right to vote, for open housing, equal pay." That tug would continue.

The struggle also involved symbols. Jackson had been quoted during his 1979 trip: "I am sick and tired of hearing about the Holocaust." The sentence would be thrown at him in the third debate; he denied saying it. Jackson was nevertheless interested in the Holocaust—in sharing it. "I identify with the Israelis," his *Post* interview went on, "because I understand persecution. My people went through a holocaust, a sustained holocaust, and suffering." Jackson usually followed such statements by appeals to forget the past and move on, but—there it was. Jews suffered? So had blacks. In a post-Christian society, suffering was honor. Jews claimed it; why not blacks?

The third debate was held February 23, five days before the New Hampshire primary, at St. Anselm's College, a small Catholic school outside Manchester. Askew ambush-

---

* At least one State Department type saw the affinity. When I was in Muscat, Oman, in the fall of 1983, a foreign service officer asked me hopefully if I thought the Jackson campaign would help change American opinion on the Middle East.

ers, still hopeful, had lined the roads with Askew posters, in the manner of Burma Shave signs. It was one of those perfect afternoons—midwinter summer—when you lug *Middlemarch* out onto the suddenly mild and visible grass, and end up playing Frisbee. Nightfall brought demonstrators—half a hundred pro-lifers, mostly students.

The eight knew they would soon be eight no longer, and their manner corresponded to their prospects. Hollings was artificially buoyed; he had targeted New Hampshire for his ambush, to the extent of going to Dixville Notch, the little town which votes at one minute after midnight and makes all the morning papers, to ride the ski lift. Mondale looked calm, McGovern smiling and benignant, Cranston tired and spent, Askew glum, Glenn dead. Hart grinned like the cat that ate the canary.

Jackson seemed suddenly subdued, with good reason. Moderator Barbara Walters's first question to him brought together "Hymie" and the "sick and tired of the Holocaust" line. Jackson thought the situation "unfortunate"; we should "put the matter to rest and move on to higher ground. . . . I am not anti-Semitic," he said, twice, then repeated his hope that the quarrel could be put to rest. "Let's put it to rest right now," said Walters. "I am not anti-Semitic," Jackson said a third time. "Did you ever say Hymie?" Walters pursued. Jackson gave a garbled answer (this was before his Manchester clarification). What about the other statement? "Do read that again," he asked. Walters did so. That was "taken out of context," Jackson insisted. "Both Jews and blacks have suffered. I believe in Israel's right to exist. I'm a human-rights activist . . ." He rambled, and Walters cut him off. His subsequent preacherly flights—"we have forgot the least of these"—knocked and sputtered.

McGovern came up with nothing as riveting as his Des Moines finish, but he was still having the time of his life. Would he accept the number two slot? (Hollings had categorically refused, vowing, if it was offered, to flee the country and fight extradition.) "When I was in the Senate, I might have said no, as Fritz did. But I don't have a job now. My apartment burned in May; I don't even have a place to live." Jackson and Glenn made a plug for a woman running mate. "With all due respect . . ." McGovern came back in, "the real things women are worried about are comparable pay and day care." Talk of women vice-presidential candidates was "a form of tokenism."

The most interesting answers of the evening, though, came to a pair of hypotheticals. Candidates are instructed never to answer such questions, since the mental ambles they prompt often end in disaster. Hypotheticals keep getting asked, because a good one can indeed illuminate a candidate's cast of mind (maybe disaster is where he's headed). Would you, as President, consider the use of force, Walters began, if Iran threatened to cut off the West's oil by closing the Strait of Hormuz?

Hollings answered simply. "Yes, I would use force." Glenn and Mondale said they would also consider it; they both gave sober, longish responses (Mondale proposed to go in with NATO allies; Glenn found that unrealistic, since "we have the major force in the area"). Jackson, while insisting that we could have better relations with both Iran and Iraq, said that "some things are worth losing lives for." Hart's answer put his ideas about maneuver warfare into a political context. "If I were President, this country would not find itself with the stranglehold of Persian Gulf oil around its neck." Meanwhile, ships and planes would do the dirty work, and "not one American life" would be "put ashore."

Suppose, Walters went on, a leftist guerrilla movement appeared in Mexico, "seeking to establish a Communist government"? Hart gave a second change-the-universe answer: America must address the true cause of Latin American unrest, which was poverty. Mondale thought "those to the south of us" should work out their own destiny. Cranston warned that "our efforts to block social revolution" in Central America would *cause* a Mexican blowup. McGovern dismissed the problem on the grounds that the Mexican government was "responsive to the needs of its people," unlike Somoza, who had been a "miserable crook." (Next to the Mexican graftocrats, Somoza looked like Aristides the Just.) Jackson declared that we were embracing the wrong side of history and called for derecognizing El Salvador's "killer regime." Only Askew showed any knowledge of Mexican politics—he called the country, correctly, a one-party state—and only Hollings said, "Under no circumstances would we allow a Communist regime to arise in Mexico."

After the debate, some of the candidates went to a banquet hall down the road for brief remarks. The organizers of the event wanted to charge the press fifteen dollars a head for beer—a sad sign of the decline of the Democratic party. Mondale was hearing "Hail to the Chief"; he spent his whole time talking about the nature of the presidency.

Gary Hart was hearing the theme from *Rocky* (it was, in fact, his campaign song). The day after the debate he went to Meredith, a summer resort on a lakeshore lined with abandoned pleasures—miniature golf courses, rides, beached, hooded boats—to rally his supporters. It rained and rained; the hollows smoked; trucks sent up clouds of mist.

The New Hampshire Democratic party attracts two types. There is a wing of New England Nice People—educated liberals, environmentalists these days, anti-Vietnam when that was happening. John Anderson had rounded them up in herds. There is also a blue-collar wing, often immigrants or their descendants, chiefly from French Canada. Socially, they tend to be even to the right of Granite State Republicans. They hearken to the state's premier paper, the Manchester *Union-Leader;* its candidate-eating editor, William Loeb, died in 1981, but his spirit lives on. (Loeb was an original—hard-core conservative on almost every issue, with a few populist, even Bull Moose, quirks: he had opposed right-to-work laws and favored a 100 percent inheritance tax.) What the two groups have in common are a suspicion of dictation and a jealous regard for their own independence. Many of the workingman Democrats had already decided to support Reagan in 1984. Neither the Nice People nor the blue-collars that remained had any disposition to love Walter Mondale.

The Hart rally was in the Studio Cafe. It was chic over funky—a few deco motifs, spider ferns in the windows, a pressed-tin ceiling. The Hart workers put up his posters— cool compositions in blue and silver. Soon, there was only standing room inside; thirty extra people clustered on the sidewalk.

Hart came, late, radiant. He introduced three supporters —two state legislators and Stephen King—"one of the most talented writers in America." (For his third academic degree, Hart can do a thesis on *The Shining.*) "I've said before, if you don't support me, Stephen King will scare you to death.

"There are those in Washington who say the debate is over," that "the only choice before the voters of New Hampshire is to ratify a choice" that was "already made." Standard rhetoric—but it can play in New Hampshire. These were the people, after all, who went for Carter, McGovern, Henry Cabot Lodge, and Estes Kefauver.

"We're not only going to put the people back to work that Ronald Reagan threw out, but create jobs for people moving into the economy—young people, women, minorities. We are not only going to pull our marines" out of Lebanon, but start "supporting forces for democratic principles and human rights." We would "not only freeze nuclear weapons, but dramatically reverse the arms race. The United States will take the lead to solve problems around the world." Hart had time for nothing more; but it was a speech, such as it was, full of promise (which is a different thing from promises). There were also three *we*'s—a powerful word, if a politician can say it truthfully.

"Someone asked," said King, "if Gary Hart needed America's resident spook in his campaign. I said, the resident spook was in the White House." Then, seriously: "He represents my generation. I want to feel like I felt when Kennedy was President again."

Mondale visited a shopping mall outside Portsmouth the following day, with all the intimacy of a royal levee. He arrived after a fashion show—"We like these ladylike attitudes; very twenties, very Gatsbyesque"; a Dixieland band set up on the platform to tootle his progress. He was surrounded by a flying wedge of Secret Service, still photographers, television crews with boom mikes. Outdoors, he could still have been seen through the cocoon; under a low ceiling in a tight hallway, he was virtually invisible. Word passed back through the crowd of his doings: He had bought a cookie. "You can see him better on TV," someone complained. After venturing fifty feet into the mall, he retired. The band played the "Washington and Lee Swing."

Hollings's Dixville Notch strategy paid off in Dixville Notch; three Democrats voted for him and five Republicans wrote him in. Statewide, he got three thousand votes more, for a seventh-place finish, at 4 percent. Ronald Reagan, on a write-in campaign ballyhooed by the *Union-Leader*, finished sixth, with 5 percent. McGovern and Jackson each got another 5 percent. Glenn received 12 percent; Hart, 37 percent. "Hail to the Chief" was second, with 28 percent.

For the next two weeks, the sun would not rise on Walter Mondale. He pushed all his resources into the Maine caucuses on March 4. He lost them, 50 percent to 45 percent. "I'm in trouble," he joked on "Good Morning America" on March 5. "I need your help." On March 6, the Vermont preference primary, which Mondale had abandoned in favor of Maine, rejected him 71–21. On the tenth, he dropped the Wyoming caucuses, 61–36. Sober folk thought it possible that he might be shut out on Super Tuesday.

Super Tuesday, a collection of eleven primaries and caucuses all held on March 13, was a thing of Mondale's own devising. The thinking, back when the schedules were being drawn up and when Mondale and Kennedy were the likely front-runners, was that a heavy load of early contests and a quick rhythm would overwhelm any little renegades,

anyone who would work day and night for a fluke victory in
Iowa or New Hampshire and then hope to struggle on from
there. Well, the victory had happened, and instead of being
crushed down by the sudden rush of voters, it looked to be
spreading by contagion. Mondale was down to his last as-
sets: the black mayor of Birmingham; the unions of the
Alabama industrial belt; and the thirty-ninth President of
the United States.

PLAINS WELCOMES JOAN & FRITZ. The banner stretched
across one street; a high school band and a speaker's platform were parked in the middle of the other. The peach
blossoms were bursting, and birds sang like hinges, though
in the shadows it was still winter. The unions had bused
down a crowd from Atlanta, which was supplemented by
locals less interested in the candidate than in the former
President. *"They* said, we got to get that evil man out 'f th'
White House. Well, Jim Carter was a Christian." "Yes." "Jim
Carter was a good man." WALTER AND JOAN, read another
sign, THE WHITE HOUSE NEEDS YOU-ALL. It felt more like a
campaign kickoff than a desperate attempt at political heart
massage.

Carter and Mondale came to the rally on foot. Left to
himself, Mondale preferred suits and tightly cinched ties,
but down-home gear was part of the Carter style, and for
the occasion Mondale had donned a pair of jeans and an odd
pepper-and-salt cardigan. Chip Carter began by introducing his mother, "maybe the best campaigner onstage,"
which didn't sound like much of a compliment just then.
She in turn spoke of Joan Mondale and their years at the
top. "I learned to love and admire her." But then, who
didn't the Carters love and admire? It all came back, the
emotional inflation of the Carter presidency, as corrupting
as the inflation of the currency. It was enough to make
Francis of Assisi become a gangster.

What benefit could Mondale wring from such an association? The lieutenant governor of Georgia, introducing
Mondale's introducer, gave a clue: History, he said, would
record that Carter made a great President, but "more than

anything else, to those of us who were born and lived in the South, he gave a sense of pride." Appomattox, after all these years. And Mondale was rallying the Confederates.

"We've heard a lot recently," Carter said, "about changing times, and new, and new ideas, and so forth. . . . You have to adjust to changing times, but you have to hold to unchanging principles." No quarrels about who had supported which decisions now. "When I searched for peace, Fritz Mondale was tha. When I went to Camp David, Fritz Mondale was tha. When I sat across the table from Soviet ambassador Dobrynin and plotted our strategy on SALT II, Fritz Mondale was tha . . ." The list of his collaborations was long, and included plans to increase defense spending and reduce the deficit.

"He knows our country as well or better than any man alive. In some strange way in the last few days and weeks, this knowledge of our country—of teachers, farmers, workers—has been twisted by the press and some of his opponents as being a detriment. I can tell you from experience, the White House is not a place to go to school. I don't know the theory of politics; I've been involved in it. [The Carter presidency in a nutshell.] Let's pause awhile. We're not making a frivolous decision. We're looking at the futa of our country."

Mondale spoke last. "We need a President who understands we must be strong, but who will use that strength to keep the peace . . . who will get these deficits down, but fairly. We need a President who understands justice in America, who understands when people are hurting, when people are old, when people are unemployed, when people are sick, when people are handicapped . . ." A pause; had he run out of unfortunates? ". . . Who understands when people need a President who understands and cares for them.

"I'm a people's Democrat. Nothing fancy. No new hair spray." He spoke warningly of Washington, where there were "the finest-dressed lobbyists you've ever seen in your life," wearing "the sweetest perfume you ever smelled. You need a President who remembers who sent him there."

His father, he finished, had been a minister, his mother a music teacher. "They were good Americans, good friends. They're being forgotten. Give me the chance to carry that struggle for what you believe to the nomination and to the White House."

Balloons rose, fireworks shot, and the Carterites partook of a barbecue. At a Hardee's in nearby Americus, one of the band members reported on the event to his family.

"Get a crowd?"

"Yeah. Hart'll tear him up."

But in the fourth debate, on March 11 in Atlanta—the day after the Class of '76 reunion in Plains—it was Mondale who finally got in a damaging question. The location of the debate was the Fox Theater, an old movie palace and the former national headquarters of the Ancient Arabic Order of the Nobles of the Mystic Shrine. Of all the venues of all the debates, it was the only one appropriate to the occasion —that is, if beauty and dignity were unavailable. The Fox Theater didn't have an ounce of either, but it had imagination, energy, and conviction by the cartload. There were crescent moons, Stars of David, onion domes, crenellations, Moorish windows, canopies on pikes, gold-and-rose wastebaskets, lounges like Oxford common rooms. It was a Rainbow Coalition of architecture. The candidates sat with John Chancellor on a vast stage beneath a towering proscenium in the form of battlements and a night-blue ceiling pricked with twinkling lights.

They were five by then. Cranston had folded his tent on February 29, followed by Askew and by Hollings, who threw his support to Hart. Not that Hart would pick up any legions thereby, but Hollings's justification chimed with what a lot of people were thinking—if the Democrats nominated Mondale, they would be crushed. Glenn and Jackson looked grim on the Fox stage—if Jackson did not win at least 20 percent of the vote in one of Tuesday's primaries, he would by law lose his federal matching funds. If Glenn could not win something, he would have to hang it up. Then there was the man of the hour. Analysts, scrambling to figure out how Hart had done it, decided that he had uncovered a class of young, liberal, professional voters. John Anderson had in fact done much of his spadework four years earlier; an old Anderson slogan, "Heart on the left, wallet on the right," seemed perfectly to capture their impulses. They had now been christened "yuppies"—young urban professionals—which spawned an entire family of unfortunate acronyms: guppies (gay urban professionals), muppets (middle-aged urban professionals). The Hart campaign was in danger of resembling the joke about Bush's 1980 effort: How do you know you're at a Bush rally? Because everyone has nicknames like Poppy, and Muffy, and Boopsie—and those are the men. Hart was excitedly tense; he looked as if he had spent odd bits of the last ten days learning how to smile inoffensively.

His fellow candidates tried to wipe it off his face. "Gary," said McGovern (who was concentrating on Massachusetts and had vowed to drop out if he did not finish second or better there), "has posed [the election] as a contest between the past and the future." But McGovern, "an old history teacher," asked, "Does the past include George Washington and Thomas Jefferson, Franklin Roosevelt and John Kennedy . . . ? Then I want to be a part of it." Glenn, in answer to a defense question, read off a list of weapons both Mondale and Hart had voted to cut, then singled out Hart for special attention. "I've fought in wars when my life depended on" technology. "I do not agree with this smaller is simpler is cheaper is better." Replying to the same question, Mondale called the Soviet Union "a powerful military force using its power irresponsibly in Poland, Cambodia, Afghanistan, and Syria"—not a world, the catalogue implied, for neophytes. "We don't elect momentum," he said in his opening answer, "we elect a human being. We better elect someone who's committed" to improving things "and knows how to get them done."

Hart turned all these attacks aside with good-natured

laughs, or with earnest rebuttals—"I don't see," he told his former boss, why paying an ensign fourth class "to make a career of defending his country . . . should threaten the Russians"—and developed themes of his own. Why, Chancellor asked, should people vote for the Democrats? Because of toxic wastes, Hart answered, the "fundamental problems" of the economy, and the "anguish of our children over nuclear holocaust."

He got into minor trouble on a hypothetical. It's 2 A.M., said Chancellor; a Czech airliner has flown into American airspace, heading for Colorado Springs (site of the Strategic Air Command) and ignoring all efforts to make it land or determine its purpose. What does the man in the loneliest job in the world do? Chancellor was trying, of course, to construct a dilemma to match KAL 007. But since the Soviets aren't amateur tricksters, and since we don't casually shoot down civilian airliners (however far astray), the problem was inherently absurd. Mondale, who gave the second answer, saw it right away. "You think if the Soviet Union were after us, they'd fire up an old 707 and send it putting up there?"

Hart, though, took aim at the Czech mystery plane and let fly a dud. He would instruct American fighter pilots to look in the windows. "If the people they saw . . . had uniforms on, I'd shoot it down. If they had civilian clothes on, I'd let it go."

Glenn thought it was a howl. ". . . saying we'd go up and peek in!" He mimed an airborne Peeping Tom. "I've flown wing on these things; you don't go peeking in!" (Hart claimed later he had been joking; if he was, he had a better poker face than Buster Keaton.)

Should the Democrats, Chancellor continued, decrease federal intervention in the nation's affairs, or "return to the way things were before Ronald Reagan"? Mondale did not hesitate. Only "a strong federal government" could manage budget, trade, a "renaissance of learning," civil rights, ERA, and medical care. The President had to "lead us." Hart agreed. Ronald Reagan "says he loves our country but

hates our government. I don't hate our government." He
began his own list of legitimate government tasks with the
stimulation of small entrepreneurs.

Mondale made his move. For almost two weeks, he had
been trying to damage Hart, without effect. His ads for the
Maine caucuses picked at Hart's record. Hart had cast a
vote once in favor of decontrolling oil prices that, Mondale
charged, would have raised oil prices ten dollars a barrel. It
hadn't stuck. Why should it? Hart had made a mistake,
perhaps. Was Mondale trying to pass himself off as infallible?
Unless he could fit Hart's actions into some unattractive
pattern, he was simply flailing.

"What's new about entrepreneurs?" Mondale broke in.
"You know, when I hear those new ideas, I'm reminded of
that ad, 'Where's the beef?' " Mondale aides had thought of
the query; he had never seen the Wendy's commercial from
which it was taken. He trusted their antennae for popular
culture, though—wisely. He caught the ad at the peak of its
omnipresence. The house laughed.

In the next breath, Mondale seemed to throw it all away.
"Another thing," Hart went on sourly, a President "can't be
tied to special interests." "Wait a minute," Mondale jumped
back in, exhilarated, getting "deficits down" was not a "special interest. I've said I'd stand up for—*against* special interests . . ." There are, as Freud observed, no accidents. The
audience gave another laugh.

"My ideals," Hart said in conclusion, "are as deeply
rooted in this party as anyone's." But it was also necessary to
change. "When this country wanted change, it turned to
this party. We cannot go back."

"It takes someone," said Mondale, "who knows what he's
doing."

Hart supporters gathered after the debate in another up-
scale boîte, down Peachtree Street. Campaign workers,
mostly young, gave the campaign chant: "Gar-*y*, Gar-*y*."
"One of my problems," Hart told them, "is I can't smile and
think at the same time. Other people smile and don't think.
. . . We must be boldly experimental and innovative, and

launch this country into the eighties and nineties. . . . We must not send our sons to die in Lebanon and serve as bodyguards for dictators . . ." The *Rocky* theme played on a tape, too loudly. Hart shook hands. Ten girls in short skirts and tap shoes shivered on the stoop. A pale half-moon hung in the twilight. "Gar-*y*, Gar-*y*" followed him outside. "Okay, dance," said the girls' handler. "Do your little thing." Hart reached the car, put one foot in on the floor, hoisted himself up for a wave, was gone.

Hart took the Nevada, Washington, and Oklahoma caucuses, and the Florida, Rhode Island, and Massachusetts primaries. George McGovern, finishing third in Massachusetts, pulled out as he had promised. Jackson won 21 percent of the vote in Georgia, enough to keep the federal money flowing. Glenn finished fourth there and third in Alabama, and pulled out that Friday. Mondale, though unopposed in the Hawaiian caucuses, came in second to "uncommitted." He won a write-in primary for Democrats Abroad and the caucuses in American Samoa. He also carried Georgia (31 percent to Hart's 27 percent) and Alabama (34 percent to Hart's 21 percent). Hart had torn him up, as his supporter in Americus had predicted—but not in sufficiently small pieces.

From a seat in the Fox Theater, the fourth debate looked like a draw, Mondale's Freudian slip canceling out his hamburger commercial, and Mondale had needed to do better. As time passed, though, his faux pas faded. Obviously Mondale would not repeat it. It also revealed nothing that was previously unknown. Hart had made the point in Des Moines—Mondale was the soul mate of special interests. Mondale had built his campaign around the point (he did not call them "special," of course, and denied that there was anything invidious in serving them). Mondale's question, though, was new, and not senseless. What *were* Hart's new ideas?

Hart helped him in several important ways. Hart said, as often as his supporters played *Rocky*, that he was the enemy

of "old arrangements and the policies of the past." What
could be more antithetical to the new era than political
bosses? (And indeed, most of the party's bosses were lined
up behind Mondale.) So, for the Illinois primary, which
came a week after Super Tuesday, the Hart campaign ran
an ad attacking Chicago alderman Edward Vrdolyak, who
was supporting Mondale. But there are limits even to the
politics of the future. Hart might conceivably reform the
military and lead the nation into a Second Industrial
Revolution, but to purge Chicago of bosses was utopian.
Chicago was the last big American city where old-style boss-
ism flourished; it was where it *worked.* He might as well
have attacked caste in India, or tenure on a campus. The
machine, to make matters worse, had its blood up. A year
earlier, an upstart black boss, Harold Washington, had
seized City Hall. The ensuing hand-to-hand fighting was
like the battle of Verdun. Washington, who was running his
own slate of independent delegates, had no interest at all in
supporting Hart, so Hart's attack lacked even the excuse of
venality. Hart had the ad withdrawn.

The press also helped create its second story of the campaign, this one at Hart's expense. It managed it by the
simple journalistic feat of checking biographical facts. Gary
Warren Hartpence, it turned out, had not been born November 28, 1937, but one year earlier. Hart had given the
correct date on his college and graduate school transcripts.
He first became a year younger in February 1965, on his
application to the Virginia Bar, and thereafter, with a few
relapses into accuracy, kept the new date. (His book, his
driver's license, his Naval Reserve commission, his biographies in Who's Who and the Congressional Directory, and
his campaign literature, all said 1937.) The Washington *Post*
had the true birth date, and an outline of the discrepancies,
as early as January; but the story was slow to catch on.

When it did, in mid-March, Hart gave it impetus. The
reason for the confusion, he explained, was a childhood
family game, a form of teasing. (A game he was still playing
when he was forty-six—or forty-seven?) He cast his change

of name—an unexceptionable act; changed names are as American as self-improvement—into prominence in the same way. It was a family decision, he said, in which he had acquiesced. But relatives told the press that he had been the prime mover; he had gone to court himself to get it done. The candidate added that "Hart" was the original form of the name, which he had simply restored. A helpful genealogist then pointed out that in the nineteenth century the name had been "Pence." It got so the Hart campaign told jokes about it. "I'm forty-eight," Lee Hart began one interview. "I *know* when I was born." Hart's only truly new ideas, said Frank Mankiewicz, one of his aides, were his name and his age.

Hart was in no joking mood when he heard from his staff that Mondale was running ads in Illinois harping on the discrepancies. He went on the attack against what he took to be a personal assault. The only problem was, there had been no assault. Some Mondale people had discussed a name-related ad, but it was never made. Hart's Illinois staff had simply picked up a rumor. Hart was forced into a second, embarrassing Illinois retreat.

The problem with Hart's name and age, it must be emphasized, was not the revelations, which were trivial, but his reactions to them, which were bizarre. A third instance never received general notice. One Hart campaign ad showed the candidate and his wife together over a chessboard. Gary, his people gave out, had always loved the game. On closer inspection, the pieces were incorrectly placed; the board had been rotated ninety degrees. Had a techie made the blunder in setting them up? The Hart campaign returned with the answer that that was how Hart had first learned to play, and how he had played ever since. But who could he have found to play with? The man who reminded Stephen King of John Kennedy was showing the defensiveness of Richard Nixon. (Like Nixon's, Hart's defensiveness was self-damaging.) Even this might not have mattered if he had had a long record or a strong profile—as long and strong as, say, Nixon's in 1968, or Mondale's in 1984.

But the candidate of new ideas could not afford weird behavior.

Mondale, meanwhile, stressed his familiarity. He was not afraid of oldness; he gloried in it. Michigan had a caucus on March 17, four days after Super Tuesday, three days before Illinois. Mondale campaigned as the savior of Chrysler. "I voted for that loan," he chided Hart in a debate in Chicago, "you didn't. That's why they voted for me." (Here's the beef.) He visited a Chrysler plant in Belvidere, Illinois, where he rode in the millionth Omni car. "It was a thrilling experience."

He continued as well to emphasize that the world was a dangerous place. Hart, he charged in a debate at Columbia University on March 28, "learned the wrong lesson" from Vietnam. "There is a proper role for American power in the world." He cited Central America (where Mondale "differ[ed] . . . on just pulling out the plug and walking out of there") and the Persian Gulf (where he accused Hart of telling our allies, at St. Anselm's, that "they're on their own"). "We should not imply to the Soviet Union that there is an area in the world where we're not involved." This sounded hawkish, though it was not. On Central America, for instance, Mondale made it clear that he would stop aid to the Contras, end American military exercises in Honduras, and hitch our diplomacy to the Contadora group's tail pipe. He could also play the dangerous-world theme in an overtly pacific key. "The night before I was sworn in as Vice-President," he told the Columbia audience in his summation, he had been given a briefing on the "football"—the mechanism that would enable him, should he be thrust into the position, to respond to a nuclear attack. "For four years that person"—its carrier—"was never more than a few minutes away, even when I went fishing. . . . Ask which of us you think is best prepared to lead us to a safer world. Vote as if your life depended on it, because it might."

Michigan gave 50 percent of its votes to Mondale, and Illinois followed, 41 percent for Mondale, 35 percent for Hart. Hart completed his New England sweep with a 53 percent win in the Connecticut primary, a week after Illinois, but since the presidency of New England has not been a viable option since the Hartford Convention, serious attention shifted to April 3 and New York. Five days before the primary, Hart was scheduled to appear at a fund-raiser at the Red Parrot in Manhattan. Discos haven't been at the cutting edge for seven or eight years. (I don't know where the cutting edge is now. I would have said punk, until I overheard a young man at a book party speaking of a "post-punk sensibility.") Hart was late, and a live band, Girls' Night Out, took up the slack. The lead girl wore a black tank top, a short leather skirt, and pink stockings; some of the others ran to glitter. The drummer was introduced as "a girl who has a terrible crush on Gary Hart." The room stretched back long and low, in the manner of converted industrial space. A red-and-gold neon parrot hung on the wall, and a few live ones huddled solemnly in huge cages. Young men in red neckties moved about, sweeping up litter.

For New York, Hart had to face a second Mondale question to go along with "Where's the beef?" Where's the embassy? The embassy in question was the American embassy in Israel, located in Tel Aviv. The policy supported by both Mondale and Hart was to move it to Jerusalem. The question was, when had Hart adopted the policy, and what did this signify about his staunchness for Israel? Ideally, he should have been able to prove that he had adopted it when he was still Hartpence, but it seemed that he had waffled as late as March. Mondale, for his part, made it the Chrysler of the Middle East.

The band at the Red Parrot played "He's So Fine" and "Leader of the Pack." *Is that Gary's ring you're wearing? Yeah, I'll be wearing it for the next four years.* The crowd danced. They had the look of young lawyers at play, unwinding after a hard day of antitrust. Outside, it had begun snowing and sleeting; the candidate was caught in a traffic jam, and his estimated time of arrival kept getting pushed back.

Hart probably would have been better off not announc-

ing a new embassy policy at all; the switch only drew attention to a deviation on what was, after all, a symbolic issue.
But the rules for discussing the Middle East in Democratic
presidential primaries are clear and, unless one has, like
Jackson, powerful reasons for breaking them, strict. Candidates must not only support Israel's security; they must
accept Israel's maximum definition of its own security
needs. These strictures ran right across the spectrum, from
unreformed cold warriors like the late Henry Jackson to
peaceniks like Cranston. Hart accepted them too, and
joined Mondale in an unseemly scramble for pro-Israeli
brownie points. Jackson, observed columnist Murray
Kempton, may have called New York City Hymietown;
Hart and Mondale treated it as if it were.

An hour and a half late, Lee Hart arrived at the disco and
took to the dance floor. Cameras swarmed around, mere
yuppies sat down. It is all rather horrible, the way would-be
First Relatives are expected to perform. But I reflected that
she had made the bargain willingly. A starlet sang "New
York, New York," that hymn of Big Apple bumptiousness,
and the light man covered a wall with projections of Hart's
face. It was announced that Hart would be another half
hour late. Reporters have some self-respect, so I left.

Even Jewish organizations finally sickened of the embassy controversy. But it served Mondale's larger strategic
purpose—to portray Hart as an unknown quantity. For the
rest, Hart met Mondale's foreign-policy challenge forthrightly, and he met it on the left. On Central America, he
appeared to believe a peculiar bit of folklore. Somoza, he
told an interviewer, kept a cage of panthers in the basement of his residence, to which he would occasionally throw
a hapless opponent. There was a grit of truth at the center
of this pearl, which was that Somoza's father once put an
opponent in a cage *next* to a cage that contained a lion.[1] But
the Sandinistas had embroidered the tale, and Hart repeated it.

In his longer addresses, there were still dissonant notes,
like echoes of forgotten melodies. He told a meeting of the

Foreign Policy Association that America "must not retreat to protectionism" and that it was "vital" to "support democracy." A few sentences later, though, he chided the Reagan administration for "pumping guns and ammunition" into El Salvador (then in the midst of its own presidential campaign). He ended with a statement whose parallelism bore the failing touch of Theodore Sorensen. "We have confidence that our allies will be tough on the battlefield; we must also be confident they will be tough at the negotiating table."

On the stump even the grace notes vanished. Hart held a rally on Washington Square in Greenwich Village, which he was able to make. Winter's rains and ruins were over. He stood on the south side of the park, facing SoHo; at his back, the square was filled with joggers, Frisbees, refuse, crocuses, bums, pot. We needed, Hart said, a "foreign policy to make Americans proud of something other than our invasions." He wanted guaranteed student loans, and he knew how to pay for them. "When I debate Ronald Reagan and he asks, where is the money coming from, I intend to say, from the cancellation of the MX and the B-1 bomber." He wanted to "bring the troops out of Central America" and "bring the doctors and teachers and agricultural experts in." A yell: "Isn't he cute?" Hart condemned old politics and Ronald Reagan and brought his speech to a close, then added, "I was the first candidate to say I would not accept a penny in PAC money, and I am the only candidate who has done so."

Three days before the primary, Jesse Jackson marched through Harlem. Before he got there, he passed through other bands of the Rainbow. He came to a little square in the Village, popularly called Sheridan Square, after a green, pigeon-stained statue of General Sheridan (not knowing, one assumes, what to make of it all), though the true Sheridan Square is another triangular sliver around the corner. At ten o'clock on a Saturday morning both the real and the ersatz squares were empty. The Village Independent Democrats had a table set up—"Can't get rid of Reagan and Koch unless everyone registers!" The park benches were stacked with old vodka bottles, bums' empties. Two press buses came, with seven TV cameramen, numerous still photographers, and pencil press; then the police, then Jackson, and the crowd, now detectable, made their way to a church a block and a half to the east. An accordionist in a beret joined in. Jackson stood on the church steps.

"The old minorities in coalition are the new majority. . . . All of us are somebody. We must be counted.

"We're going through a flood. Reagan has drowned education. He has drowned Headstart. He has drowned school breakfast programs. He has drowned school lunches. He has drowned food stamps. It's better and cheaper to feed a child than to jail a man or a woman." Jackson wanted more money for AIDS research. "How can a civilized people discriminate against a disease? The human family must destroy disease before it destroys the human family.

"The richest nation in the history of the world must stop building MX missiles and B-1 bombers and educate our children and house the homeless. . . . Mr. Mondale and Mr. Hart cannot have a missile in one hand and a dove in the other. Martin Luther King said, give peace a chance. We must not have our boys dying in Honduras. Give peace a chance. We must end the nuclear industry," encourage "solar power, and weatherize our homes. Give peace a chance. There must be no more missiles in Europe. Give peace a chance." The little crowd was chanting by now. The accordionist, a pale-complexioned white girl with red hair, shouted, *"Que viva!"*

"In East Harlem, there are large heaps of garbage, rats running the streets. We must challenge our city to pick up the garbage. We must train our youth to end the slums and build America." "Get the garbage out of the White House!" someone yelled.

At the next stop, the corner of Bayard and Mulberry streets, Asian-Americans for Jesse Jackson had produced a dragon—a little one, one boy in the head, another in the tail —and appropriate music (which sounds to Western ears like noisy garbagemen, though one billion Chinese seem to like it). Jackson was introduced by two local politicians, and shook the dragon's hand. The street was filled with shoppers, examining fish, squid, and vegetables, and pausing occasionally to listen impassively.

Jackson's two hooks for the Chinatown audience were the internment of Japanese-Americans in World War II, which required "reparations," and the bombing of Hiroshima, which served as an all-purpose metaphor for American aggressiveness. "The American government," he said, "must stop its program of intervention and destruction of Third World people. Never again, as it were, must we drop a bomb on the Japanese people. My campaign will reach out for the locked out. We'll make room for all of you. We should learn the lessons of Nagasaki and Hiroshima. We must bury nuclear bombs, not let nuclear bombs bury us.

"Give peace a chance. I am somebody, I am somebody. Respect me, protect me, never neglect me. I am somebody. Red and yellow, brown, black, and white, we're all precious in God's sight. Everybody's somebody, everybody's somebody. We've been down too long. Our time has come, our time has come. The rainbow is alive, the rainbow is alive. The rainbow is doing well, the rainbow is doing well. On to victory. On to victory." This was the regular Jackson chant, every phrase or half-phrase of which was to be shouted back by the crowd. Translation into Chinese slowed it up some (what did they do with the rhymes?). A core of Jackson supporters started a thin chant of "Win, Jesse, Win." The shoppers ignored it. It was noon, they'd only been up six hours; no time to let the grass grow under their feet.

When the Jackson campaign got to East Harlem, though, there was a parade in earnest. An entire extra-wide block of 104th Street, off Third Avenue, had been blocked off for assembling. There were designated areas for labor, women, and seniors and disabled. The dragon came up from Chinatown. There were flags for an independent Puerto Rico, signs (STOP U.S. AID TO ISRAEL), a table selling pamphlets on "The Political Meaning of the Assassination of Stalin." A procession of speakers, as various as the crowd, trickled across a reviewing stand located in mid-turmoil. A black woman, who was the National Coordinator of the All People's Congress (a group of free-lance Leninists), flayed Koch and Reagan. "Social services have been cut to the bone" by a "racist administration" and "militarists in the White House." She was followed by a self-described "feminist" and "writer," who said "the human race has been a misnomer," and offered a parable which she implied was folkloric, though it bore the unmistakable traces of her own style. A young Asian man announced "a song of blues, but the words are going to be played by the violin," and he tucked one under his chin. Through the PA system, it sounded like a buzz saw. The president of the Village Independent Democrats had also come uptown, and she told a joke, the single one of the afternoon. "How do progressives form a firing squad? By standing in a circle." They weren't, she said, in a circle today. Averting their eyes from this uproar were the Fruit of Islam, Louis Farrakhan's corps of bodyguards, detailed to Jackson events since the year before. The Muslims wore gleaming white shirts, chesterfield coats, stony faces, and black shoes buffed to a mirror shine which even the Army has abandoned. PS 22 had sent its marching band, with majorettes in cowboy hats and white fringed skirts, and the lone American flag. On Third Avenue, a station wagon had parked, with a rooftop sign, JESSE THE MAN / FOR GOD'S PLAN.

After two and a half hours (given the impressionistic quality of the Jackson campaign's scheduling, it would be rash to say "two and a half hours late"), the parade heaved into motion. East Harlem—primarily Hispanic, with a sprinkling of Asians, blacks, and whites—lined the curbs. But the sidewalks were clear. For all the determined ecumenicism of the paraders, the Rainbow Coalition had remained monochromatic. Had Hymie hurt? Not in East Harlem. But it had knocked some of the gilt off, and may have knocked Jackson off his stride. Only a prophet could lead humanity into an ark, and prophets don't tell ethnic jokes. Most humans do, but prophets can't. The banner, avenue-wide, at the head of the parade was borne by fourteen blacks, one white, one Asian, and one American Indian. That seemed about right.

The parade flowed, five blocks long. Some Pentecostalists —Cristo Viene Pronto—looked out of their church. "Who do we want?" *Jesse.* "When do we want him?" *Now. April 3rd, spread the word, Jesse Jackson will be heard.* The chants clashed, the band played Sousa. At 116th Street, the mass swung west. The street was solid shops, mostly discount clothes. The hard-core leftists, who always seem to have a bullhorn handy, took up a new chant. *Hey hey, ho ho, Cowboy Ronnie has got to go.*

Jackson himself had not appeared. He was waiting for Harlem proper. Beyond the Penn Central railroad tracks, past Park Avenue (no Park Avenue addresses here), came Lenox Avenue, and a different world. Whole lots and sites, whole quarter blocks, were scooped out, flattened, like bare gums; but around the gaps was sumptuous frontage, streets of town houses with intact stoops, like rows of Victorian typewriters. Blank boarded windows stared from the brownstone façades. Like a chemical solution when it precipitates, the crowd doubled, quadrupled; the Fruit of Islam came to the fore. A man stood on the sidewalk waving a piece of paper, drunk or spoofing, or both. "This card takes you anywhere in this country. This is your *voter registration* card. This card is the bottom line. Like the rain, like nature, like the weather, it's funky. So let's get funky too." He did not make much disturbance. Young men hauled themselves up traffic poles, into the crisp air, for a look. Jackson arrived, to a joyous roar. "He be taking the whole city."

It did look like it. The march rolled up Lenox Avenue, swelling and swelling. The roar continued like a surf. The traveling press corps had been packed into slow, bulky trucks, rolling ahead, like Rumor. Cameramen scrambled up steps, over car hoods, clambered into Dumpsters for a view, a shot. "I haven't seen him yet." "There he is."

"Jesse!" Jackson turned, beamed, waved. Someone shouted at the news truck, "You've got a lot to tell."

They swept west again, on 125th Street. The Muslims had trouble holding things together. The crush was so thick it may have creased a shirtfront. The crowd joined a second crowd, standing at the base of the Harlem State Office Building (a slab as incongruous as the stone in *2001),* and awaited the candidate. More warm-ups. Imamu Amiri Baraka, né LeRoi Jones, had some blues of his own, written "on the spot," though unfortunately the words were not spoken by a violin. "Black people don't care what you say, America. . . ." Hart and Mondale "only want seven trillion murders, not ten trillion. . . . Only Jesse speaks for us against your freaky fascism. . . . No matter what you death-freaks do, look to the Rainbow. . . ." The amplifiers roared off the modernistic walls. The only competition came from a drunk, stretched out on a stone embankment, looking wretchedly at the fading light: "You see how beautiful you are? You so beautiful, they send sunshine. Lord, you see this shit down here? Ah, God *damn."* Having Baraka speak was like letting Céline introduce a Reagan rally. (Then why did Jackson have him?) A soul group, a minister, Barry Commoner, Mr. Abdul Kareem Mohammed of the Nation of Islam, all followed. Mohammed spoke of "all those from George Washington to Ronald Reagan" who had "done nothing to help us." "Look what they've done to rebuild our black community—absolutely nothing!" An untruth—but a complicated one. The building beneath which he stood was not nothing; on the other hand, it was nothing effective. At five, in the gloaming, came Jackson.

> "I am
> somebody,
> I am
> somebody."

(It was all in the original now.)

> "I may be poor
> But I am
> somebody.
> If my mind
> can conceive it
> and my heart
> can believe it,
> I can achieve it.
> I may be born
> in a slum,
> but the slum
> was not born in me.
> I am
> somebody.
> Give peace a chance.
> Give peace a chance.

"As I stand here today, I am mindful of Marcus Garvey; of Malcolm [X]; of Mr. [Elijah] Muhammad; of Adam Clayton Powell; mostly of Martin Luther King; of Kwame Nkrumah and Sékou Touré—all those leaders whose work led to this day. It's time for us to move to a new dimension of our struggle. It's time for us to provide leadership to our world. . . .

"Poverty has no color, no sex. A baby crying in the night without milk, a child in school without lunch, has no color, no sex; it has no food. We must remind our nation over and over again, there is danger in locking somebody out just because they don't have a big name. The followers of Jesus had no big name. Jesus himself was born in a slum, but the slum was not born in him.

"The poor of our nation are mostly hardworking. Most poor folks are not on welfare; they have too much pride to be on welfare. Poor folks raise other folks' children. They can't raise their own. Poor folks clean other folks' houses. They cannot clean their own. A rising tide does not lift all boats. There are boats stuck on the bottom. . . .

"We must make America the great nation America was

supposed to be for everybody. . . . When I walk these streets, there're two sides to the story. The seamy side, and the sunny side." A broken wall, a broken door, a busted water main—those were "the seamy side. But train a child" to be a mason, a carpenter, a plumber; "that's the sunny child. That same child, that can't learn, they join the Army, and drive tanks and build bridges. When they say new generation—I'm not talking about forty- to fifty-year-old men, I'm talking about fourteen-year-olds. Train them—not to pickle their brains with liquor. Train them to turn that TV off at night. Train them to choose education."

His voice was screechy and crackly. How did his throat hold up? "We need to see the whole world. . . . America has six percent of the world population. One-half of all human beings are Asians. One-eighth of all human beings are Africans; one-quarter of them are Nigerians. . . . When we win this election in New York on Tuesday we will make it clear to the world that South Africa has nuclear power, and therefore threatens the world."

Hart and Mondale "are not mean men. But that's not the issue. At a time when we need liberation, they want to stop at liberalism. We need to go a little further.

"Let nobody fool you—a change is going on. April 3rd will be a mighty great day. On April 4, 1968, Dr. King was crucified. On April 3, 1984, we will roll the stone away, and go from crucifixion to resurrection."

Attempts were made, throughout the campaign, to account for the power of Jackson's oratory by analyzing it as verse, while a minority denied that he had any power or skill at all. The latter position was absurd, the first beside the point. Jackson's rhyming jingles, even his chants, were verbal punctuation, commas and underlining; they did not create the sense of flow, they only marked it. His power came from describing, in plain and vivid language, the problems of his audiences. (Nine thousand politicians have talked about "poverty"; Jackson talked about poor black maids.)

But Jackson also sought to mobilize. The "new dimension" of his struggle, the "little further" beyond liberalism that he wanted to lead people to, was, it became more and more clear, some strange conception of the Third World. The world was big; so focus on South Africa. A civil rights leader (Martin Luther King) belonged on a list with a black separatist (Marcus Garvey), a religious fanatic (Elijah Muhammad), a crook (Powell), and two dictators (Nkrumah and Touré). The Rainbow Coalition put on its podiums a ragtag and riffraff of communists and lunatics, who thought of white Americans as fascists, and of Walter Mondale as a mass murderer. Into this stewpot were somehow heaved the aspirations of American blacks.

The sun set. I went to the subway to go home. "You sightseeing?" a voice asked.

"My mother always told me," the mayor of New York, Ed Koch, said, shaking his great bald head for emphasis, "it's always better to *win* than to *lose.*" He was at Mondale headquarters on primary night with the winners. Hart barely came in ahead of Jackson, at 27 percent. Mondale took 45 percent (two-thirds of the vote in New York City). The erosion had been stopped and reversed. It was now Hart who began running like a blocked gutter.

Mondale won the Pennsylvania primary on April 10. ("I helped work the arrangement," he boasted in a Pittsburgh debate, to get Wheeling-Pittsburgh Steel "back on their feet" during the Carter years. "When labor, management and government work together, anything can happen." *Here's the beef.)* Hart lost out in the Missouri caucuses eight days later. The next big contest was the Texas caucus on May 5; it did not look very good for him either.

For one night, Hart tried to talk like a hawk. Speaking at Texas A&M, April 30, he told a crowd of Aggies that the hostage crisis had been "days of shame" during which America seemed an "uncertain power, unlikely to stand up for its own interests." He had only been talking about our unreformed military, he backtracked later, and its ineptitude in maneuver warfare, but as with his Czech-airliner answer at the Fox Theater, his explanation came as news to everyone who was there. Mondale expressed dignified hurt ("that was a tragic situation") and Hart never tried running to the right again. It was a lesson in the limits of pandering; it only works when you're sincere.

The debate before the Texas primary, in a hotel at the Dallas–Fort Worth airport two days after the Texas A&M speech, yielded Hart no gains—or anyone else, for that matter. The format was becoming frayed. The three candidates that were left were by now well known, and they weren't coming up with anything zippy. The moderator, Sandor Vanocur, did ask Jackson what he thought about Louis Farrakhan's deportment. (The discussion, interestingly, focused on the threat to Coleman. To accuse an entire race of being demonic half-breeds is apparently ho-hum stuff. Threaten a reporter, and out come the cops.) Hart and Mondale, who had shared several platforms with Farrakhan's patron without themselves raising the issue, expressed their disapproval.

There was one new question. Vanocur asked if English should become the official language of the United States. The idea had first been proposed by former Senator Hayakawa of California, and it was intended, not as a *Kulturkampf* against lesser breeds, but as a symbolic gesture to avoid well ahead of time the maniacal bureaucratic even-handedness of officially bilingual societies, like Canada and Belgium. The three were unimpressed. America was the "only industrial nation," declared Jackson, "with only one language" (Germany? Japan?).

Hart flew the next morning to San Antonio, where the issue came up again in an elementary school on the Mexican end of town. He sat with a dozen or more teachers and administrators in the school library, looming over the child-sized table. Hart had the only mike, but the teachers in fact had some interesting things to say. "We don't want a dual system. We're proud to be American citizens." If Spanish-speaking kids weren't started out in their own tongue, they would drop out of school. Hart summed it up: bilingual education, he said approvingly, "built a bridge" to a "largely non-Hispanic society." Across the hall was a room-ful of first-graders. Hart lowered himself into a chair next to two wide-eyed little girls. It wasn't clear how much traffic was going over the bridge; every word on the classroom wall—one fox, *uno;* two dolphins, *dos;* three turtles, *tres*—was in Spanish. The symbol for *invierno,* though, was a snowman, and the month of *marzo* was illustrated by a shamrock. The kids, meanwhile, were taken with the mo-torcade, particularly the network cars, station wagons with a cameraman standing on the rear door, shooting over the roof. That was something worth being a grown-up for.

While Hart was in school, Mondale made his pitch to the parents. He began the fourth of May with a rally in Corpus Christi, in a park fronting the heavy, hazy Gulf. Mondale had long-standing ties with Texas Hispanics, and he was calling in all chits. (The Mexican-American Democrats of Texas endorsed him over Jackson by a 12-to-1 margin.) Away from Plains, he reverted to type—a black suit, a dark red necktie. The crowd was sown with union banners on standards, looking rather feudal, like props from an old-fashioned production of *Parsifal.* The warm-up speakers (in Corpus Christi, the term seemed singularly inappropriate) included the governor of New Mexico. "Governor Anaya," said his introducer, "is one of us. He speaks Spanish, just like you and I." To prove it, Anaya said that *nuestra raza* would make the *diferencia* in Texas, California, and other states. The man for bilingualism, he concluded, was Walter Mon-dale. "You are here," the local state senator followed, "among real Democrats—people whose path to upward mobility was the New Deal of Franklin Roosevelt" and the "Great Society of Lyndon Johnson: loyal traditionalists of great innovators. You do not disparage a tradition of innova-tion and compassion." Mondale asked permission to remove his jacket. His shirt blazed like a searchlight.

"I've been criticized for having the support of people who work for a living. I don't defend it. I'm proud of it. . . . Our future is made in heaven for us. Ours is the best and most beautiful nation on earth. We have everything we need except the leadership to take us into that future."

The Gulf was hot, the Rio Grande Valley was hell. The Mondale rally in Laredo was held (good planning) on a blacktop parking lot. The grass in a neighboring baseball field was the same color as the dirt. Mondale removed his jacket here without asking, though the tie still flew at full mast. A mariachi band in neckerchiefs and sombreros stood out in the pounding sun and blared. Mondale mentioned Central America, where the administration was "militarizing, Americanizing, and widening the dispute. They're forgetting that the people [there] have hearts and souls and families, just like us." But he returned to more central themes. The local unemployment rate—20 percent—was "sinful." "I'm a people's Democrat." His candidacy was "not just for me. It's for us."

The little town of Donna produced the biggest crowd— five thousand, the organizers said; maybe half that in fact. Leafless dead palm trees lined the road like giant Q-Tips (the valley had gone three months without a ripple of rain). But the fourth had been declared Walter Mondale Day and the people were having a blast. There were balloons, streamers, piñatas, more mariachi music. Anaya said it reminded him of a good, old-fashioned rally in his home state. To say nothing of Old Mexico. The fat sun declined; the temperature stayed in the high nineties. Mondale's face had turned the color of kidney beans.

"Tomorrow is Cinco de Mayo"—caucus day, but also a Mexican patriotic holiday. "That means independence and freedom. Tomorrow let's go to those caucuses and declare independence and freedom from Ronald Reagan, Reaganomics, Reagan's foreign policy, Reagan's unemployment, and Reagan's disregard for the problems of this valley and its needs."

Reagan, Mondale noted, had flown to Dallas recently. "He talked to rich people. He should have come to Donna. That's what a President's supposed to do, help Americans when they're in need.

"I'm no stranger to Texas and the valley. You know me, and I know you. I know what you need, I know what you're saying, I know what you want for your children and your family. We'll get on with the work of our nation's business— to help the people of this country."

Aquí está el bif. The band played "On Broadway." A Secret Service agent hooked an arm around Mondale's midsection, and, thus supported, he leaned off the speaker's platform, grabbing hands two at a time.

After accompanying the mayor of San Antonio to the polls in the morning, he flew to Ohio. "You can almost be sure," he said, that "where people are suffering, Ronald Reagan will be somewhere else." Mondale himself was somewhere else when he said it, specifically at a party on the back lawn of the governor's mansion in Columbus. But for his second stop in the state, he inspected the Cleveland waterfront.

WE CAN'T ALL BE COMPUTER PROGRAMMERS read the sign of a friendly demonstrator. PUT AMERICA'S BASIC INDUSTRIES BACK TO WORK (a machine-printed sentiment, courtesy of the Maritime Trades Division of the AFL-CIO). Mondale boarded a tug with Representative Mary Oakar, and slid past rotting piles, rusted spans, cyclopean brick shells. "They're putting in condos here for a hundred fifty thousand dollars," commented a member of the congresswoman's staff. "The whole industrial belt," said Mondale of Reagan, "is getting nothing from this guy." When he had seen enough desolation, he returned to shore for a press conference. "If the steel industry is sick—we all suffer." Its sickness was "a dagger in the heart of the Midwest." The government had to "invest in science and technology and the arts so young people of this region can be on the cutting edge of technology, and the rest."

He repeated a prediction he had made in Rochester, New Hampshire, eleven months earlier, that the combination of temporary recovery and deficits would drive up interest rates. "I don't see why we risk it." Representative Oakar compared Mondale to his mentor: "Hubert Humphrey devoted his life to full employment. So will he."

There was a literal sense in which Walter Mondale was the most conservative candidate in either party. The cutting edge was a nice place to talk about, but the bedrock of Mondale's position was that he, and his supporters, wanted people to be able to stay put. They *couldn't* all become computer programmers; and to the extent they did, the ranks of such as the Maritime Trades Division of the AFL-CIO would dwindle (along with their clout). When the Corpus Christi state senator spoke of FDR and LBJ as "great innovators," he was indulging nostalgia; but when he described the "real Democrats" who reverenced them as "loyal traditionalists," he was on the mark. Politically, it worked, at least in the primaries. They might be "special interests." But Mondale had real things to offer them, and they were really interested.

Hart tried a last major countermove to catalyze new support: hitting Mondale's campaign finances. Glenn, in his final days in Iowa, had raised the issue, complaining about labor union phone banks, burning their wires for Fritz—a vain complaint, since it had the flavor of sour grapes (if the unions had backed Glenn, would he have made them use smoke signals?). When the same phone banks failed so conspicuously in New Hampshire, that particular charge withered. Hart had a more serious one: that union money was flowing in an unseemly fashion into local pro-Mondale political action committees set up to evade the election laws.

The limit that any group or individual could legally give to a campaign was $5,000. After Hart unexpectedly surged, though, Mondale supporters found a loophole: Suppose each would-be Mondale delegate were treated as an individual campaigner, with a PAC of his own? The proliferation of delegate PACs allowed Mondale fans, particularly unions, to make multiple contributions far in excess of the one-shot limit (the American Federation of Teachers gave $54,000 to thirty-eight different committees, while the automobile, communications, and public employees' unions together kicked in a hundred thou). The day after the New York primary, Hart filed a protest with the Federal Election Commission; on April 25, he left a message for Mondale with a Nashville audience: "Give the money back, Walter."

Mondale replied, in part, that he was playing by the rules; if Hart didn't know them, too bad. "This upcoming convention is not the first we've had in the history of America," he told a press conference in Dallas. "The farther you're behind, the more you try a trick to get what the voters have denied you." "I'm just doing what the other guy is doing," he had told an interviewer in 1983. "As long as the system exists, you have to use it."[2] There were two problems with this line of defense. The first was that many of the Mondale delegate PACs weren't playing by the rules. To qualify as separate entities, each entitled to a full contribution, the committees had to be independent of Mondale headquarters, and of each other. They seemed to have a strange way, however, of forwarding leftover money, once their particular struggle was done, to fresh committees farther down the primary trail. The same Mondale operatives kept popping up on their organization charts. (On December 4—too late to help Hart, of course—the FEC ordered the Mondale campaign to return 400,000 misraised bucks.)

The real problem, though, was rhetorical. It suited the demonology of a certain kind of Democrat, going right back to the Reverend Mondale and every other Plains state populist, to believe that big money, usually corporate, bought and sold public servants like fish bait. Big election money was evil. It was Mark Hanna; it was the Devil; it was Nixon. The campaign-spending laws of the post-Watergate era had restricted the sums that might be contributed. When it was found that they permitted the existence of political action committees, the purer Democrats felt obliged to disdain these too. Gary Hart boasted that his campaign took "not one penny" of PAC money. So had Reubin Askew. And Mondale? "It's time, fellow Democrats," he had said in January 1983, "that we declare war on special-interest money in American politics. . . . Let's plant controls on these PACs. Let's end the loopholes of so-called independent committees." Government "belongs to the American people, and we want it back." But when the "special-interest money" came from the tribunes of "the American people" —what then?

Mondale confronted his hypocrisy with aplomb. (Hypocrisy on procedure is rarely fatal; people know politics is a contact sport.) He insisted, first, that the PACs were beyond his control (those wacky Mondale folks—what free spirits); next, that he would disband them; finally, when they had done their work, that he would give back the money. "Now," said Jackson, "give me back my share of delegates." Hart began to speak of "tainted primaries"; there were rumors of challenges at the convention. All idle. There had not been a decisive delegate challenge since the Republican convention of 1952, when the Eisenhower forces managed to throw out marginal delegates pledged to Robert Taft, and that had worked only because the two sides had been almost exactly balanced. Winners do not allow their juggernauts to be stopped. If Hart wanted to derail Mondale, he would have to do it by winning.

The first week of May was a draw. Mondale took the Texas caucuses on the fifth and the Maryland and North Carolina primaries three days later. Hart won the Colorado caucus on the seventh and the primaries of Indiana and Ohio on the eighth. The last and largest bloc of delegates would be picked on a second Super Tuesday, June 5. The five primaries that day included New Jersey and California. Hart had to win them both to prevent Mondale from reaching a clean majority.

First, there were debts to repay—George McGovern's campaign debts (and the party's to him, though this was inexplicit). Five days before the last Tuesday, the leading contenders—Jackson stayed away—attended a fund-raiser in the sculpture garden (the lawn, to you) of a longtime McGovern supporter in Brentwood, just across the San Diego Freeway from Beverly Hills.

Jacarandas dripped purple petals. Reporters swarmed around the debarking famous. (I recognized only Ed Asner, O. J. Simpson, and Hugh Hefner, but my celebrity antennae are blunt. One of the blond, waif-haired beauties I pegged as a starlet turned out to be an anchorwoman.) Waiters served the guests satays; the press huddled on the driveway, satayless, though the liquor was generous. A pair of neighbors, Republicans perhaps, stared at the sleek stream of incoming Cadillacs and Mercedes-Benzes.

The sound of a low-flying chopper signaled the arrival of the Secret Service. In a sunrise of flashbulbs, Mondale came up the grass, then Hart. The theme of the evening was unity, prompted by the talk of tainted primaries and delegates; prompted also by the elder-statesman persona that George McGovern had crafted for himself.

Hart spoke first. "This country is in dire circumstances"— he hadn't known how dire until he saw recently a bumper sticker: CAP WEINBERGER FOR PRESIDENT / LET'S GET IT OVER WITH. He seemed tired and a little dazed, and he was tanned an unflattering hue, like the color of an odd shoe polish. He joked awkwardly about Mondale, and Reagan. "When was the last time a President owned more tuxedos than books?"

Mondale was more amiable. "It's nice to be here, with just plain folks." He hit three themes, all suited to the general election (four months after New Hampshire, he was hearing "Hail to the Chief" again, with more reason): deficits— crippling; interest rates—sure to rise; the state of the world —parlous. "Under [Reagan's] leadership, the world is becoming far more divided and dangerous."

The host then introduced the guest of honor. McGovern's campaign that year, he said, had "removed for a lot of us the pejorative use of the phrase 'McGovern Democrat.' " Also the distinguishing use; who wasn't anymore? McGovern stepped up between his former campaign manager and the protégé of his former opponent and spoke with well-earned satisfaction. "This year, I come in third in Iowa, and everyone says, 'Isn't George wonderful?' I tie for fourth in New

Hampshire, and everyone says, 'Isn't he a great statesman?'" Any permutation of the remaining candidates
would suit him as a ticket, or one that included a woman
(applause). "My main goal is the defeat of Ronald Reagan.
The enemy is not Gary Hart . . . but the virtual collapse of
Soviet-American relations, to the most dangerous position
since fifty years ago. The enemy is not Fritz Mondale's delegate committees; the enemy is Reaganomics" and unfair
taxes. "The enemy is not Jesse Jackson's view of Israel, but a
President on the verge of taking us into war in Nicaragua
and El Salvador.

"Now praise the Lord and pass the ammunition."

What issues did Hart and his supporters hit in the home-
stretch? He spoke on the first of June to a rally in downtown
Los Angeles. A rock band, whose lead singer was a Chicano
in dreadlocks, sang a song about Lebanon. "Gary Hart cares
about what women want," his first introducer declared,
which was "first and foremost" passage of the Equal Rights
Amendment. "He has distinguished himself," said the second, "in the fight to ban nuclear weapons from the face of
this earth." "This nation has not passed its prime," Hart
said, "its leaders have." ("What about abortion, Gary?" a
man in a goatee called loudly. *Why don't you shut up, son
of a bitch?* But the man did not shut up, and yelled the
question repeatedly through much of Hart's talk, claiming
the privilege of "free speech." *You idiot, you don't know the
meaning of the word.* It would not be the last such confrontation.)

Hart went on to San Jose, to be questioned by a panel of
students at Yerba Buena high school. Reporters ask questions about their own stories, and sound like idiots. The
students asked what was on their minds—school prayer,
space exploration—and sounded like Socrates. There was
also a question on human rights around the world; the peg
was Sakharov.

Hart gave a long, detailed answer. "We have," he began,
"a lot to do on human rights in this country"; he cited poor
people, women, the elderly. The Democratic party also

"shuts people out," and would have to adopt new rules for its delegate-selection process. Looking abroad, he criticized "dictators of the right and left," mentioning Marcos, Somoza, and the governments of South Korea and South Africa. In a Hart administration, "so-called allies" would have to "liberate and liberalize their systems." A long answer; and not one word about Sakharov.

The Hart press bus drove through rush-hour traffic to San Francisco; some of his supporters in the music industry came along. (Names? Blunt antennae.) One carried a lap-size synthesizer, the shape of an electronic mandolin or a huge coke spoon, and composed a song, a sort of calypso, as the bus crawled on.

He's got an eye for the people, a nose for the news.
He's got charm and charisma, he's the one you should
    choose.
And to top it all off, he wears good shoes.
Vote, vote for Hart.
Vote, vote for Hart.
Please do your part,
Vote, vote for Hart.

His fellow musicians performed this composition with descants and obbligati.

The night's rally was in the St. Francis Hotel. "We cannot afford to go back to the imagined time in which Ronald Reagan is living. We cannot afford four more years in which he might appoint" a new "Supreme Court. We cannot afford four more years in which he might perhaps engage this nation in an unnecessary war in Central America, the Persian Gulf, or elsewhere. We know we cannot afford four more years of a costly arms race. We can do better."

"We have a vision," he said next day in San Diego, of putting "unemployed people back to work, rebuilding our cities. We have a vision of workers, trained to produce the most efficient products on earth. We have a vision of a new environmental decade" in which we would "end acid rain and clean up toxic waste dumps once and for all . . . of a

President totally and unqualifiedly committed to ratifying the Equal Rights Amendment . . . of the diplomatic and moral leadership to negotiate a freeze. . . . Let's negotiate an end to the production of nuclear weapons all around the world." Let's "not just end the nuclear arms race, but strengthen our conventional forces." He had a vision of a mission in Central America and the Third World, which was "to combat the enemy, which is not Communism, but poverty."

There, over two days, was the Essential Hart, the Compleat Yuppie. What was he? A new leader, he said, in his prime. What was new about him? What had been new at first—a commitment to beefing up the conventional arsenal in imaginative ways and a handful of haphazard economic proposals. What else did he have to offer? Nothing—ERA, acid rain, no foreign wars, and freeze, freeze, freeze—that Walter Mondale didn't also endorse with, it must be added, less stiff-necked dogmatism than Hart. Hart's Sakharov non-answer was typical of his reflexive leftism. It would be wrong to make too much of it. But it would also be wrong to make nothing. The worst pitches are the fat slow ones a batter doesn't swing at. Hart didn't even waggle at Sakharov. He could have plugged détente and quiet diplomacy, as Henry Kissinger would have done ten years ago; he could have blamed Reagan for incensing the Russians and goading them to new heights of cruelty, as columnist Anthony Lewis, among others, was then doing. Hart presumably cared about Sakharov—because every decent man did, and Hart was a decent man. But at the end of a long campaign, on the second stop of the day, with the third to go, the brain switches to automatic pilot. And Gary Hart's automatic not only did not steer him in the direction of the most famous inmate of the world's largest jail, it swerved him away. The enemy in the world was not Communism, but anything else.

"On to San Francisco, on to the White House. With your help, I intend to be the next President of the United States."

Before San Francisco or the White House, however, Hart

made a swing through New Jersey, where he found personal reason to rue toxic waste. His wife was still campaigning in California, which, he candidly allowed, was the better
deal; looking out his Jersey hotel window the night before,
he had found himself face to face with a toxic waste dump.
Pre-dump, New Jersey had been a plausible Hart state. The
local politicos had no great love for Mondale; they had been
for Glenn the preceding fall. But New Jerseyans are sensitive about the perceived homeliness of the Garden State.
They took it out on the snotty bicoastal slicker. Was Hart's
levity then the deciding factor, the slip of the lip that sank
the new generation of leadership? Yes, proximately; which
is to say, no, not at all. If a politician's defeat depends on
such a minor factor, then he was as good as beaten long
before. No kingdom is lost for the want of a single nail. Hart
had correctly picked out Mondale's weakness—special interests. But they were also a strength—they were the beef.
Hart lacked sufficient strength to overcome it. Hart swept
California, beating his combined rivals 2 to 1; but Mondale
took New Jersey, with 45 percent of the vote. It was all over
but the shouting.

Louis Farrakhan gave his last shout on June 24. In another
of his winning radio broadcasts, he called Judaism a "dirty
religion" (this was misquoted for several days, though
hardly to his disadvantage, as "gutter religion"). This time
Mondale did not wait for the promptings of Sandor Vanocur. On June 26, he called Farrakhan's statement "venom-
ous, bigoted, obscene." Jesse Jackson waited two more days
before issuing a disavowal, for he was with Fidel Castro at
the time.

Cuba was the third of a four-nation Central America tour.
American politicians do not typically make campaign
swings through foreign countries. But Jackson's trip, which
he called the Moral Offensive, marked a climax in his evolution as a self-defined figure of the Third World. It also gave a
fair demonstration of his diplomatic skills.

The Moral Offensive, Jackson said on setting out, "seeks

to promote greater dialogue and understanding." His first dialogue was with the President of Panama, who received him in his palace, a building of colonial vintage in a dense section of the old part of Panama City. The palace was mostly for show, but then, so was the President (the real power in Panama being whoever happens to be the real power in the Defense Forces at the time). Five white herons with yellow bills strolled gravely about the courtyard; statues of Law and the Laborer frowned on the stairs.

Jackson began in Panama because it was one of the Contadora countries, and hence, a moral oracle. But he had also been in Panama before, to study the Panama Canal treaties. (He had concluded that they were judicious; also that General Torrijos, the incumbent real power, was a "hero.") Jackson appeared, after an hour's meeting, with President Jorge Illueca, in a rococo salon decorated with murals of Balboa and the muse of history.

Jackson feared war by the fall of 1984. "We must move the day before so there will not be a day after. We must negotiate it out and think it out, not fight it out. We must have cease-fire, not more fire" *(cesar el fuego, no más el fuego* was what the interpreter came up with). The President was asked: How exactly had Jackson advanced the peace process? Illueca looked out at the little room, bristling with TV mikes. "He was very successful in getting all of you here." Bull's-eye. He then framed it more tactfully. "He has been conveying to the American people the realities." Jackson and the President bussed. The herons honked as the press rushed out. In the tiny park in front of the palace, a dozen Panamanians watched Jackson pull away, and an old man hawked Italian ices from a pushcart.

Illueca was a lame duck, for Jackson had come to Panama in the wake of its own presidential election. The Defense Forces had backed a technocrat picked to mollify Panama's long-suffering creditors. The other parties, chiefly the Christian Democrats, had rallied behind Arnulfo Arias, a fixture of Panamanian politics since the forties, when he had made his debut as a pro-fascist. A genuinely popular man, Arias had done many a pas de deux over the years with the military, which had deposed him after three elections, and defrauded him in a fourth. For his last hurrah, they had defrauded him once more. Such at least was the consensus of most observers, and the conviction of all of Arias's supporters. When they found out Jackson's schedule, they took to dogging him. (If the Moral Offensive was supposed to promote dialogue, why couldn't it dialogue with them?)

They stood in the street outside the ruling party headquarters, where Jackson went for an early-evening meeting with the President-elect: half a dozen chanting middle-aged women. Cars honked at them frantically, policemen took notes. It had been pouring since afternoon. ("Does it rain every day?" I had asked. "Yes." "And does the electricity go off every day?" "Often.") The women tried to hold umbrellas and signs at the same time: WE CAN PROVE ELECTORAL FRAUD. CONTADORA, DO WHAT YOU PREACH.

There was a bigger demonstration on the steps of Don Bosco Church. But the congregation, filling the pews and spilling into the aisles, awaited Jackson attentively. Cameras lined the altar rail like BB guns in a shooting gallery. "Photographers," an old black man complained, in a West Indian lilt. "They are such rude peo-ple."

Jackson plowed through a weighty text, translator in tow. Central America, he said, was plagued by debt and war, to both of which the United States contributed. Our deficit, swollen by military spending, had pushed up interest rates. Meanwhile, the International Monetary Fund—"unmerciful and voracious"—imposed "austerity measures on people who have never known anything but austerity." Blaming everything on Communism was a "reductionist argument"; the real causes of rebellion were "hunger, disease, illiteracy, repression, and exploitation." America, which should respond with "aid and trade," sent in "arms and bombs" instead. The big stick was futile as well as wrong. "Whether it is George Washington in the United States [or] Augusto Sandino in Nicaragua, the people's will cannot be stopped." That was the message—as earnest as the proceedings of a

dozen Washington think-tank symposia, and as memorable.
Then Jackson left his text and spoke untrammeled.

"I know it's tough, but there will be peace in the valley.
Feed the hungry, clothe the naked, liberate the captive.
The Lord is our light and our salvation. Whom shall we fear?
The Lord is the strength of our life. If you keep faith, no jail
cell can contain you, no graveyard can hold you down. Just
like Jesus, you may face crucifixion on Friday, but the resurrection comes on Sunday morning. Now is the time. Now is
the time. Now is the time." By this time, Jackson had left the
interpreter far behind. "Feed the hungry. Clothe the naked. Study war no more. Our time has come. Our time has
come. Our time has come."

The crowd was caught up in the swell and fall—all but the
demonstrators on the steps, who had crept in at the back of
the church and set up a chant of their own—Ar*nul*fo *Presi-
den*te—during the peroration. They and Jackson clashed
like dissonant bands. When he had finished, Archbishop
McGrath, the Roman Catholic prelate of Panama, thanked
him over the din, and expressed the hope that he would
convey Panama's desire for peace to America—"because
we depend on every action of the United States." The recessional played, the cameramen moved out. "Thank you,
Jesus," a black woman declared outside, "everything was
peace-ful."

Another of Jackson's reasons for coming to Panama City
was to pay a visit to the Panama Canal and the tomb of
Omar Torrijos. The dictator, who died in a 1978 plane crash,
has been planted on the broad lawn before a former American military headquarters. Four bronze soldiers guarded his
remains; twenty-nine live ones were on duty for Jackson's
arrival. He laid a wreath on the grave inside a small mauso-
leum of mottled marble, and spoke from the monument's
steps.

"This place," he said of the former Canal Zone, "was a
badge of disgrace to America, and a burden of shame and
pain on the people of Panama." But Jimmy Carter and
Torrijos had averted an explosion. "As you count the cost

and look at the aggregate box score, he [Torrijos] was a winner. People have dignity because he lived. Let's join hands, and bow our heads in prayer.

"We thank You for the life of General Torrijos. Let us build on the tradition of the freed zone of the Panama Canal and let the freedom bell ring everywhere, from Canada to Cuba. We will beat our spears into plowshares, and our swords into pruning hooks. Peace is possible; now is the time. Amen."

Nearby was Lake Miraflores, a man-made sheet eighty-two feet above the Pacific. If engineering has works of art, the Miraflores Locks are one of them. They move 26 million gallons of water in eight minutes; the original control board, installed in 1905, still works (computerization was recently considered, but rejected as less reliable). Jackson greeted the tourists at the observation deck, and ascended to the control tower to turn the knobs himself. The 700-ton gates pivoted, the mute water rushed. Jackson and his entourage watched from the balcony.

Jackson held a second press conference that afternoon, with representatives of the civilian franchise which the Salvadoran rebels maintained in Panama City. The most prominent of these was Rubén Zamora, leader of the Revolutionary Democratic Front (FDR), bearded, bespectacled, pale. In a cloth jacket and cap instead of his safari shirt, he could have passed for a chum of Raskolnikov's. The rebels, Jackson announced, embraced the Contadora process, and were willing to go to San Salvador to meet with the government. This was not a new proposal; the government was even willing, in theory, to meet with them. The hitch, now as before, was that the government wanted the shooting to stop before the talking started; the rebels wanted talks first. Zamora, who had not budged, was asked if he thought the government had. "There must be some flexibility," he speculated, since the government was about to receive Jackson. There would be more details, the press was told, at a second press conference that night, after further discussions.

The lights went off again in the afternoon. The press conference was canceled.

On the third day, the Moral Offensive moved to El Salvador. The streets of the capital were brisk with morning business. Of all the cities on the trip, it seemed most vibrant. People drove, ate, drank, walked, worked, ran errands— half a million of them, about the same size as Cleveland. There were also soldiers on every corner.

The Secret Service put on bulletproof vests before landing. No public sermons here; no overnighting (the plane was going on to Cuba in the afternoon). After a quick meeting with the Catholic hierarchy, Jackson was whisked to the presidential palace and Duarte.

This palace looked a century or so younger than Panama's, and correspondingly uglier: a collapsed, frosted cake. Jackson and Duarte met inside, and one of Jackson's entourage—Congressman Mervyn Dymally (D., Calif.), who had joined up in Panama—let it be known that his man came "from a different perspective. He represents the poor people of America." "We have poor people in our country too," Duarte agreed. "I can identify." Outside, on the blazing portico, reporters curled into the available patches of shade like cats; locusts creaked; even the moss felt hot.

In the debate at St. Anselm's four months earlier, Jackson had called Duarte's government a "killer regime." Had he altered his views? he was asked before leaving Panama. "Yes. We all want to give peace a chance." After an hour and a half, Jackson and the ex-killer appeared together at the head of the stairs. Jackson wore an open-necked shirt with piping around the epaulettes, which gave it a vaguely semi-military cut. José Napoleón Duarte, a head shorter than Jackson, looked baggy and energetic—a Hispanic Humphrey.

Duarte took the lead. "I have received Jackson's information with great respect. I have said to him that I will present his point of view to the people of my country. . . . I believe in democracy; democracy means to discuss and talk.

Therefore, the next step is to tell my people what this concept of the Moral Offensive means."

Here was a wordslinger as adroit as Jackson. "Glad to see you; now we'll get back to work"—surely that was the substance of what Duarte had said. Yet he managed to say it without a trace of offense, subsuming himself, his guest, and the Moral Offensive under the loftier rubric of democracy. If Jackson sensed he had been bested, he gave no sign: "El Salvador means the Savior. One critical dimension of the Savior is that He endures crucifixion. But in time the stone is rolled away. After the crucifixion of bleeding, came the resurrection of healing . . ." He and Duarte restated the rebel offers. What was new in them? Nothing "in concept," Duarte replied. "It is new in the way they have said it." He wove in an anecdote involving himself and the Pope.

Jackson wanted to see a prisoner before he left, a leader of the electrical workers' union who had been jailed for calling a strike in 1980. The prison lay in the hills away from town; the warden let only a handful of press inside. Outside the gate, there was a soft-drink counter for visitors and a radio playing the theme from *Against All Odds.* When he reemerged, after an hour, the entourage was pleased. "It was very good," one said, "very sentimental."

Jackson dropped into Havana at sunset. (The Secret Service had unbuckled. No security problems here.) On the balcony of the airport terminal stood a crowd of perhaps a thousand; they had been waiting since midafternoon, victims of the Silly Putty schedule. On the runway below them stood Fidel Castro.

It was the quietest crowd I have ever seen. From time to time it cheered, but in the intervals, the silence was eerie—not a chatter, not a murmur. Jackson came down the gangway, Castro advanced to the foot of the steps to shake his hand. Shutters clattered, the antiquated TV cameras of the Cubans whirred, lights flashed like little stars. On their way to the motorcade, Castro and Jackson were mobbed by photographers. Only stray phrases floated out: ". . . turn to each other, not at each other . . . health care for the sick . . ." The dark cars rolled away, the crowd stayed put until they had gone.

Havana next morning proved to be lovely. Curiously, it has many of the qualities associated with capitals of regimes that the forces of progress seek to overthrow. The leader, when he appears in public, is always in uniform. The streets are slow and somnolent. Most of the buildings are old, charming, and slightly decayed; a few are new, ugly, and falling apart. The police are brisk and visible; the motorcycle police that accompanied the motorcades flagged over private cars with an efficient swagger.

The cars alone were worth the price of admission. Most were Fiats, made in Russia. But every tenth or fifteenth came straight out of the museum of models Detroit forgot: Buicks, Dodges, Plymouths, Ramblers, De Sotos, and, everywhere, Chevrolets (*chevy* is still slang for taxi). Some had tail fins; a few looked as if they could have flown home unassisted; most had the rounded, late-forties/early-fifties contour. They had been painted and repainted; an entire underground industry had grown up to keep them running. The motif was picked up by some of the official limousines, the cars Jackson and his entourage rode in, half of which were Mercedes-Benzes and half Chaikas, a heavyset Soviet knockoff of the 1956 Chrysler.

Jackson spent a morning of VIP tourism, starting with a historical museum, in the former Spanish governor's residence, filled with portraits of nineteenth-century Cuban patriots. Jackson asked about African cultural influence, having heard a Cuban singer who reminded him of Stevie Wonder. (Perhaps the singer listened to Miami radio. A French journalist, based in Havana, said that his maid had been greatly excited at the prospect of Jackson's visit, until she learned he wasn't Michael.) Next came a hospital, a large modern facility. Jackson's guide, the Minister of Health, declared that "no one contributes to the cost of public health," since it all came out of the national budget, though he amended this by saying that the government did draw on sales taxes. He also assured Jackson that even a poor child had a chance to become a doctor, so long as he had a high enough grade point and was a "revolutionary person."

The afternoon began with a photo opportunity. At three o'clock, the press was bused out to the Palace of the Revolution—the newest of the palaces on the trip so far, and the most unsightly—and deposited in a waiting room. The waiting ended when the wall rolled back, to reveal Jackson, Castro, and their aides seated at a long elliptical table. It was like meeting God, or the Wizard of Oz. The Cubans admonished the scrambling photographers: "With discipline, with discipline . . ." The wall rolled back, and they got down to work.

The schedule called for a press conference at seven o'clock and a reception at nine-thirty. The pressure was on Jackson, both press- and self-generated, to execute some symbolic coup. Before the trip began, he had spoken of persuading Cuba to attend the Los Angeles Olympics, but that idea was quickly dropped. The journalistic rumor mill then shifted to political prisoners. Seven, eight, nine passed without a word. At quarter of ten, the press was escorted to the party.

I had been to one buffet, at the Rockefeller home in Pocantico Hills, where the food was almost as good. Almost —the Rockefellers didn't give unlimited seconds. There was fish, caviar, shrimp, crab claws, lobster (poached tails or mousse in the half shell). There was chicken curry, corn pudding, whole roast pig. There was chocolate roulade, cake topped with bonbons, bread baked in the shape of alligators. There was Chardonnay—Bulgarian, unfortunately (if you want first-class wine from the Evil Empire, you have to hold out for dessert and Tokay), but there were a dozen bartenders pouring hard liquor with a liberal hand, most liberally of all into the *mojitos*, a concoction of sugar, mint, and rum that tasted like dew and acted like Sominex. The room was as long as a line drive over second base, and the black marble floor was bordered with rock gardens, oriental in all but scale—six-foot rocks, eight-foot ferns. It

was a long way from the Sierra Maestra. As the eating and
the evening wore on, the condensation from emptied
glasses soaked into the tablecloths like dark flowers.

The press conference got started a little after midnight.
Jackson announced the fruit of ten hours' work: Castro
would release twenty-two Americans in Cuban jails. Jackson invited him to the United States, and they condemned
South Africa.

Castro listened while Jackson spoke. He is getting on. He
is stout now, and the hair is graying, which pictures convey.
The surprise was the face—lined, softening, the face of an
English eccentric, Mr. Dick perhaps. He could still give five
speeches before breakfast. Would he accept Jackson's invitation? Castro noted that it was not official; it "must be
examined and meditated in a careful manner." Under what
terms would he pull his advisers out of Central America?
But Cuba had none—only teachers and health workers.
"Professors, that's what we have there."

After a mango-juice nightcap, the buses pulled out at
quarter of two.

Jackson was up early next morning for a flight to the Isle
of Youth, formerly the Isle of Pines, where all the African
nations in which Cuba has stationed troops have sent children, to work in the fields and become revolutionary persons. The kids danced, the few reporters who were able to
wake up and go got bags of souvenirs. Back in Havana,
Jackson visited the American prisoners he was repatriating.
(The New York *Times* reported, days later, that the prisoners had played a "visitor's game" of baseball—so-called because it is a recreation permitted them only when visitors
come. Since Jackson was his usual hour or so late, the game
went seventy innings.)

Castro took Jackson to the University of Havana in the
afternoon. The crowd there at least was lively; they stood on
the baking steps of the Aula Magna and hollered, "Fi-del,
Fi-del," also "Jes-se, Jes-se." The hall steamed; Jackson's text
was "The Dream of Today's Youth."

"It dreams that human rights be measured by one yardstick. We cannot tolerate apartheid. Injustice to one of us is an injustice to all of us. . . . It dreams of nuclear disarmament. We must bury the weapons before they bury the people. Youth dreams of the day when the United States and the Soviet Union come together to wipe out forevermore hunger and disease and illiteracy. If both of the superpowers were to stop building arms today, we could end hunger tomorrow. . . . We must dream of doctors more concerned with public health than with personal wealth. Of lawyers more concerned with justice than judgeships. Of artists who convey music with a message, and rhythm with a reason. Of priests and preachers who prophesy, instead of profiteer. . . . No matter how difficult the day or dark the night, there is a promised land somewhere: in Mozambique, in Angola, in Nicaragua, in El Salvador, in Harlem. With *eye*sight, we see misery. With *in*sight, we see the brighter side. In the end, faith will not disappoint; faith will prevail.

"Long live Cuba. Long live the United States. Long live President Fidel Castro. Long live Martin Luther King. Long live Martin Luther King! Long live Che Guevara. Long live Patrice Lumumba. Long live the cry of freedom. Our time has come [repeated three times]. Bless you."

Cheering again, quickly coalescing into chants. Castro patted his hands gravely. A few blocks from campus was the First Methodist Church of Havana. Nine musicians and a women's choir tried without much success to get the congregation to sing hymns. They perked up when Jackson and Castro arrived: *Fi-del, Fi-del.* Castro said a few words from the pulpit, hailing Jackson as an "example of Christian force," and sat on the altar beneath the cross.

"Our Father God," Jackson began. "We thank Thee this day for the church, for the Holy Bible, for powerful words, for redemption, for forgiveness, for hope, for Jesus Christ, for resurrection, for the promise of eternal life. We thank Thee for the spirit of Martin Luther King, who must be smiling in heaven this day. . . .

"Dr. King was not a liberal who settled for reform, but a liberator who believed in change. Like Jesus, Martin Luther

King was a revolutionary—a Christian revolutionary, a martyr, who did not wear the cross around his neck, but bore it on his back. He climbed Calvary and faced crucifixion. When he died, tears ran down our faces. Our hearts were heavy. But we have been taught to stand still, and see the salvation of God. We had been taught that in time the stone would be rolled away, and we could take the wings of morning and fly somewhere, and rise above our circumstances. So we came to Cuba. . . .

"We came to Cuba to talk, to share, to love you, to affirm our relationship. We must end war, we must save the children, we must love our enemy. If you love your enemy, you will talk to your enemy. If you talk, you may lose an enemy. You may find that you yourself made your enemy your enemy. We must begin the search for common ground. We will not kill each other, but cure each other. We will go another way."

Castro looked as if he was drifting. "My brothers and sisters in Cuba. Weeping may undo us for the night. But hold on, for joy is coming in the morning. The Kingdom of God is within you. Call upon that God; rise, go home with your thoughts. Use your spirit to free the Sandinistas. Use your spirit and power to end war in El Salvador, to get the military bases out of Honduras. [Applause] Use your spirit. I'll fear no evil, for Thou art with me. Thy rod and Thy staff comfort me. Hold on, Cuba! Hold on, Castro! [Applause] Hold on, Nicaragua!"

Then, the recessional.

> We shall overcome,
> We shall overcome,
> We shall overcome some day.
> Oh, deep in my heart
> I do believe
> We shall overcome some day.

Castro did not sing along.

Diplomatically the Moral Offensive was a farce. Corrupt democrats, scheming front men, the beleaguered socialist, the aging caudillo—every leader and would-be leader Jackson met with played him like a banjo. One after another, they thrust themselves into the beam of the media spotlight that tracked him, and picked out the same old songs they had been performing for months, sometimes years. One of the Salvadoran rebels-in-exile was quite frank about it: Jackson, he said, represented "a new effort to try to achieve what we have been trying to achieve for two years." The Panamanians plugged the Contadora process. The Salvadoran rebels wanted in. Duarte wrapped himself in the *vox populi*. Castro, as he has done before with honored or at least impressionable guests, dipped into his capacious jails and doled out wretches like party favors. (Reacting perhaps to early stories along the lines of CASTRO UNLOADS DOPE PEDDLERS, he presented Jackson with twenty-six Cuban political prisoners in addition to the Americans.) Didn't Jackson notice?

Did he care? It wasn't only Duarte and Castro who were using the press backdrops. By hobnobbing with bona fide international leaders, on however unequal a footing, Jackson was certifying his own status as a transnational figure. Jackson's experiences as a Third Worlder may have begun, in his mind, in Greenville, South Carolina, but they had now encompassed, in six days, the presidential palaces of three countries.

Jackson spent the last morning of the trip in the fourth country, conferring in Managua with Sandinistas, including some members of the junta, the most prominent of whom was Ernesto Cardenal, the Jesuit and poet (you knew he was a poet because he wore a beret). Jackson addressed the Council of State and compared their experiment in democracy favorably to America's, for Nicaragua was to have elections only five years after their revolution, whereas we had waited thirteen, until 1789 (no one having told him about the Articles of Confederation).

He landed back in Havana that evening on the heels of a

storm, to pick up his prisoners. The airport crowd had been brought down to the still-wet runway, and he and Castro worked the fence. Wherever the two were, the crowd cheered, but before them, and behind them after they passed, it kept silence. When they retired to the airport lounge, half a dozen men stepped out at even intervals and spoke to their sections: the cheerleaders.

Inside, a second buffet. Castro can cater any party of mine he wants. A bus rolled up to the plane and the prisoners were loaded. In the darkness, there was a final press conference on the runway. Castro rocked back and forth slightly on the balls of his feet as Jackson talked, gazing into space. Occasionally, he took a puff on a cigar. Jackson spoke earnestly; his face glistened. The smoke from Castro's cigar curled in the camera lights.

During the whole time abroad, Jackson got criticized only once to his face. As the plane left Cuba, he walked down the aisle of the press section, shaking hands, something he did at the beginning and end of trips. But one cameraman wasn't shaking. "You know," he said meditatively (he was black), "you really pissed me off."

5
Funny Hats:
San Francisco

The sky was cloudless and gleaming. The flag at the top of the Fairmont Hotel hung limp in the warm air. As the cable car slid to the crown of Nob Hill, three middle-aged, middle-class tourists got on, wearing large buttons: FUCK REAGAN. The Democrats had found their hearts in San Francisco.

The political convention is a ceremony which gets short shrift these days. For 1984, the networks announced that they would no longer provide gavel-to-gavel coverage, leaving the task to CNN and C-SPAN. For viewers, this was no great loss, for over the years Walter and David and Chet had given inordinate time to sidebars, to interviews (the camera picks out a man in antennaed earphones, an extraterrestrial, who turns to his bareheaded earthling prey: "I'm here with Senator Stump. Senator, what does this latest development mean [in a nanosecond or less]? *Thank you*, Senator. Back to you"), to their own musings—to anything, it sometimes seemed, but the business of the convention itself. The indifference of the networks reflected a fundamental misunderstanding of the convention's purpose.

Indeed, one role which conventions used to serve has all but disappeared. The selection of nominees is finished before the first delegates check into their rooms; there hasn't been a second ballot for either of the top slots since 1956. But another role remains. For four days, conventions hold together, in one spot, hundreds of politicians, who want to do nothing but talk. Why shouldn't the attentive citizen have the chance to listen? It means more for the republic than the wit of Dan Rather.

San Franciscans attributed the weather to Mount St. Helens, to El Niño, to they didn't know what. They practically apologized for it. Usually, every summer's day the fog comes in on big cat feet, leaving the unwary outlanders shivering over their cappuccinos in Ghirardelli Square. The Democratic delegates would not suffer that fate. For whatever reason, July in San Francisco felt, remarkably, like July.

Politics (and weather) brought out more than delegates. A hundred aging hippies set up a totem pole in Golden Gate Park. Two days before the convention opened, there was an All Species parade, with folks dressed up as trees, birds, and crustaceans. (A lobster confessed to one of the local papers that his costume was impractical for a march. "It's more for standing in place and doing a little break dancing. It's hard to be a lobster in the city.") Tapping through the local cable stations, you could hear a woman explaining that "prostitution has been a personal-growth workshop for me" and a man declaring that "Walter Mondale is a blatant homophobe, as everyone knows." Even some conservatives crept out. On July 12 and 13, there was a meeting, "I Am My Brother's Keeper," at the Union Square Holiday Inn, cosponsored by the Moral Majority and the Free Congress Foundation. On the second morning, a pair of radical feminists slipped into a session, in the course of which they rose from the audience and kissed passionately; while outside, in Union Square Park, a bunch of transvestites in nun costumes, led by a professional astrologer, performed an exorcism of Jerry Falwell.

But that was the kind of effluvium that is to be found, in

more diluted form perhaps, in half a dozen other large cities, that is drawn to other sorts of events. Sunday, the fifteenth, the day before the convention formally opened, two mammoth parades, both political and semi-official in character, made their way along Market Street.

Labor came first. The AFL-CIO had organized a march called "We Can Do It!"—meaning: elect the party's nominee, presumably Walter Mondale. They had to hope they could, because they had promised to. For the first time in its history, the AFL-CIO had endorsed a candidate during the primary season. They sought thereby to show their clout, and they had been vital to Mondale (yet how perilous it is to step down into the arena; so many others—southern blacks, Jewish New Yorkers, Jimmy Carter—had an equivalent claim on his gratitude). Now they had to show that the candidate they had sown, watered, and reaped could win an election. At ten in the morning, the union troops stepped off from the wharf end of Market Street and headed south. Not another creature was stirring. They passed beneath the silent skyscrapers of the financial district, cheering and music-making, like a rattle in a pail.

Lane Kirkland led the way; or was he simply at the front? The ambiguity had permeated his tenure as president of the AFL-CIO. Kirkland was the protégé of George Meany, and he would be the last president in Meany's mold. Meany had practiced the beliefs that once animated Walter Mondale—fundamentalist economics at home, fire-breathing anti-Communism abroad. Kirkland, in his unimperial way, shared them, but he had to maneuver within the realities. The reality that morning was a union parade speckled with signs (NO GUNS TO CENTRAL AMERICA). Meany would have clapped them in Coventry. Marching with a group of unionists from New York State, farther down the line, was Senator Patrick Moynihan, another symbol of changed times, who had avoided the pathos of Kirkland's dilemma by abandoning the embattled half of his position. Nine years earlier, when Moynihan was ambassador to the UN, he had called the thugs of the world thugs; after the Grenada invasion, he

had skipped onto television with a denunciation faster than
Gary Hart.

The parade was enormous, and clumpy—a long gap, then
a hoplite phalanx from a particular union, in matching jackets and gimme caps. The hospital workers had seven bag-
pipers, and the carpenters brought a banjo and a concertina
and three girls on a truck doing hornpipes. There was a
Chinese dragon dancing over firecrackers (you thought lob-
sters had it hard). The most elaborate float was a long, two-
headed alligator, a protest against double-gating (the practice of allowing union and non-union workers to work on
the same construction site). 2 GATES = OPEN SHOP, a sign
explained. It did not seem like an issue to excite the nation's
sympathy, but the creature's keepers were proud of it. "So
far, we got on NBC, ABC."

In fact, the nation's sympathies have been less and less
excited. Apart from defections at the polls—44 percent of
union households had voted for Reagan in 1980—the union-
ized proportion of the work force has been dropping since
1950. As organized labor declined in size and clout, would it
move further left, and so decline yet more?

That was a problem for Kirkland's successor. For at least
three hours, the parade made its way to City Hall. The
marchers drank, ate fast food—Polish sausages, burritos—
stretched out on the grass, while on an unregarded podium
sat exhausted, spare-tired, capped labor leaders. The PA
system read off lists of union locals and lost children.

As that parade dispersed, down from the other end of
town came the second, the National March for Gay and
Lesbian Rights. The police had predicted 100,000 marchers; the New York *Times* estimated 50,000; so make it
25,000. No matter, it was huge. They had assembled in a
trough of Castro Street, a mainline of the city's homosexual
arrondissement, and at two o'clock in the afternoon, they
rolled.

Their signs were at least interesting. The religious right
was a popular subject. NOW PLAYING, read the best-hu-
mored, LA CAGE AUX FALWELLS. Others were less pleasant:

IF GOD IS GREAT AND GOD IS GOOD, WHY DOES HE HAVE MEN LIKE JIM JONES AND JERRY FALWELL REPRESENTING HIM? THINK ABOUT IT. Another placard linked Jones and Falwell, and threw in Reagan and Hitler for good measure. The whole quartet together WON'T KILL FREEDOMS.

The media had looked forward to a carnival, a Walpurgis-nacht of faggotry. There were glimpses. One marcher in leather leggings sported a chain hooked through his nipples, and there was a drag queen in a tight gown with a sequinned bodice and a boa trudging along under the afternoon sun. *Il faut souffrir pour être belle.* But on the whole, except for a greater number of T-shirts than was perhaps statistically likely, and, of course, the pairings, it was a thoroughly normal-looking crowd. Which was the point.

Marchers coming over the first crest in Market Street saw what they were a part of, exclaimed, "My God, look at that." "Did you see how long this is?" one asked scribbling me, belligerently. It took an hour and a half for the whole line to flow under the Route 101 overpass. Signs identified homosexuals from Arizona, Denver, Texas, Toledo, Utah, Minnesota, Pittsburgh. A group called "Enola Gay" announced itself as GOMORRAH FOR TOMORRAH. There were the "People with AIDS Alliance" and "Hi Tech Gays"; the "Gay Atheist League of America" and "Presbyterians for Lesbian/Gay United." There were homosexual Mexicans, Indians, mothers, fathers, yuppies, Jews, Catholics, Mormons (the angel Moroni on a lavender banner). The Gay Men's Chorus of San Jose sang "God Bless America" in a key out of its range. GAY, LESBIAN AND BISEXUAL VETERANS HELPED DEFEND OUR COUNTRY. WE PAY TAXES TOO—WE WANT THE SAME RIGHTS AS YOU. A general question, to the cameras, to the air: HOW MANY OF US DOES IT TAKE FOR YOU TO BE CONVINCED?

Convinced of what, of course, was the question. The proposition that anti-sodomy laws are neither proper nor practical would require no more than two marchers; in theory, it requires none. The proposition that sodomy is normal would require at least sixty or seventy million. What the sexual politicians who organized the march wanted to convince the nation of was that homosexuals should join blacks, women, and Hispanics as an officially recognized minority group, entitled to the full cornucopia of affirmative action and government patronage. The nation might take a long time convincing, but the Democratic party had already agreed, or was in the process of agreeing. The rules committee had passed, and the convention the day after the march approved, a rules change requiring state parties to develop "outreach" programs to draw homosexuals into the delegate-selection process. Delegate quotas, such as were already in place for women, beckoned as the next step. The march was as much a victory celebration as a call to arms. Henceforth, homosexual activists were to be on a par, in status if not numbers, with shop stewards. We are part, declared San Francisco supervisor Harry Britt at parade's end, of "the problem-solving family" of the Democratic party.

The George Moscone Center, where the delegates convened on Monday, was a new building, low-slung and ugly. Delegates and press—the latter outnumbering the former by a substantial proportion—entered at ground level, then reached the hall by descending escalators and stairs, like groundhogs who had seen their shadows. If Reagan started a nuclear war during a session, they could emerge to repopulate the political landscape. To the left and right of the speaker's podium, in the middle of the hall, sat two enormous ziggurats—the control booths of the major television networks. Along the rim of the ceiling hung the smaller eyries of lesser media. The band was plunked at the back end of the hall, the lights on their music stands shining like distant glowworms.

Conventions have one other function, besides talk—giving delegates the chance to dress up. The definitive pro-funny hat argument appeared in *The Economist* in 1976, which reminded its English readers at convention time that, however odd it might seem to see grown men and women wearing stuffed toy donkeys and elephants on their heads, it was all in all a healthier social symptom than "the more mature demonstrations of the recent European past." The funny hats on these heads were sparse—yet another sign of the party's decay. The Democrats had made one compensating improvement this year, however; they had returned, for the music played during the posting of the colors, to Sousa marches. At the 1980 convention in Madison Square Garden, it had been Aaron Copland's "Fanfare for the Common Man," a thirties period piece that was "maturity" with a vengeance (all those post offices, decorated with muscled steelworkers). It was also the cause of some ludicrous contrasts: it was played, outside the convention proper, to hail the arrival at the Waldorf-Astoria of Edward Kennedy. Much better Sousa.

The Democrats had a problem of convention etiquette, not unlike the Republicans' problem with Richard Nixon. The Democrats' problem was what to do with Jimmy Carter. In many ways theirs was the harder. Carter was not a criminal, who could be trusted out of simple decorum to stay away—he was an unpopular failure, a stickier social situation. The Democrats ended up doing the noble thing, but barely. Carter went to the podium the first day, almost the first speaker, when many people on EDT were still eating dessert.

He began with a line which, if taken seriously, could have cleared the room: "Here I go again." But he wore the put-down that had put Reagan over in their 1980 debate as a badge of loyalty; to "nuclear survival," "human rights," and "equal opportunity" (meaning, chiefly, ERA). Of the three, human rights came closest to being a Carter administration property, and he elaborated on it: "We Americans oppose Communism . . . not because it is Russian, but because it is a tyranny that oppresses human beings." Meanwhile, supporting "oppressive dictators around the globe" did "not enhance American ideals."

There had been several problems with this in practice. Carter had not treated Communism as if it were all that tyrannous (indeed, he said, we had an "inordinate fear" of it). Aside from an early White House visit with a Russian dissident, the Carter administration focused all its human-rights fire on weaker and less noxious countries. It took the invasion of Afghanistan to open Carter's eyes to a crucial distinction: the Soviet Union exports tyranny; Paraguay does not.

He spoke for fifteen minutes to light and indifferent applause. He responded with his smile that, over the years, had become more and more like a snarl, with little Christian charity in it; though in fairness the martyrs only had to face lions, arrows, and griddles, not dead houses.

In the event, he could have read an open letter on nuclear proliferation by Amy; it would have been forgotten, for New York's Governor Mario Cuomo was next with the keynote, and he carried all before him. Cuomo had given inklings of his talents in 1982. He had had, up till that point, a fairly beige career, losing the New York City mayor's race in 1977 to Ed Koch, and then serving as lieutenant governor. In 1982, Koch, fresh from a landslide re-election as mayor, decided to move up to the governorship, and Koch and Cuomo met again. Their last debate before primary day had been held in the Waldorf, under the aegis of the *Daily News*. Koch usually is a ham, a scene stealer, an incarnation of the actor's joke about a two-man show, in which the lesser character has nothing to do but sit silently downstage at a desk, writing with a quill. (So why was the lead glum after opening night? The scrivener drank the ink.) But Koch that morning was stumbling and defensive. Cuomo had a sharp, mean streak, which he put to good use. "You have changed your mind, Ed," he hectored Koch. "You have gone where fifty-one percent of the vote went." Koch tried to interrupt, but the moderator held him to the format of the debate. "Unless you want to change that too," Cuomo put in; game, set, and match. But what he did most effectively was something quite different: He showed a knack, exceeded by only one other American politician, for uttering the pieties piously; as if he believed them (and so he must have, if he could carry it off). He closed his summation with boilerplate out of a social studies textbook: Voting is Important. Cuomo gold-plated it thus: "the high holy day of our political process." *Yes, Mario,* you wanted to tell him, *I will vote.*

That race was politically significant. Koch, who had already wandered from the liberal reservation on a number of issues—he supported capital punishment, and he was skeptical, not to say contemptuous, of the savvy and the character of the city's black political establishment—had lately been pushing the notion that the Democratic party had become the prisoner of its own constituency groups. (One of his favorite examples was a federal requirement to retrofit the New York subway system for the benefit of the handicapped. It would be cheaper, he pointed out, to give all the handicapped cab fare.) Cuomo met this creeping responsibility head-on; Koch's argument "cut our throats." Had the Democrats done too much for their special interests? "Hardly enough." In the gubernatorial primary, piety beat doubt, 53 percent to 47. Cuomo's victory in the general election was equally sweet in liberal nostrils. His Republican opponent, Lew Lehrman, had a stiff stance and, at forty-four, a balding pate, which made him look like the red-headed drinking birds that used to be sold at cheap fairs and seaside cotton-candy stands. But he was also a committed supply-sider and a self-made millionaire (from the family drugstore business) with no anxieties about expenses; clearly, a man to be stopped. Cuomo did it, just (the margin was 2 percent). Tipsters took note.

Two years in Albany had not improved Cuomo's looks. Here in San Francisco, his eyes sagged, his cheeks drooped, and in general, his face made Mondale's look bright. But his delivery was both rapid and feeling, a tone of urgent plaint.

"Please allow me," Cuomo began, "to skip the stories and the poetry [a sure sign that the muse was upon him]" and "deal immediately" with the vital facts. The most vital fact in any war is to know the mind of the enemy; Cuomo had peered into Reagan's, and found Darwin. More exactly, "social Darwinism. Survival of the fittest. Government can't do

everything, we were told, so it should settle for taking care
of the strong and hope that economic ambition and charity
will do the rest. Make the rich richer and what falls from the
table will be enough." Democrats believed in "encouraging
the talented"; but they also believed that "while survival of
the fittest may be a good working description of evolution, a
government of humans should elevate itself to a higher
order." We would rather have laws written by St. Francis of
Assisi—"the man called the 'world's most sincere Democrat' "—than "laws written by Darwin."

Against Darwinism, Cuomo held up the family. This was
an important effort; the family had become a rhetorical
weak spot for Democrats since, roughly, the Gay Atheist
League began regarding the party as its home and forum.
Cuomo made a bid to retrieve the family by expanding it to
the size of the country. "The Republicans believe that the
wagon train will not make it to the frontier unless some of
the old, some of the young, some of the weak are left behind
by the side of the trail. The strong, the strong, they tell us,
will inherit the land." Democrats believed "in something
else . . . that we can make it all the way with the whole
family intact."

His chief counter-model to the struggle for survival,
though, was class warfare. He did not call it that, naturally,
but that's what it amounted to. He confronted the trope at
the core of Reagan's finest perorations, the "shining city on
a hill"—"city on a hill" courtesy of John Winthrop, "shining" courtesy of Ronald Reagan—and tore into it. "The hard
truth is that not everyone is sharing in this city's splendor
and glory. . . . There's another part to the shining city, the
part where some people can't pay their mortgages . . .
where students can't afford the education they need";
where "elderly people . . . tremble in the basements of
houses" and "people . . . sleep in the gutter, where the
glitter doesn't show . . . ghettos where thousands of
young people give their lives away to drug dealers every
day. There is despair, Mr. President, in the places that you
don't visit in your shining city. In fact . . . the nation is

more a tale of two cities than it is just a shining city on a hill."

Was there a middle class in this Manichaean America? Yes, and Cuomo called it "the heart of our constituency": "the middle class, the people not rich enough to be worry-free, but not poor enough to be on welfare . . . those who work for a living because they have to, not because some psychiatrist told them it was a convenient way to fill the interval between birth and eternity."

But Cuomo could not dwell on the middle class, for then his implicit image of Reagan sipping champagne on the Pacific Palisades while the rest of the nation toiled in sweatshops would be weakened. So he proceeded to enumerate the party's constituents: "minorities"; "young people demanding an education"; "senior citizens terrorized" by threats to "their social security"; women for ERA ("thou shalt not sin against equality"); friends of the environment; foes of "macho intransigence" in foreign policy. It was a list more or less composed of the friends of Walter Mondale. It was for them that the rhetorical engines of misery were stoked.

The "struggle to live with dignity," Cuomo concluded, was "the real story of the shining city. . . . I watched a small man with thick calluses on both hands work fifteen and sixteen hours a day . . . a man who came here uneducated, alone, unable to speak the language, who taught me all I needed to know about faith and hard work by the simple eloquence of his example. I learned about our kind of democracy from my father. I learned about our obligation to each other from him and from my mother. They asked only for a chance to work and to make the world better for their children and . . . to be protected in those moments when they would not be able to protect themselves. . . . They were able to build a family and live in dignity and see one of their children go from behind the little grocery store in South Jamaica . . . to occupy the highest seat in the greatest state in the greatest nation in the only world we know. . . .

"And I ask you now, ladies and gentlemen, brothers and sisters, for the good of all of us, for the love of this great nation, for the family of America, for the love of God"— vote for the Democrats. "Please make this nation remember how futures are built."

Cuomo had booked a seat on the first flight to 1988.

All the men who had contested for the nomination in 1984 seemed pallid by comparison. Cranston, marooned in a four o'clock (Pacific Daylight Time) slot on Wednesday afternoon, got one chorus of "California, Here I Come" from the band; he spoke of "hellish" nuclear weapons, and rejoiced that "we can now slam the door on the cold war mentality that has dominated Democratic thinking for thirty years." McGovern, withdrawing his name from nomination several hours later, wondered avuncularly what "our Creator think[s] as He looks down on His creatures. He sees a little band here in one corner of the globe digging holes in the ground for missiles to blow up another little band doing the same thing." He also observed with a smile that Reaganism was "at odds with the Judeo-Christian heritage."

The Democrats had spaced out their big guns over the last three nights. Jackson came first, on Tuesday. Farrakhan's last little fling had gotten Mondale out of a tight spot. Jewish pressure to put some distance between him and Jackson had been intensifying steadily, until "dirty religion" gave him a chance to make an unequivocal blast; Mondale followed quickly with an announcement that he really could not consider Jackson as a running mate because of his views concerning the PLO, a Palestinian state, and the defense budget. Once that was clear, it was safe to do what had to be done to avoid revolt in the other direction— give Jackson a prominent and honorable place on the podium.

Those who had heard him seldom or not at all were impressed with his performance, but it was not vintage Jackson. He was weary, and his pipes sounded as if at last they had been abused past the point of usefulness. He saw

Cuomo's Dickensian evaluation of the state of the nation, and raised it: his constituency was "the damned, the desperate, the disinherited, the disrespected, the despised." He tried to salve some of the wounds he had opened. "If in my high moments I have done some good, offered some service, shed some light, healed some wounds" (from the hall: *all right*), "rekindled some hope" *(yes)*, "stirred someone from apathy and indifference" *(yes)*, "or in any way along the way helped somebody, then this campaign has not been in vain. . . . If in my low moments, in word, deed, or attitude, through some error of temper, taste, or tone, I have caused anyone discomfort, created pain, or revived someone's fears, that was not my truest self. If there were occasions when my grape turned into a raisin and my joy bell lost its resonance, please forgive me." Cheers. "Charge it to my head, not to my heart." Cheers. "My head, so limited in its finitude, my heart which is boundless in its love." Applause. Still not quite an apology (yes, I was a boor, but that was my *false* self), but the hall was impressed. He spoke for fifty minutes, and was interrupted thirty-five times by applause.

For Gary Hart, the pre-convention weeks had been a varied but unbroken string of frustrations. He had run back and forth, like a base runner in a hotbox, from expedient to expedient; all in vain. Mondale gave him an opening on July 12, by deciding, in seclusion in Lake Tahoe, that he would fire the chairman of the Democratic National Committee, Charles Manatt, and replace him with none other than Bert Lance. Mondale was acting in simple justice; Lance, more than Carter, had done the actual mustering of the Johnny Rebs who had saved Mondale's neck in March. Gratitude, however, had warped his judgment. Lance had, as they say, left Washington under a cloud. He had been the Democratic party's oblation to the Watergate morality (and a cheap one, too: a measly Budget Director, in payment for a three-year political jackpot). In addition, Manatt was popular. Delegates from his home state of California were particularly outraged at his ouster. Hart hoped to pick them up, but on July 15, Mondale gave Lance his second ticket back to Georgia.

For the convention, the Hart team offered a minority report on foreign policy, setting forth a list of conditions in the absence of which the United States would never send troops abroad: clear objectives; acceptable costs; "all" diplomatic means exhausted; allied support; and "local forces . . . working to resolve the causes of conflict." (If Roosevelt had applied any one of four of these, Churchill would still be waiting.) The Mondale forces did what all front-runners do when faced with a foreign-policy fight; what Gerald Ford had done when confronted by a right-wing revolt at Kansas City in 1976—they gave in (time enough to fine-tune Latin America after you've won).

Hart's chances for the vice-presidential nomination—not that he ever seriously wanted it; he lacked the temperament of a number two man, and if his judgment of Mondale was correct, number one was headed for defeat—had meanwhile been scotched by a final indignity. The pre-convention issue of *Vanity Fair* had carried an article, "The Hidden Hart," which drew on the testimony of an unusual source, a Comanche healer named Marilyn Youngbird. What did she know about the new generation of leaders? Nothing, except that Hart communed with her for spiritual counsel. In breathy prose, she described a sunrise ceremony he had attended. Gourd dancers "brushed the front and back of our bodies with eagle feathers. . . . It was sensual, oh yes." The Hart camp responded that she was not a *close* adviser. All the puzzlement that had been provoked by his name and age changes flooded back. The Mondale campaign needed a vice-presidential medicine woman like a hole in the scalp.

Hart's moment came Wednesday night, before the balloting. With him, alas, came Copland. The band put up its horns, and the hall was filled with canned music, loud enough to make the earwax run. It was dreadful, painful. While the super Dolby system or whatever it was rang with gongs, screens suspended over the delegates' heads showed

Hart on horseback, riding the range. Copland gave way to the "Marlboro Man" theme. When the cacophony finally spent itself, Hart appeared in person. But his supporters, who had not spent themselves, shouted, "Gar-*y*, Gar-*y*," and "We want Hart"; shouted it for ten minutes. He did not enjoy it. In defeat, the Hart signs were bold red and white, not cold, confident blue and gray. At last Hart gave them what they and he deserved, a smile. "Think where man's glory most begins and ends," he quoted Yeats, "and say my glory was, I had such friends."

His speech was a reprise of the last primaries. The election would be a referendum on the future, "perhaps on whether our children will have a future." "Millions of children" in Central America who should see the "hand of America bearing gifts of friendship" saw it instead "brandish[ing] instruments of death." Reagan's "gang of greedy polluters" had "scarred [America's] face, poisoned her air," and "corrupted her waters." There was a politician that had read and thought, all right. His supporters cheered him ten minutes more while the Muzak cassette blasted the theme from *Chariots of Fire*. He had fought till the end, but not all out. It had been the struggle of a fish landed on a dock. In desperation, he could have challenged Mondale's tainted delegates, caused a commotion on the floor. Counsels of unity had prevailed; unity, and calculations of the likely results. Hart went to his end quietly, if not silently.

The nominators of Walter Mondale came out around quarter after eight. The best was the treasurer of the state of Texas, a lady named Ann Richards. She had the appearance and manner of female politicians who had graced the conventions of a past era—the national committeewomen who took the roll calls of the states with schoolmarmish fussiness, making prim jokes whenever the vote totals came back garbled. But Richards made her points with a simplicity that was not much less affecting than Cuomo's histrionics. Her theme was the invisible men and women of America. Her "momma and daddy in Waco," who had lived through the depression: "Now you see it happening again.

. . . You paid Social Security all your lives and now they say they can't afford to pay you." Her two daughters, whose constitutional rights were not guaranteed. Her sons: "There's not a mother in America" unaffected by Lebanon. (She managed, unlike most politicians who refer to their children, to sound as if she had not bred them solely for the purposes of speechmaking.) "Walter Mondale sees the unemployed, and feels their pain. He'll make sure Social Security checks keep coming, as sure as the sun is coming up in the morning. . . . He sees you, he hears you, he has the wisdom and experience to understand what you're saying."

He had made her "proud to be a woman," she concluded, by naming Geraldine Ferraro.

Mondale had done something genuinely imaginative, though he made himself foolish in all but the final stages of doing so. The rigors of his vice-presidency, he was fond of saying, began with Carter's careful scrutiny of possible nominees. Mondale naturally believed that the process had borne excellent fruit, and he was determined to repeat it. He began interviewing on the twenty-first of June, with Los Angeles mayor Tom Bradley. Senator Lloyd Bentsen of Texas and San Francisco mayor Dianne Feinstein came by on the twenty-third; Philadelphia mayor Wilson Goode on the twenty-eighth; Ferraro on July 2; San Antonio mayor Henry Cisneros on the fourth; and Kentucky governor Martha Collins on the sixth.

Very soon, though, the process stopped seeming rigorous and began to look absurd. There was the strained ecumenicism of the participants: three women, two blacks, a Hispanic, and one white male. It looked like a James Watt joke. Four of the possibilities had no experience beyond the level of city government. Two—Goode and Collins, both in office for less than eight months—were tyros. Did Mondale seriously propose to put them in line for the presidency? If he was not serious, then wasn't the whole thing a PR cattle call, demeaning to the qualified and unqualified alike?

The most prudent choice available to Mondale would

probably have been Bentsen. He had been in the Senate since 1970 (when he had beaten one George Bush); standing to the right of Mondale, he would have given the ticket some ideological balance. More to the point, he was from Texas. The importance of Texas was cold electoral arithmetic. With Republicans sure of the votes of the western states (which they had failed to carry only once in the last eight presidential elections), and Democrats strong only in the industrial Northeast and Midwest (and weak even in spots there—e.g., Indiana, New Jersey), the balance of votes was in the South and the border states. Texas alone had 29 electoral votes, and Mondale would need them badly.

But there were other pressures on him. In the midst of the running-mate "Gong Show," the National Organization for Women held its annual convention in Miami Beach. Seven months earlier, Mondale had received the endorsement of the governing board. But endorsements do not simply reward past services, they presume future ones. NOW now resolved, on July 1, to nominate a woman from the floor of the convention if Mondale was so insensitive as to pick a man. Gary Hart had also been making noises that he might announce a woman running mate (empty noises— what politician, male or female, would want to jump aboard a sunken ship?).

The best justification for Mondale's audacity, though, was that it was audacious. The same cold arithmetic that pointed to Bentsen as the best choice also suggested that Mondale had little chance at all. Prudent losers end up losers. The first woman on a major party ticket might shake things up. If Mondale could find a female politician who was personable, qualified, and had no skeletons in the armoire, he could do himself no harm, and might do a great deal of good.

On the night of July 12, Mondale called Geraldine Ferraro to give her the news. "Can you imagine," she said later, "if he'd gotten a busy signal?"

The picture of Mondale's choice that emerged over the next few weeks was of a liberal Democrat sprung from a traditionalist ethnic background. She was born August 26, 1935, to Dominick and Antonetta Ferraro, immigrants who ran a restaurant in Newburgh, New York. Two years earlier, the Ferraros' youngest son, Gerald, had been killed in a car crash while sleeping in Antonetta's arms. The grieving mother buried his toys and continued to launder his clothes, until the family doctor advised her to have another child. The Ferraros named their daughter Geraldine.

Mr. Ferraro died when Geraldine was eight, and the family's circumstances, comfortable until then, took a downward turn. Mrs. Ferraro moved to Queens and took a job crocheting beads on wedding dresses. "You'd better go to college," she told her daughter after watching her try the work, "or you'll starve." Geraldine went to Marymount, a Catholic girls' college, and became an elementary school teacher after graduating. She put on her own wedding dress in 1961 to marry John Zaccaro, a real estate dealer.

Mrs. Zaccaro had also put herself through Fordham Law School at night, and though most of her time was taken up with homemaking, she performed legal chores for her husband's business, which was doing well. In the sixties, the Zaccaros moved to Forest Hills. ("I thought," Tip O'Neill said when he first visited their home, "you told me you lived in Queens.") In 1974, a cousin who had become district attorney appointed her an assistant DA. Three years later, she was named head of the Special Victims Bureau.

Her shot at the big leagues came in 1978. James Delaney, Queens's congressman for three decades, stepped down, and the Republicans put up a conservative Italian, Alfred DellaBovi. Ferraro ran under her maiden name (it "flowed better," her first campaign manager decided) and her record as a prosecutor ("Finally, a Tough Democrat" was her slogan). She upset DellaBovi, 54 percent to 44.

Ferraro's district, it would be pointed out several thousand times, was the residence of Archie Bunker (the houses in the trailers for "All in the Family" stand on Steinway Avenue in the Astoria section of Queens). Her voting record in Congress, though, was more like the Meathead's. Her

first year on the Hill, she supported a constitutional amendment to ban busing. It was the lone jag on her chart. She
voted against the MX missile, under both Carter and Reagan, and against the B-1. She opposed military and economic aid to El Salvador, and supported cutting off the
Contras. She backed the freeze, and a budget resolution of
the Congressional Black Caucus which called for a lower
level of defense spending than that supported by House
Democrats. She voted against the Kemp-Roth tax-rate cuts,
for the resubmitted Equal Rights Amendment, and for federal funding of abortions. Withal, she could speak the idiom
of her upbringing. Her first press conference with Mondale
in St. Paul was like a Mother's Day homily. She had been
shaped, she said, by "neighborhood," "faith," "work," and a
"strong, loving family"—"straightforward, solid Americans
trying to make ends meet." Mondale had found a running
mate who could deliver liberalism in an outer-borough accent.

The roll call began at 9:15. After all the aggravation it had
caused him, New Hampshire ended up casting 12 votes for
Mondale, 10 for Hart. California announced itself as the
future "retirement home of former President Reagan," Virginia as the birthplace of Thomas Jefferson, Patrick Henry,
and Governor Charles S. Robb. The closest thing to a surprise was 16 votes cast from Minnesota for Missouri senator
Thomas Eagleton. It was not nostalgia for McGovern's first
running mate, but a symbolic right-to-life gesture (Eagleton
was anti-abortion). Hart moved to make it unanimous, the
Reverend Jackson gave the benediction, the band played
bits of the "1812 Overture."

The last day's festivities began with an "Anti-Interven-
tionist Funeral Procession" through downtown, to mourn
the deaths caused by one side in the Salvadoran civil war.
("Wear black," said the notices, "carry coffins.") These
marchers spoke for the undeceived left, which knew that
the Democratic party was as steeped in lucre and blood as
the Republicans. Still, the target of opportunity was Reagan,

represented by a mannequin with gory hands; also Duarte, a smaller mannequin trailing puppet strings. The marchers, about three hundred of them, tramped through downtown to the beat of funerary drums, and they sang Slavery in Ancient Times music, a low monotonous drone. A woman carrying a coffin in memory of four American nuns murdered by a right-wing posse burst into a passion of shrieks and wails. As spontaneous as a professional mourner. It was just possible, of course, that she was related to one of the nuns, and so genuinely distraught, but that was the trouble with such demonstrations: you couldn't have told the difference. At levels of discourse so crude, everything became hokey.

Over at the Moscone Center, in an adjacent parking lot, was a concert, "Rock Against Reagan." A reggae singer under a topknot which, together with his dreadlocks, looked like a hat-sized tarantula, was explaining his provenance. "I come from Afreeca four hundred years ago. It was a fantastic cruise—only twenty million of us died on thee way. *Afreeca, oh, Afreeca, be free . . ."* Kids in green and purple spiked hair lounged on the asphalt, soaking up rays. Off to one side sat a sculpture, an assembly of hair dryers, toilet seats, and other artifacts, labeled the "Amerikan Lobotomy Machine" (America with a *k*—talk about your snows of yesteryear). REAGAN HATES ME, declared a T-shirt.

A mile and an Alpine ascent away, Speaker of the House Tip O'Neill presided over a fund-raising luncheon at the Fairmont. There was no blood in evidence, but plenty of lucre: red plush, old gold, mottled columns of devil's-food-cake marble. O'Neill himself was booked into the presidential suite. He had risen to compassion from a background in Boston machine politics. "Show me a boy," said George Washington Plunkitt, "who hustles for the organization, and I'll show you a comin' statesman." O'Neill began hustling for Al Smith in high school. He slipped into Jack Kennedy's congressional seat in 1952, after an already substantial career on Beacon Hill; altogether, he had been in public office longer than most people in America have been alive. The political system that nourished him was, in its own way, a conservative force, drawing its strength from its attention to the needs of what Burke called the "little platoon." The drawback was that it did its attending with public money. From the little platoon to the vast salvific visions of the Great and post-Great Society was but a step. O'Neill took it with ease. One young representative of a later generation whose down-the-line liberalism had impressed him was Geraldine Ferraro, and his recommendation had counted for much in Mondale's decision.

Over the years, and perhaps most visibly during his one-on-one confrontations with Ronald Reagan, O'Neill had become a conscious and deliberate parody of a blarneying pol. Given his white thatch, red face, and corporeal amplitude, he could hardly have done anything else. O'Neill moving toward a lectern looked like the *Hindenburg* coming into Lakehurst, New Jersey. He struck a note of reminiscence and recalled his first convention, 1948. "Thank God we won," he said, thankful not for the Truman Doctrine but for the GI Bill, which "made middle America." The woman of the hour spoke, briefly. Ferraro still seemed to be in the nervous stage, naturally enough. Until now, she said, women "hadn't truly become part of the process." O'Neill looked back on similar breakthroughs: Branch Rickey, "a man of cahrage," putting Jackie Robinson on the Brooklyn Dodgers. "You know, in the thuties, I was a baseball buff."

Inside the Moscone Center, the Democrats filled the time before the formal invocation with hopeful Senate candidates: "Freud asked long ago," said Libby Mitchell, who was challenging incumbent William Cohen of Maine, "what do women want? We answer loud and clear"—an end to tax cuts, toxic waste dumps, and the arms race. The parade was mercifully halted by the Reverend Cecil Williams, of Glide Memorial Church. "If you know the melody of your life like jazz, you can improvise, like Coltrane, like Miles, like Monk." A singer rendered "The Star-Spangled Banner" in a version that sounded improvised, and the convention set about its final business.

The first order of business was to elaborate on Geraldine Ferraro's qualifications, which was no easy task. Nearly every other major-party running mate of the last quarter century had had higher and broader experience. Mondale, Dole, Eagleton, Muskie, Humphrey, Johnson, and Lodge had all been senators, and held other offices besides. Bush had served in Congress, Peking, the UN, and Langley. Sargent Shriver had been a utility infielder for Camelot. Even William Miller, a veteran of the American Express card commercial, was a seven-term congressman and chairman of the Republican National Committee when Goldwater tapped him. One had to go to Spiro Agnew—six years in Baltimore politics, one year as governor of Maryland—for an equally skimpy résumé. But Agnew, in his brief time at the state level, had made decisions of political weight: he had successfully backed open housing, a liberal move for Maryland, and chided urban rioters, a hard move for a liberal. It is not hard to fade into the mobs of the House, and Ferraro had not stood out. She had looked out for her district (her first foreign-policy speech was a blast at Turkey, tailored for the Greeks of Astoria) and looked up to Tip O'Neill. Jim Wright, the House Majority Leader, met the challenge head-on. "Let me tell you about her experience," he began. It turned out to be "the experience of living"— daughter of an immigrant (from whom she "learned the passion of love of America"); daughter of a seamstress ("love of family"); teacher ("it's a wonderful thing to pray for better schools," but you "also have to pay for better schools"); mother (she had "pray[ed] for the safety of her children"); and finally, member of Congress, where she had gotten six years of "exposure to national problems"—two years more, Wright pointed out, than Reagan now had. Barbara Kennelly, a freshman congresswoman from Connecticut, noted that Ferraro had been to Nicaragua, Israel, and Lebanon, where she had told officers that the Marines at the Beirut airport were vulnerable.

Second business, touched on by Wright, was to repeat as many times as possible the words "country," "God," and "family." New Mexico's Governor Anaya lengthened the tally by one. Ferraro, he stressed, was an "Italian Catholic . . . deeply religious and deeply patriotic. Being religious means living, not just quoting, the word of God." Cuomo, though he had flown back to New York on the day before, was the source here. His speech had become the party's common property, which lesser talents rifled for themes and paragraphs, like builders carting off chunks of field-stone.

The delegates had come with Ferraro signs, the most interesting of which reflected the local patriotism of the New York delegation: FULTON COUNTY FOR FERRARO; CO-OP CITY FOR MONDALE-FERRARO; GRAND CONCOURSE BRONX 76 AD ♡ MONDALE-FERRARO. In the aisles of the delegation, Bella Abzug and Betty Friedan took interview after interview. The band played a little Tarantella, a little "New York, New York," a chorus of "YMCA." In the Minnesota delegation, the cadre of anti-abortionists held up a few orange-and-white signs, lettered simply: LIFE. They were an inconsiderable discordance. At last, Ferraro presented herself for her formal debut. She made an attractive figure, handsome rather than pretty. When she smiled, her eyes crinkled and flashed; at rest, her mouth had a stern set to it. The aisles filled with cheering bodies, bulbs flashed like fireworks.

She began with a trip to Cuomo's quarry. "Tonight, the daughter of a woman whose highest goal was a future for her children talks to our nation's oldest party. . . . Tonight, the daughter of working Americans tells all Americans that the future is within our reach. . . . Tonight, the daughter of an immigrant from Italy has been chosen to run for President." A Freudian slip; maybe that's what women really want.

"Last week, I visited Elmore, Minnesota, the small town where Fritz Mondale was raised." A cheer: *Yay, Elmore.* "Soon, Fritz and Joan will visit our family in Queens." A much lustier cheer. "Children walk to school in Elmore past grain elevators. In Queens, they pass by subway stops. But no matter where they live, their future depends on education. . . . In Elmore, there are family farms; in Queens, small businesses. But the men and women who run them all take pride in . . . hard work and initiative. On the Fourth of July in Elmore, they hang the flags out on Main Street. In Queens they fly them over Grand Avenue. But all of us love our country."

With the Grant Wood mural firmly in place, she moved into the main theme of her speech: Americans believe in playing by the rules, but under Reagan "the rules are rigged against too many of our people. . . . It isn't right that" the proportion of taxes paid by individuals rose while the corporate share had sunk. "It isn't right that this year Ronald Reagan will hand the American people a bill for interest on the national debt . . . larger than the entire cost of the federal government under John F. Kennedy. The rules say: we must not leave our kids a mountain of debt." A tepid cheer. "It isn't right that a woman should get paid fifty-nine cents on the dollar for the same work as a man." These were the figures commonly cited in discussions of comparable worth—the belief that women were underpaid, not for doing the same work as men, but for performing jobs that were judged (by supporters of comparable worth) to be equivalent. It had become the hottest feminist issue, and for this the delegates cheered from the heart. "It isn't right that young people today fear they won't get the Social Security they paid for, and that older Americans fear they will lose what they have already earned." Probably more young people feared paying for the Social Security that their elders had been told they had earned. But such thoughts could not be uttered by any politician, Democrat or Republican, radical or Tory. Ferraro was not about to make *that* kind of history. "Social Security is a contract between the last generation and the next, and the rules say, ya don't break contracts."

Here and there, the patois of Queens peeked out. But for the most part, her delivery was measured, a little choppy, with a modest sense of the occasion. She slipped in, as every nominee must, little valentines to special voters, Castro Street for instance ("to those concerned about the strength of family values, as I am, I say we are going to restore those values . . . by including, and not excluding, those whose beliefs differ from our own"). "The generation before ours," she finished, "kept faith with us, and like them, we will pass on . . . a stronger, more just America." The band did more "New York, New York," some "Celebrate," and the happy Democrats boogied.

There followed one of the more doleful features of the modern convention agenda, the film short on the life of the candidate: all the techniques of *cinéma vérité* lavished on scenes that were strictly *posé*. In fact, the films may be a moral step up. In 1840, when there were only broadsheets and campaign songs, the Whig party pretended that William Henry Harrison (son of a governor of Virginia and a signer of the Declaration of Independence) had sprung from a humble cabin. The relative integrity of films did not make them any easier to watch. Mondale split wood, grilled steak, lectured his staff (you knew it was a private staff meeting because the knot of his necktie had been lowered one quarter of an inch). Deficits, he was saying, had bad effects. "You can't put the future on hold for four or five years." The staff listened attentively.

After the film came Senator Kennedy. Under normal circumstances, this would not have been an improvement. One of the facts demonstrated most strikingly by Kennedy's 1980 campaign was what an inept speaker he was. He either dithered, as in the manner of his Roger Mudd interview, when he had been stumped by such tough questions as "Why do you want to be President?" or roared in stentorian tones like a hot-dog seller at a ball game. Sometimes he did both in the same speech. Tonight, though, he was right on: funny, impudent, pointed. (My admiration for his performance was diminished on learning that he had been practicing it for ten days.)

The Democratic party, he began boldly, was "the tribune of the people" and the "enemy of the interests. The greatest collection of special interests in all American history is now assembled in that cold citadel of privilege, the Republican party." Mondale would "demand a spirit of sacrifice"; Republicans "run from this reality. Where, oh where, is their balanced budget? If twenty-billion-dollar deficits were wrong under Democrats, then two-hundred-billion-dollar deficits under Republicans are at least as wrong." But it wasn't just the money, it was what it went for. "Cancel that needless missile without a mission," Kennedy urged, of the MX. "A just society cannot be tough on poor mothers and easy on Pentagon contractors." When Reagan goes to the hospital, "all he has to do to call a helicopter is push a button. (And I hope it's the right button.) Ronald Reagan should not be the only senior citizen who does not have to worry about the cost of medical care."

He took up a theme that Mondale had played a year ago in New Hampshire—Reagan the radical. Every President "since McKinley" had supported a progressive income tax —"except Ronald Reagan." Every President since Harding had picked a Secretary of the Interior who was not "an enemy of the environment—except Ronald Reagan." Every President since Hoover, "even Richard Nixon, has negotiated with the leadership of the Soviet Union." By this time, the crowd had learned its part. *Except Ronald Reagan.* It was great fun. "Ronald Reagan never met an arms-control agreement he didn't dislike." He should return to Hollywood, where both he "and Star Wars belong."

If re-elected, Reagan would "stand even closer to right-wing dictators abroad" and to "the racist regime of South Africa," and "sell even more sophisticated weapons to the enemies of Israel." Will you be my valentine? "Under the leadership of Walter Mondale, there would be "no room in the Democratic party for bigotry of any kind or bigots of any stripe."

Mention of Mondale brought him to the consummation. Hubert Humphrey and his own brother Robert both "sore in him very special promise." So at long last, after three and a half years of ceaseless effort, the thirty-ninth Democratic

convention was presented with "Walterrrr Mondaaaale."
The band played the theme from *Rocky*—to the victor belongs the melodies—and Mondale stepped forward.

He started where Ferraro had, with origins. "I grew up in
the farm towns of southern Minnesota. My dad was a
preacher, and my mom was a music teacher. We never had
a dime.* But we were rich in the values that are important
. . . to work hard; to stand on my own; to play by the rules;
to tell the truth; to obey the law; to care for others; to love
our country; to cherish our faith. . . . My presidency will
be about those values."

But first he had to secure the office. This meant attacking
Reagan. He had been doing that for months, of course. But
all these attacks had been primarily partisan: designed to
outshine the attacks of his Democratic rivals and to appeal
to Democratic voters and power brokers. After the New
Jersey primary put him safely over the top, however, Mondale had to begin fashioning arguments that would seem
effective in the give-and-take of a general election. Tonight,
he came up with two.

"In 1980, Ronald Reagan beat the pants off us. So tonight,
I want to say something to those of you across our country
who voted for Reagan . . . I heard you. And our party
heard you." This was the closest Walter Mondale had come
to acknowledging the possibility that the 1980 election
might not have been a fluke, an inexplicable aberration. It
was not very close. He cited as evidence of his and the
party's attention the platform. "Look at" it. "There are no
defense cuts that weaken our security; no business taxes
that weaken our economy; no laundry lists that raid our
Treasury." But this was asserting that which was to be
proved. Mondale passed, without further demonstration, to
a consideration of Reagan's failures. "One last word to those
of you who voted for Mr. Reagan." Hissing from the hall. "I
know what you were saying. But I also know what you were

* Only five Presidents were born, as Harrison professed to have been, in
poverty—Fillmore, Andrew Johnson, Garfield, Nixon, and Reagan. Mondale would have become the sixth, and the first Democrat.

not saying. You did not vote for a two-hundred-billion-dollar deficit. You did not vote for an arms race. You did not vote to turn the heavens into a battleground. You did not vote to savage . . . destroy . . . trash . . . poison . . . [and] assault" Social Security, family farms, civil rights, the environment, and the poor. "You did not vote to pay fifty bucks for a fifty-cent light bulb."

Each of the nine derelictions was greeted with a tremendous "no." But these were applause lines from stump speeches. Mondale set out a more definite and accessible bill of particulars, according to which Reagan had failed in four areas: taxes, trade, the deficit, and the arms race.

"First there was Mr. Reagan's tax program." Mondale had earlier quoted the tag line of the Gettysburg Address, and added: "what we have today [instead] is a government of the rich, by the rich" (the crowd picked it up), "and for the rich. . . . What happened," Mondale went on, "was this. [Reagan] gave each of his rich friends enough tax relief to buy a Rolls-Royce—and then he asked your family to pay for the hubcaps. . . .

"Then they crimped our future. They let us be routed in international competition. . . . By the start of the next decade," Mondale said later on in his speech, "I want to be able to walk into any store in America, pick up the best product, of the best quality and the best price, and turn it over and read, 'Made in the U.S.A.' " With protection, that would be easily accomplished; better, cheaper foreign products wouldn't get into the store.

Arms control, the fourth item, brought out real passion; indeed, the only real passion of his speech. "We know our deep differences with the Soviets. . . . But between us, we have the capacity to destroy the planet. Every President since the bomb went off has understood that and talked with the Soviets and negotiated arms control. Why not this one? Why has this administration failed?" Here Mondale left his text. "Why haven't they tried? Why can't they understand the cry of humanity to control these god-awful

weapons? Why? Why?" The crowd cheered WE WANT
FRITZ.

His third item was the deficit. "We are living on borrowed
money and borrowed time." Deficits "hike interest rates,
clobber exports, stunt investment, kill jobs, undermine
growth, cheat our kids, and shrink our future. Whoever is
inaugurated in January . . . the budget will be squeezed.
Taxes will go up. And anyone who says they won't is not
telling the truth to the American people. . . . Let's tell the
truth. Mr. Reagan will raise taxes, and so will I. He won't tell
you. I just did."

This was Mondale's second attempt to engage Reagan
directly. Tactically, it was interesting, in that it struck at a
presumed difference, not in behavior, but in awareness and
honesty. President Reagan and President Mondale would
both inevitably do the same thing, raise taxes; but Mondale
would set about it as a clear-eyed judge of budgetary necessity, Reagan as a denier and a deceiver. Working from
Mondale's assumptions, a hefty tax raise in the next term
was indeed inevitable. It was not because he was uncon-
cerned, at least at the level of rhetoric, with the tax burden.
All politicians, Democrat and Republican, care about deficits, taxes, and programs. They differ in the hierarchies in
which they rank them. Mondale's hierarchy went: programs, deficits, taxes. Programs—aside from a few weapons
systems—could not be touched; they were sacred. (A few
moments later in his speech, Mondale said that his message
to Congress would be that "we must cut spending and pay
as we go. If you don't hold the line, I will. That's what the
veto is for." This was sad fustian, as incredible as Hart rat-
tling his saber at Texas A&M had been. In a three-year
campaign, and a thirty-year career, Mondale had yet to veto
the demands—or just needs—of anyone. He would not be
starting now. The echo of John Glenn—*pay as we go*—was
also unfortunate.) Deficits were a concern of the day,
prompted, Mondale would argue, by Reagan's huge ones.
Tax relief came last. Mondale was only saying so; and since

he could not imagine the world working any other way, it
made sense to dare Reagan to say so too.

There would be debate, throughout the campaign, on the
wisdom of Mondale's avowal. That could only be shown by
the result. But it reflected the logic of his position. Expressing it showed clarity and forthrightness.

"My friends," he finished, "America is a future each generation must enlarge. . . . For the rest of my life, I want to
talk with young people about their future. And whatever
their race, whatever their religion, whatever their sex, I
want to hear some of them say what I say, with joy and
reverence, tonight. 'I want to be President of the United
States.'"

The convention adjourned, and Mondale, Ferraro, and
lesser luminaries attended a party given by the mayor.
Over the bay, the mild sky filled with blue, green, red, and
gold rockets.

Like every party at the end of a long, tough internal fight,
the Democrats were about to enter that strange and unfa-
miliar country, America. The perils of turning outward and
submitting to extra-partisan judgment are always, at least
potentially, grave. At the extreme, the language you have
been speaking for months may turn out to be as incomprehensible as Lettish or Volapük. Arguments that have bulked
huge dwindle to disputes between Big and Little Endians,
while issues dismissed as beyond concern or beneath con-
tempt suddenly swell. Everyone is not anyone, and you may
be the odd one out.

At the extreme. It may also be that a party at the end of its
thrashings finds itself quite comfortably placed, and that
with little modulation or none, it can talk what seems like
sense to the majority of voters. It is not true, as mechanistic
and symmetrically minded political scientists would have it,
that both parties move in the general election toward some
mythical "center." For two decades, the years of Roosevelt
and Truman, the Democratic party did not have to move
much at all. It was the "center"—the center of the loyalties

of a majority. It was the Republicans who moved (Senator Taft, the New Deal's most principled critic, failed three times, from 1940 to 1952, to win his party's nomination).

In 1984, the Democrats had decided not to move. "If Mr. Reagan wants to rerun the 1980 campaign," Walter Mondale had said in his acceptance speech, "fine. Let them fight over the past." But the Democrats were the past. Their nominee had claimed to have understood the reasons for the party's defeat four years earlier, then showed that he had no idea. Their keynote speaker had not even claimed that much (that the "disastrous quality" of the Republican record, Cuomo had said, "is not more fully understood by the American people is attributable, I think, to the President's amiability"). The vice-presidential candidate agreed with her running mate in every significant particular. The Democrats had stayed with their past—because of its inherent attractions (to them, at least) and because of the feebleness of the alternatives—Glenn, Hart, Jackson—which they had been presented. They now had fourteen weeks in which to present it once more to the American people.

6

Not Built in a Day

On a crisp January afternoon, the local volunteers working for the 1980 Reagan for President campaign in the neighborhood of Florence, South Carolina, had assembled at a VFW post off a country road in the pine trees to meet their man. There had been other bad weeks in the life of Ronald Reagan, but this one would do until the next came along. Reagan's latest—and, if he failed, last—try for his party's nomination had been moving with all the stateliness of a dreadnought. No coy shallying as in 1968, no bitter fight with an incumbent as in 1976. Going into 1980, Reagan had had to his credit a sizable war chest, a trunkful of endorsements, a famous and familiar face, a long record, and a longer lead over a field of half a dozen challengers, none of whom had managed to raise a ripple. Every incipient swell so far had been duly smoothed—an attempt, pushed primarily by supporters of former Texas governor John Connally, to break the California delegation's unit rule; a Florida straw poll, intended as an ambush by backers of Illinois congressman Phil Crane. Nothing had come of either gambit, or of their intended beneficiaries. This was the struggle, or non-struggle, on the ground; at the top of the Reagan campaign, his managers had crafted for him a Rose Garden strategy—calm, confident, a touch aloof—in accordance with which they kept him away from a debate held early in January under the auspices of the Des Moines *Register,* indeed away from Iowa in general, the better to distinguish him from the common herd. (Reagan had no Rose Garden yet, it is true; although he seemed to have everything but.) For the Iowa caucuses, John Sears, the chief manager, told me and every other reporter in America afterwards, the Reagan campaign had looked forward to a "large caucus vote"—about 50,000 Republicans altogether. Reagan accepted Sears's judgment because the strategy had worked so far; because Sears was in fact a skillful tactician; and most importantly because Sears, skillful or not, was the man to whom Reagan had delegated the strategic chores, and the cardinal administrative principle to which he had always adhered, up to and often beyond the point of failure, was delegation. In the event, Reagan exceeded the number of Iowa votes his masterminds had expected. The difficulty was that so did everybody else, most particularly George Bush, who exceeded Reagan's final tally as well. It had been, Sears explained calmly, "a small primary vote." The tide in the affairs of men which, taken at the flood, leads on to fortune suddenly began to piddle.

The driveway, dirt and pine needles, was packed solid with parked cars all the way to the road. The Reaganites, over a hundred of them—rowdy men (many plaid work jackets); some young people; some ladies, middle-aged and up—filled the small all-purpose room. The day before, two days after Iowa, Reagan had been in St. Charles, Illinois, to speak at a fund-raiser for the congressman in the Fifteenth District. "I'll be honest," he'd said almost modestly at the end of his talk. "I'd like to be his neighbor in Washington." (Modestly, or wistfully?) He had flown to Florence that morning, where he read a reaction to President Carter's State of the Union message at an airport press conference— shakily, stopping in mid-sentence and bobbling words. He had never been comfortable sight-reading manuscripts; in 1937, he had almost washed out of his first movie at the preliminary script reading, and he had preferred ever since to talk from memory or note cards (but could it be age?). There was also a rasp in his voice, which he had blamed at his next stop, Francis Marion College, on the Los Angeles smog (he *was* pushing seventy). Nemesis lurked in every gesture. Reagan came to the volunteers' rally from the college, made an arc through the crowd, and clambered up onto a small stage. The student body president of another local college gave him a toy bear wearing the school jersey, and Reagan began again. The hostage crisis, the polite name for America's being at the humiliating mercy of a mob of swaggering Iranian goons, was in its eighty-third day, and Reagan started off with a contrasting vignette: During the Greco-Turkish war after World War I, the USS *Arizona* docked in embattled Constantinople, where, every morning, a sailor with a flag, a marine with a mailbag, and a marine with a rifle would march to the American legation and back, untouched, unmolested. As the years lengthened, Reagan liked to joke, of his remoter historical references— to the Revolutionary War, to ancient Rome—that he was sure of the facts because he had been alive at the time; in this case, he had been. "We can have that kind of America again," he assured his listeners.

Carter, a man asked, had been saying a lot about poor people; what did Reagan have to say? "We Republicans have to show people we're not the party of big business and the country-club set. We're the party of Main Street, the small town, the city neighborhood; the shopkeeper, the farmer, the cop on the beat, the blue-collar and the white-collar worker. Now, a word we hear a lot is compassion. If someone is genuinely helpless, of course we should be compassionate, and Americans are the most compassionate people on earth. But what about the man who gets up every morning, gets his kids off to school, goes to work, pays his bills, supports his church and charity, and pays his taxes? We have some compassion for them." The entourage wanted to push on to the next state, but Reagan took two more questions. What did he think of the SALT II treaty, still before the Senate? "Ship that thing back to the Soviets in Mos-

cow." Did he believe in God? "If I didn't think I could turn
to God for help, I wouldn't be running for this office." As the
crowd left, a few Reagan workers stood at the door holding
buckets for contributions.

There was no need for buckets at the next stop, only
envelopes: a $250-a-head buffet at the Tropic Room of the
Miami Intercontinental Hotel. The nippy weather, maybe
65 degrees, had sent bare female arms and shoulders under
cover of furs. Reagan acknowledged the cost of the affair—
"If we don't win, that's gonna be a regular price for a drink"
—and went immediately to questions. Social Security? The
system, he said, was several trillion dollars out of actuarial
balance. He intended to appoint a task force—a favorite
Reagan remedy, going back to his days as governor—to
suggest ways of shoring it up. A Cuban supporter wanted to
know about Cuban freedom, and got a favorite Reagan answer, going back to President Monroe. "There are no foreign colonies in this hemisphere." The most urgent question of the evening had come first. Tell us, a woman had
asked, that you are saying the same things you said in 1964.
"It wasn't exactly a question," Reagan observed. But another supporter pursued it. Was he moderating his views?
"The hell I am." More questions, more affirmations, and the
crowd retired into the silvery night.

Reagan left Miami next morning for New Orleans, and a
meeting of the Southern Republican Leadership Conference at the Fairmont Hotel. The Republican South—at least
that portion of it on view at the conference—for sixteen
years a Reagan stronghold, was sown with Bush and Connally buttons; Connally had rented a steamboat for a Mississippi cruise over the weekend, and Crane would also be
showing up later. Reagan had a new speech to give, devoted
mostly to foreign policy. Reagan in person was an unusual
speaker; in fact, the Republican field in 1980 made a good
contrast. The challengers covered the forensic spectrum,
from John Anderson, who was a practitioner of old-style
oratory, about the last left, wending his way through involved, leisurely sentences (a pompous and unappealing

practitioner, but a practitioner nonetheless), to John Connally, a stand-up, play-the-crowd stump speaker, who exhaled parallel constructions like a baby breathes, or a jogger gasps, the best in America till the advent of Jesse Jackson. Between them lay all the other Republicans, representatives of the vast middle class of speakers, making do with meager, short-winded texts in which, at their best, a few good things might be suspended, like fruit in Jell-O—jokes, jabs, chunks of near eloquence—but which, for the most part, were perfectly suited to bear the operations which had to be performed on them: grafts, amputations, adding a new paragraph for a stop in Oregon, cutting an old one because the foreign-policy adviser vetoed a reference to Ouagadougou; no *petite musique* at all, at most a *petite* tinkle. That was the Standard American Speech; the speech of Bush, Baker, and the rest. Also of Reagan. What was unusual was the way he delivered it: There exists, behind and above every lectern, a center of attention which all speakers seek to occupy; some draw it to them, some crowd it, most just occupy it stiffly, as if they were driftwood. Reagan, uniquely, *kept back* from it—just a touch; the distance of a duck of the head—and so drew his listeners in. The enemy buttons eyed him and each other suspiciously.

He finished the swing that night in St. Paul. The bare shoulders would have cracked in this cold; the radio was predicting highs of zero. Reagan went first to the Minnesota Club, a dark wood-and-leather-lined nest of the kind burghers of the last century built for themselves, to read the political entrails. These were confused. Connally had finished only eleven percentage points back in a straw poll of the state central committee; Bush was coming on strong in the suburbs of the Twin Cities.

The rally was not at the club, but at Stem Hall, a down-homier place, basically a big bare room with a stage. The crowd was well wrapped in scarves, tweeds, wool shirts, fur and felt hats (as well as plastic boaters with Reagan bumper stickers pasted on the crowns). Some had come over from Wisconsin; a Mr. and Mrs. Buddy Jensen had driven one

hundred miles from upstate. The warm-up speaker labored
to cover for Reagan's lateness, declaring that "a political
speech with jokes and homilies wouldn't seem quite right"
in a time of crisis like the present; so he cited Milton Fried-
man, the ancient Greeks, and poor Santayana on history
instead. Three clarinets, eight brass, and two laconic men
behind bass and snare drums took over after he ran through
Bartlett's, playing "There'll Be a Hot Time in the Old Town
Tonight" in a warmish tempo, two, four, six times. The
crowd looked puzzled; finally Reagan came, with an introduction by freshman Senator David Durenberger, who was
all praise and no endorsement, though the crowd paid no
more heed to Durenberger than they had to the ancient
Greeks; it was Reagan they'd been waiting for. The band
gave it another shot, boaters fluttered. Reagan repeated the
speech he had given in New Orleans that morning, in the
same way, and with the same effect, ending, here as there,
with the conviction that America might be what John Winthrop had told "the small band of pilgrims on the tiny ship
Arabella" they could become: "a shining city on a hill."

Back in Miami, one of the Reaganites had asked point-
blank about his age. Phil Crane, Reagan answered, had
been saying as an argument for his own candidacy that he
was Reagan, only twenty years younger. "That's too bad,"
Reagan went on, "because twenty years ago I was a New
Deal Democrat." He had slightly misled his audience, for
twenty years ago Ronald Reagan's conversion from New
Deal Democracy, which he had indeed believed in, was
already complete. He had been bringing much the same
message he had given in St. Paul and New Orleans (and
Miami, and South Carolina, and Illinois, and hundreds of
other places) to audiences for years. Sometimes he had
brought it in the same words: "city on a hill" went back to
the previous election; his description of the average American went back at least sixteen years. ("We represent the
forgotten American," he had written in a symposium after
the Goldwater debacle, "that simple soul who goes to work,
bucks for a raise, takes out insurance, pays for his kids'

schooling, contributes to his church and charity, and knows there just 'ain't no such thing as a free lunch.' "[1]) "Reagan's stature with Republican voters, and particularly with conservatives," wrote his biographer Lou Cannon, "was not built in a day."

Neither was the conservative movement to which he appealed. It had been gestating, first as a body of thought, then as a political faction, for twenty-five years. By the 1980 election it expressed what had become, in many areas of American life, the prevailing climate of opinion. Reagan and the conservative movement had met when it was still at the beginning of its life and he was midway through his.

Ronald Wilson Reagan was born February 6, 1911, the second of two sons, in Tampico, Illinois. The Panama Canal was under construction, Arizona and New Mexico were applying for statehood, and the President was William Howard Taft. There was a Hapsburg in Vienna, a sultan in Constantinople, a Manchu in Peking, and a czar in Moscow. Reagan was never aware of these foreign relics; his earliest memory of public affairs was World War I, the convulsion that swept the last of them away. Of Tampico, he remembered a park, a Civil War cannon, stacked cannonballs. By the time he was nine, the Reagans had made five moves, all in northern Illinois, ending up in Dixon.

John Edward (Jack) Reagan, Ronald's father, made a slender income selling shoes. He was an Irish Catholic and a confirmed Democrat, northern style: he forbade his sons to see *Birth of a Nation* because it was sympathetic to the Ku Klux Klan. He was also an alcoholic. The second vignette in Reagan's autobiography is of Jack, lying on the front porch, "dead to the world . . . his hair soaked with melting snow." The boy was grieved and (we must assume) angry. The man blotted the anger from his recollection: "I could feel no resentment." Ronald helped Jack to bed. "In a few days he was the bluff, hearty man I knew and loved and will always remember." Nelle Reagan (née Wilson) bore with her husband's periodic benders, acquiesced in his politics, and devoutly attended the Christian Church. Neither of the Reagans had gone beyond grade school, but they enjoyed books, and Nelle led the dramatic readings in the local ladies' societies.

In 1928, Reagan entered Eureka College, a small Christian Church school twenty miles south of Dixon. Eureka gave him a job washing dishes in the girls' dormitory to cover his board and an athletic scholarship for half of his tuition. Reagan lettered in football, swimming, and track. He also joined the dramatic society. In his junior year, Eureka entered the Eva Le Gallienne Competition, sponsored by Northwestern University, for one-act plays. Eureka's production of *Aria da Capo* took a second, and Reagan was one of six actors singled out for a good performance.

He didn't act again for five years after leaving Eureka. "Broadway and Hollywood," he felt, "were as inaccessible as outer space," and he went to Iowa instead, broadcasting the games of the Chicago Cubs for station WHO in Des Moines. His break came in 1937, when he traveled with the Cubs to spring training on Catalina Island. A former colleague at WHO, living in California, recommended a screen test with Warner Brothers (provided he removed his glasses—Reagan was nearsighted). Warner Brothers took him. When the studio brass met to decide what his name should be, the new acquisition suggested "Ronald Reagan." "Ronald Reagan, Ronald Reagan," mused the casting director. "I like it."

There followed fifty-two movies, some of which still lead a flickering TV afterlife in the small hours of the morning. His best-known role was George Gipp (whence "Gipper," as in *Let's win this one for the),* but his best was Drake McHugh, a small-town playboy in *King's Row* whose legs were amputated by a vengeful doctor. Reagan had to wake up, discover his mutilated body, and cry, "Where's the rest of me?" That scene provided the first vignette in his autobiography, as well as the title. For the rest, he played engaging characters who sometimes did, sometimes didn't, get the girl. "Reagan for governor?" Jack Warner is supposed to have asked in

1966, when the actor first became a candidate. "No. Jimmy Stewart for governor, Ronnie for best friend."

Reagan spent World War II in Hollywood, making training films (his eyes made him unfit for active service). In 1940, he had married one of his first leading ladies, Jane Wyman. They had a daughter and adopted a son before she divorced him in 1948. Both had been taciturn about the breakup in the years since. When Reagan came to write of it, it was almost as something external, which had simply happened to him. "I suppose there had been warning signs, if only I hadn't been so busy," but "small-town boys grow up thinking only other people get divorced."

What kept him busy, as much as and soon more than his career, was Hollywood's actors' union, the Screen Actors Guild. Reagan's first brush with politicking had come at Eureka, when he helped lead a student strike against a belt-tightening president. The Guild offered him an opportunity to practice at the adult level, and Reagan liked it. Guild members liked him, electing him president five years running.

It also offered him a firsthand view of Communist tactics. From 1945 to 1947, Hollywood suffered a crippling series of strikes. The question at issue was ostensibly jurisdictional: should stagehands be organized by the International Alliance of Theatrical Stage Employees (IATSE) or by a variety of craft unions? In fact, the craft unions were being egged on by Communist organizers. "The Communist Party in Hollywood," concluded a committee of the California Senate in 1959, "wanted control over everything on wheels. . . . They moved Communist units into those unions having jurisdiction over carpenters, painters, musicians, grips, and electricians. To control those trade unions was to control the motion picture industry." The AFL soon disavowed the craft unionists, but their strikes persisted. Cars were trashed, strikers rioted, IATSE members were mugged, their houses bombed. Some of the ugliness washed over Reagan, who, as an outsider, had been trying to mediate. While filming *Night unto Night*, he got a call on the set threatening that he would be "fixed" so that he would never act again. The police issued him a .32 Smith & Wesson and put a guard on his house.

It was no ah-ha experience (food, perhaps, for later thought). Reagan had inherited his father's Democratic loyalties and added an idealistic overlay of his own. He joined the ADA and Alan Cranston's World Federalists. In 1948, he campaigned for Truman and (along with Walter Mondale) for Hubert Humphrey. Two years later, he supported the Democratic slate, including Helen Gahagan Douglas in her Senate race against Richard Nixon. But his days as a liberal —sentimental and unreflective, perhaps, but sincere— were drawing to a close.

American liberalism does not need historians. For much of the last forty years, its history coincided with the country's; its wars—against poverty (lost), Jim Crow (won), and the Vietcong (changed sides)—were America's wars. Conservatism had a more subterranean existence.

When William Rusher, a line officer in conservative journalism and politicking since the fifties, came recently to write an account of the modern-day right wing and his career in it, he considered what his inspiration had been and came up with three books: *The Road to Serfdom* by Friedrich Hayek, *Witness* by Whittaker Chambers, and *The Conservative Mind* by Russell Kirk. He had been economical in his reading; together, the three books spanned just about everything that went into the nascent conservative movement.

It is significant that Rusher's inspiration was a handful of stray books; it couldn't have come from very many other sources. Non-liberals existed in the early fifties, but they were not a going concern. Liberalism controlled one major party at the national level and held veto power in the other. Robert Taft, "Mr. Republican," but never the Republican standard-bearer, had died in 1953 after his third and last failed attempt to win his party's nomination. The entire national career of Senator Joseph McCarthy, the net effect of which was to destroy rather than advance the issues he had taken up, lasted, from his Wheeling speech to his censure in the Senate, less than five years. The monopoly of liberalism on the American mind was virtually complete. It controlled the academies and serious journalism (and defined what was and was not serious). "Liberalism," wrote Lionel Trilling in 1950, "is not only the dominant but even the sole intellectual tradition. . . . It is the plain fact that there are no conservative or reactionary ideas in general circulation." "At the present time," wrote political scientist Kenneth Minogue thirteen years later, "most of us are, in some degree or other, liberal. It is only the very cynical, the unassailably religious, or the consistently nostalgic who have remained unaffected." Minogue was talking about the whole sweep of liberalism: about John Locke and Adam Smith as well as Hubert Humphrey. But the remark would have been about as true if he'd only meant Humphrey.

The first book on Rusher's list, and the first published, was indeed by a man who called (and calls) himself liberal. Friedrich Hayek was an economist, born in Austria, who had lived in England since the early thirties. His earliest work, on money and credit, had been only for colleagues. But in 1944 he published *The Road to Serfdom*, which was widely read on both sides of the Atlantic and even ran in *Reader's Digest* (no more "serious" then than now).

The Road to Serfdom was a book of politics, not technical economics. (Most important economics books are.) Hayek's politics were those of a pre-modern liberal, a believer in the rightness and utility of freedom, and he saw centralized economic planning, not as an extension of these ideals, but as a forerunner of totalitarian systems like Nazi Germany and (though he could not press the point in wartime) the Soviet Union. "Planning leads to dictatorship because dictatorship is the most effective instrument of coercion and the enforcement of ideals and, as such, essential if central planning on a large scale is to be possible."

Things did not work out quite the way Hayek feared. "Hot" socialism was never set up, at least not in the United

States. American liberals instead pursued an ad hoc collection of programs and promises, justified by more sweeping rhetoric: the long, long road that led at last to Mondale. But the fear was not baseless. In the thirties (Hayek noted in a foreword to a later edition) the New Deal Brain Trusters "devoted a great deal of attention to the example of planning provided by these four countries: Germany, Italy, Russia, and Japan." Planning was in the air; had been for a long time. It had even reached the minds of Amory Blaine and Dink Stover. America resisted. (Britain was less lucky. The Third World, ruled by alumni of the London School of Economics, was unluckiest of all.)

Along the way, Hayek marshaled arguments of enduring pertinence. (His fourth chapter—"The 'Inevitability' of Planning"—would have spared Gary Hart the necessity of thinking deep thoughts on industrial strategy.) He was never to be comfortable with conservative allies. "Conservatism, though a necessary element in any stable society, is not a social program. . . . Anti-intellectual, and often mystical, it will never, except in short periods of disillusionment, appeal to the young." Nonetheless, his timely defense of free-market arrangements was important to American conservatism.

"The moral force" of Whittaker Chambers, a college classmate of his recalled years later, "began with his physical appearance. This seemed calculated to negate youth and all its graces, to deny that they could be of any worth in our world of pain and injustice. He was short of stature and very broad, with heavy arms and massive thighs; his sport was wrestling. . . . When [his] mouth opened, it never failed to shock by reason of the dental ruin it disclosed, a devastation of empty sockets and blackened stumps. In later years, Chambers underwent restorative dentistry, but during his radical time, his aggressive toothlessness . . . annihilated the hygienic American present. Only a serf could have such a mouth."[2] Whittaker Chambers came to national attention in 1948 by testifying that Alger Hiss, a former State Department official and New Deal golden boy, had been a Communist and a Soviet spy, reporting to Chambers himself. *Witness* was Chambers's effort, two years later, to state the meaning of his case and his life. As a writer, Chambers was capable of a black mood and a purple prose that drove finicky critics nuts ("repulsive," wrote Dwight Macdonald of *Witness,* ". . . melodramatic, cheaply sentimental, coarse-grained, egotistical . . ."). One-third of the large book—800 pages in hardcover—detailed, with long quotations from transcripts, the ins and outs of the Hiss trial. Another lengthy chapter recounted Chambers's early life, which would have been enough to give anyone black moods. But the heart of the book was his discussion of his reasons for embracing and rejecting Communism.

What Chambers had seen in Communism was a "will to survive" historical crises: world war, world depression; more subtly (he did not say so, but the whole structure of his book implied it) the crisis of modern middle-class life as he had lived it. The "decision to become a Communist seems to the man who makes it as a choice between a world that is dying and a world that is coming to birth, as an effort to save by political surgery . . . a civilization which nothing less drastic can save." It offered a "challenge . . . to end the bloody meaninglessness of man's history—by giving it a purpose and a plan."

The plan took Chambers openly into the party and the *Daily Worker* (where his first assignment was to write a puff of Augusto Sandino); finally, into the underground. The underground, he knew, engaged in worse than espionage. ("Any fool can commit a murder," ran one of its sayings, "but it takes an artist to commit a good natural death.") The tide of deaths unleashed by the Purge Trials was Chambers's proximate reason for breaking. But in *Witness* he wrote that he had detected the earliest impulse in "a very casual happening."

> I was sitting in our apartment on St. Paul's Street in Baltimore. . . . My daughter was in her high

chair. I was watching her eat. She was the most
miraculous thing that had ever happened in my
life. I liked to watch her even when she smeared
porridge on her face or dropped it meditatively on
the floor. My eye came to rest on the delicate con-
volutions of her ear. The thought passed through
my mind: "No, those ears were not created by any
chance coming together of atoms in nature (the
Communist view). They could have been created
only by immense design."

The conclusion, for Chambers, of this line of thought was
that the means which Communism was willing—driven—to
employ in meeting the historical crisis were metaphysically
unacceptable. The conclusion implied a corollary: "The
only possible answer to the Communist challenge . . . is
the challenge: Faith in God."

Chambers's new faith left him in a lonely intellectual
position, even when the modern American conservative
movement had gotten itself going. The crisis of history remained, in all its implacability, and after rejecting the solution of Communism, he despaired of any other. "It is idle,"
he remarked in a letter to a friend, "to talk about prevent-
ing the wreck of Western civilization. It is already a wreck
from within." He could be scornful of those whose premises
seemed less radical than his own. ("This book," he wrote in
dismissal of the work of an Austrian economist, a peer of
Hayek's, "is not going to harm anyone above the mental age
of twelve.") At the level of tactics, he often counseled mod-
eration: when Alger Hiss applied, after his release from
prison, for a passport, Chambers supported his right to
travel.

Curiously, the most empirical part of his thesis has worn
least well. Communists might have cared, in the twenties,
thirties, and forties, about the crisis of history. The Kremlin,
in 1986, almost certainly has ceased to. The Soviet state is
run by sleepwalkers. Its strength is not its own fervor but its
enemies' confusion. To this extent, Chambers's assertions

about God and faith—which, more than any tricks of temperament or style, scandalized critics like Macdonald—turned out to be prescient. Atheism played no part in the fall of Nicaragua ("Jim Carter was a Christian"), but Washington's acceptance of sub-Marxist notions of the inevitability of revolution did. Chambers did not live to see it; the exhausted witness died in 1961.

Russell Kirk was a thirty-five-year-old history instructor at Michigan State when he published *The Conservative Mind,* in 1953. His effort was in some ways more difficult than Hayek's or Chambers's—to outline a tradition of conservative thinking broader than free-market economics and older than the upheavals of the twentieth century.

Kirk's paradigm for modern conservatism was Edmund Burke, primarily—though not solely—because of his polemics against the French Revolution. The relevance of the politics of 1790 was, in Kirk's view, that the revolution had been an assault on "the ancient traditions of humanity," of which later "radicalisms" were simply variations. Conservative resistance, Kirk believed, was by nature unschematic and diffused. But he discerned half a dozen ongoing convictions: that "a divine intent rules society" and "Providential social forces" are the "proper instrument[s] for change"; that "property and freedom are inseparably connected" and "all attempts at levelling lead to despair"; that the "variety and mystery of traditional life" should be cherished both for its own sake and as a "check . . . upon man's anarchic impulse." The bulk of the book traced these beliefs in Britain and America over the century and a half after Burke.

Kirk was conscious of the fact that he was barking up some deserted trees. His parade of conservative thinkers began with a pair of statesmen, Burke and John Adams, and petered out in a trio of bookworms (Irving Babbitt, Paul Elmer More, George Santayana). "Nowadays," he admitted, "Adams is not read; I was the first man to cut the pages in the ten big volumes of my set of his works, although they

were published a hundred years ago." Kirk originally
wanted to call his own work *The Conservative Rout.*

There were other problems. Kirk scanted the Revolution
and skated over the Civil War, the two main events in
American history and political thinking. More than one conservative found the whole project faintly unreal. "If you
were a marine in a landing boat," Whittaker Chambers
asked a friend, "would you wade up the seabeach at Tarawa
for *that* conservative position? And neither would I."

But *The Conservative Mind* was noteworthy for several
reasons. Kirk never, then or later, lost private property in
the soapsuds of Tory socialism, as English Tories are prone
to do. The way of accommodation was always open to him.
In the fifties, it was taken by the poet Peter Viereck, who
had read all the books Kirk had, and drew from them the
conclusion that the true heirs of Edmund Burke in modern
America were Adlai Stevenson and the liberal wing of the
Democratic party. As a matter of style Kirk managed to
discuss a variety of disparate men with sympathy and respect, applying his notions of manners to scholarship. Most
important was the effort itself. Other writers would find
different models for American conservatism, perhaps more
useful ones. *The Conservative Mind* was the first attempt to
define its title.

The end of the beginning came with the appearance, in
the fall of 1955, of *National Review,* a weekly magazine,
soon biweekly, edited by a thirty-year-old, William F. Buckley, Jr. *National Review* filled a gap left by the demise of the
only previous right-wing journal of opinion, *The Freeman.*
There were many similarities between the two, down to the
typefaces; several of *National Review*'s editors, including
Buckley, had worked for the older magazine. But *The Freeman* suffered from the incoherence of conservatives generally in the early fifties. (They weren't even sure about the
label "conservative"; the same issue of *The Freeman* which
discussed *The Conservative Mind* carried a lead article entitled "What Should You Call Yourself?")

The functions of journals of opinion are many. They

cheerlead, exhort, instigate. Primarily they seek influence, which they pursue by the trickle-down theory. Their direct impact on policy and public opinion is typically slight; their quarry is the policymaker a year, a decade, a generation thence. A thought that wandered across the copy desk of *The New Republic* in 1914 may have ended up in the brain of Franklin Roosevelt in 1934—or better yet, in the brains of the voters. *National Review* also provided, for conservatives, a forum in which unlike-minded people could fight it out. There was plenty of fighting to be done. Purists of various stripes were continually defecting: economists to anarchy; Catholics to Carlism. The fights also got personal. The breach between Frank Meyer, an ex-Communist, ultimately the book editor, and Kirk, who contributed a column on education, never healed. Happily for the magazine, Meyer lived and worked in upstate New York, and Kirk sent in his copy from rural Michigan. James Burnham, a former Trotskyist, philosophy professor, and CIA man, who was after Buckley the most committed of all the editors to the magazine's success, still could not forbear teasing Meyer, which he usually did by proposing that the book reviews be shortened. Meyer for his part accused Burnham at one acrid editorial meeting of never having "repudiated the Roosevelt revolution." For this insult, Buckley coaxed an apology. It was thanks to Buckley that most of the personalities meshed. So in time did most of the ideas: because the common enemies were so pressing; because there was nowhere else to go; mainly because it came to be felt that there was in fact an "instinctual consensus" (the phrase was Meyer's) that capitalism, anti-Communism, and (the American) tradition expressed.

Many of these egos and talents are still alive and producing. That is part of their relevance. The archaeologist of Walter Mondale's mind would have to dig much further back, past the ADA and the New Deal, to—what? Bull Moose and Fabians; muckrakers and John Dewey. Back most of all to Woodrow Wilson, the politician who set American liberals to watching the baggage-claim area of Prog-

ress, to grab whatever came out of history's hold next. But
the main relevance of these old first editions and crumbled
paper controversies is that they were read. In the spring of
1981, when one of the new White House speechwriters
proposed using a passage from *Witness,* Ronald Reagan suggested the description of the baby's ear, which he quoted
from memory. (Chambers was awarded the Medal of Freedom three years later.)

Five years after the founding of *National Review,* the
new conservatives made their first moves into politics. In
1960, they entered the Balkan party structure of New York,
as an explicit counterweight to the state's Liberal party.
Their greatest PR success was William F. Buckley, Jr.'s
hopeless run for mayor of New York in 1965; their greatest
electoral success was his brother James's winning run for
the Senate five years later. By the eighties, the Conservative party effectively controlled the nominating process of
the state Republican party.

At the national level, the movement sought the 1964
Republican nomination for Barry Goldwater. The Arizona
senator was till the last a reluctant candidate; the move to
draft him was the work of three men: Clifton White, a
veteran of New York politics; William Rusher, since 1958
publisher of *National Review;* and John Ashbrook, a freshman congressman from Ohio. All three had been active in
the Young Republicans in the fifties; they built the Goldwater movement out of their address books (and three years of
hard work). They also had a demographic intuition—that
the power and population centers of the party and the
country were shifting south and west. "Nelson Rockefeller," wrote James Reston in the New York *Times,* expressing
the conventional wisdom, "is in no more danger of losing
the nomination than he is of going broke." Rockefeller lost,
Goldwater won; and conservatism was on the political map
nationally.

Goldwater's defeat in the election was spectacular, almost as bad as Jimmy Carter's would be sixteen years later.
But the loss had accomplished three things for the con-

servative movement. It had generated the mailing lists which were to become the foundations of the New Right's direct-mail empires. It dislodged many liberal Republicans from their positions of power in the GOP (they would linger to serve as auxiliaries to the stand-pat supporters of Gerald Ford in 1976 and practically vanish thereafter). Finally, it launched the political career of Ronald Reagan.

Reagan's debut was a television speech, "A Time for Choosing," which he taped for the final days of the campaign. It nearly didn't run; Goldwater's managers—Clifton White had been shoved aside immediately after the nomination—feared it might be extreme (as in "in defense of liberty is no vice"?). Reagan had to assure Goldwater over the phone at the last minute that it was "not really that bad." The speech raised a million dollars, a record; David Broder judged it the splashiest political debut since William Jennings Bryan and the Cross of Gold speech in 1896.

Like Bryan's, Reagan's speech had been polished over years of practice. In 1954, with decent movie offers becoming increasingly scarce, he had accepted an offer to host a television series sponsored by General Electric. The deal also included speaking tours to GE plants as part of the company's employee and community relations program. Reagan began by talking mostly about Hollywood, but the GE audiences wanted to hear more, and he found himself developing opinions on other subjects. "We marinated him in middle America," said his GE handler years later. Among the places he began turning to for congenial opinions were *Human Events*, a weekly conservative tip sheet on Washington politics, and *National Review*.

Another factor in his rightward shift was his second marriage. Reagan met Nancy Davis, an actress and an actress's daughter, in 1951 on Guild business, and married her a year later. She had come by her own conservative disposition from her stepfather, a successful Chicago neurosurgeon. (A minority view holds that Nancy had no effect on Ron; she was only, insists one biographer, a good listener. This seems to reflect a rather naïve view of marital dynamics.)

Reagan campaigned as a Democrat for Nixon in 1960. He marked a turning point after Kennedy's election, when a union paper in Illinois branded him an "extremist" and a teachers' federation in Minnesota asked that he be removed from a winter carnival parade as a "controversial personality"—all on the basis of what had become his standard GE talk. Reagan finally left his father's party in 1962.

The Republican party of California had fallen on evil days, and after "A Time for Choosing," Reagan was recruited to take on Governor Pat Brown in 1966. In a famous enthymeme, Brown noted that both Reagan and John Wilkes Booth had been actors. Reagan turned out to be an assassin; he beat Brown by nearly a million votes. Two years later, Governor Reagan made a run for the Republican presidential nomination, which he now remembers as having been unserious. Hesitant, perhaps (a Reagan trait, every bit as much as delegation). But quite serious. Clifton White, Reagan's manager this time around, came close to assembling enough open commitments and secret pledges to force the convention roll call to a second ballot—closer, perhaps, than on any other occasion in the last thirty years. White was working against the man he had drafted seven years earlier, who had committed himself to Richard Nixon as early as 1965. Goldwater and his allies held the waverers in the South, which was crucial, and Nixon headed for his one and a half terms.

Reagan's stickiest problem as governor had come up at the beginning of his first term—a clique of homosexuals on his staff, who were alleged to have held an orgy at Lake Tahoe. Reagan fired the ringleaders without publicity and rode out the storm after columnist Drew Pearson broke the story. The situation had arisen as a result of that Reagan propensity to delegate, and at times overdelegate; he learned about the indiscreet aides only from other staff members who had been investigating the matter for several months on their own. Reagan did not change his style, for delegation was in fact the vice of a virtue—a disposition to focus only on a few essentials. Reagan responded to the homosexual scandal, not by taking daily business into his own hands, but by consigning it to new, more trustworthy ones.

His greatest accomplishment was at first a short-run political failure—a ballot referendum, Proposition 1, offered at the end of his second term. A dry run of all future tax and spending revolts, Proposition 1 would have limited tax-funded spending to a percentage of state personal income and required a two-thirds vote of the legislature to raise taxes. It was noteworthy as a first attempt to discipline the spending constituencies by limiting the size of the pool of revenue they could draw from. The wording of the proposition was forbidding, and the entrenched interests of the state united successfully against it. (They were rewarded, five years later, with the passage of the far sterner Proposition 13.)

The 1968 presidential elections were a moment of conservative opportunity. Hubert Humphrey had been defeated, and hence Richard Nixon elected, by precisely the kinds of voters which White and Rusher had targeted as conservative since the early sixties. (The complicating factor, in the election and the sentence, was George Wallace. It is impossible to say how the Wallace vote would have split had he not run; Nixon and Humphrey would each have gotten some. The significant fact, in retrospect, was the near-permanent defection of the Wallace vote from the Democratic party.) Richard Nixon did not, as far as conservatives were concerned, seize the chance—largely, no doubt, because he had never been a conservative on domestic issues, and domestic policy bored him in any case. Abroad, he inaugurated a détente with the Soviet Union and China whose etiquette—toasting Mao Tse-tung in Peking like a long-lost father—upset the right as much as its substantive concessions—the loopholed SALT I treaty. Nixon would write in his memoirs that he had intended, after the 1972 election, to "revitalize the Republican party along New Majority lines." Watergate got to the GOP first.

The leaders of the conservative movement—the laymen, not the politicians; Governor Reagan stuck by Nixon as long as it was decent—protested his derelictions. But they had acquiesced in his nomination in 1968 and supported him—after a nearly invisible protest candidacy by John Ashbrook—in 1972. While they suffered sullenly, conservatism enjoyed two important accessions.

Neoconservatism was less a body of new thought than a new idiom. Its spokesmen were overwhelmingly academics, mainly Jewish. Many had once been Marxists, or at least dialecticians. (One Trotskyist debate that Irving Kristol attended as a college student took two whole days. "The most succinct presentation, by James Burnham, lasted only two hours, and caused many of those present to question his 'seriousness.' ") But all had spent the bulk of their adult lives as liberals, which was their strength. They commanded the attention of "serious" publications, and controlled two of them *(The Public Interest* and *Commentary);* they knew at first hand, and could explain with authority, the failures of many of the programs which the paleoconservatives had predicted on purely philosophical grounds.

The New Right represented, in part, a new approach to political technique. Several of its leaders had cut their teeth in the Goldwater campaign, but they concluded, in the early seventies, that conservatism had to do more than struggle for power at the top of the Republican party. They aimed to expand the movement's base, among unconverted voters and in Congress. To this end, they pioneered the use of direct mail. Direct mail now fills many mailboxes, and wastebaskets; it is easy to mock ("But that, Mr.   Jones   , is exactly what James Watt/Castro wants to do to our wetlands/Canal"). But it meets the main test of politicking—it works; and so long as liberals continue to be over-represented in organs of opinion, it will continue to work best for the New Right (the news is already full of wetlands, less full of Castro).

The precipitating cause of the New Right was Gerald Ford's nomination of Nelson Rockefeller as Vice-President. Congressman Ford had always stood, in his stolid, unimaginative fashion, on the GOP's right. His selection of the faded billionaire liberal was a total misreading of the party's, and the nation's, dynamics. It also stimulated Ronald Reagan, ending his second term as governor, to think about challenging the incumbent.

The 1976 campaign was a revue of Reagan's mannerisms. He hesitated, over 1974 and early 1975, to make the irrevocable decision: because he hesitates, and because of loyalty, in this case to the idea of a united Republican party. The conduct of the campaign was marked by delegation, some of it disastrous and probably fatal (his local managers in the New Hampshire and Florida primaries cheerily predicted decisive triumphs, so that Ford squeakers—narrower than the margins which Eugene McCarthy, losing to Lyndon Johnson in 1968, was able to count as moral victories—were seen as Reagan defeats); some of it well done (the John Sears ploy of picking, six weeks before the convention, liberal Senator Richard Schweiker as Reagan's running mate staved off the recognition of the inevitability of Ford's victory). It was marked, finally, by persistence. After Florida, Reagan dropped primaries in Massachusetts and Illinois. His aides were discussing terms of surrender with Ford. REAGAN VIRTUALLY CONCEDES DEFEAT IN NORTH CAROLINA ran the New York *Times* headline about the next primary. Reagan won, on the strength of a last-minute TV appeal ("A Time for Choosing," twelve years later), and went all the way to Kansas City; 60 delegates shy of all the way.

Ford's loss confirmed the demographic instincts of the first conservative political pros. In an election so close, every vote is decisive. But the greatest shifts, from Republican to Democrat, were registered among the "Wallace vote," concentrated in an arc that swung from Appalachia to East Texas. (Psephologist Kevin Phillips, studying twenty key counties, guessed that the slippage might have cost Ford 6 percent of the national vote.)

Reagan kept his hand in over the next four years. His biggest issue was one which had worked well for him in the 1976 primaries, the Panama Canal. It kept him before his public—the New Right also mobilized legions—and since the treaties ultimately passed, he avoided the responsibilities of victory. (William F. Buckley, Jr., who almost alone in the conservative movement endorsed the treaties, and who debated them with Reagan, believed that if he had not made the argument, he would never have been nominated, and that if he had won it, and a Salvadoran-style insurgency had resulted, he could never have been elected.) No politician was better positioned to take advantage of, or credit for, the tax revolt. Proposition 13 had not been a California peculiarity, like mesquite or psychobabble. Similar proposals made the ballots, and the law books, across the country, even in the McGovernite bastion of Massachusetts.

No Republican, finally, was better suited to take on Jimmy Carter. Carter was an able campaigner but a bewildered President, feebly serving an exhausted ideology; almost any Republican could have beaten him. But he was made for Reagan. President Carter responded to the energy crisis by lecturing the nation on its spiritual health; Reagan had never dwelled on the gloomy side of things since he had hauled his father in off the porch. Carter fussed with everything and had no solutions for anything. Reagan's very torpors coincided with—in face, sprung from—a conviction that there were answers, and that he saw them clearly.

The Republican field that lined up for 1980 spanned the party's political spectrum. Howard Baker, the Senate Minority Leader ("assistant to the Majority Leader," ran the crack), was the sort of old-boy officeholder who believes that presidential nominations go to old shoes. He had no definite positions, did no work on his campaign, and faded fast. Robert Dole, who at that time appeared to have many of Baker's weaknesses and none of his strengths, faded even faster. John Connally was Richard Nixon all over again, in a Titan's body. Phil Crane was the conservative backup in case Reagan disintegrated.

There was a time when John Anderson had stumped the country as a young congressman for Goldwater, but that time was long past. The journalistic phrase for the process Anderson underwent is "growing in office." The intended meaning is that one arrives in the big city, with straw behind the ears and unworkable notions between them; over years of experience and education, one learns the world's complexities and matures as a politician and a leader. Ideally, one does. But since those who use the phrase are generally liberals, for whom "complexities" are reasons for doing things in a liberal way, "growing" always means moving left (Ronald Reagan, between 1950 and 1960, did not "grow"). By the end of 1980, Anderson grew out of the Republican party altogether and ran as an independent.

There was finally, far back in the pack, George Bush, who made up for lack of name recognition by sheer industry. In 1979, he spent 328 days on the road, in forty-two states. Ten men, according to the Talmud, are sufficient to hold a service; ten Republicans, according to Bush, were enough to justify a speech. "The next night," the Washington *Post* reported on one of the lesser ones, "in Clanton, Alabama, speaking at a $6-a-plate county Republican fundraiser, [Bush] was given a series of tokens by the Possum Growers and Breeders of America, Inc. . . . Then to the surprise of all, the mayor of Clanton thrust at George Bush a baby possum, which Bush dangled by the tail."

Slowly, Bush's labors bore fruit. Late in 1979, Howard Baker flew up to Maine with the national press corps to record a Baker triumph in a local straw poll. Bush won instead. Two weeks later, he did unexpectedly well in another straw poll in Florida. Connally was squandering money and staff, Baker was trying to build a house from the roof down, Reagan was as visible as the Man in the Iron Mask—and suddenly, the week of Iowa, there was George Possum, jogging across the cover of *Newsweek*.

Bush's vigor was not just the affectation of an aging yuppie. He had been a Navy combat pilot in World War II, enlisting on the morning of his eighteenth birthday. In 1944, he was shot down over the Bonin Islands, and afterward awarded a Distinguished Flying Cross. That was the most gallant page of his résumé, but all the others were glittering. George Herbert Walker Bush, born June 12, 1924, in Milton, Massachusetts, was moved, a year later, to Greenwich, Connecticut. George went to Greenwich Country Day School and Phillips Andover. At age seventeen, he met Barbara Pierce, age sixteen, at a Christmas party, and married her when he got out of the service. Bush completed his education at Yale, where he made Phi Beta Kappa and Skull and Bones and played first base on a championship team. Out of Yale, Bush went to Texas, where he started an offshore-oil-drilling company in 1954, and made his first million.

Bush's father, Prescott, had served as Republican senator from Connecticut from 1952 to 1962, and in 1964, George decided to run for a Senate seat of his own. He assailed Texas liberal Democrat Ralph Yarborough's "left-wing radicalism" and ran 200,000 votes ahead of Goldwater—stronger than any local Republican in the history of Texas. He lost by 300,000 votes nonetheless. Two years later, he had better luck: running against a right-wing Democrat in a new district carved out of a wealthy Houston suburb, Bush won a seat in the House.

He spent four moderately conservative years on the Hill, opposing dovish policies on Vietnam and big spending at home, and supporting open housing, pollution control, and the establishment of a congressional committee on family planning. In 1970, he had another try at the Senate. Yarborough lost the primary to conservative Democrat Lloyd Bentsen, to whom Bush lost by fewer than 160,000 votes.

Bush left the pursuit of elective offices for a series of appointive ones. He served as UN ambassador, then as chairman of the Republican National Committee, in which posts he tried to keep Taiwan in the General Assembly and to shore up the Watergate-weakened GOP. "People come up to my mother," Bush observed of the second job, "and say, 'Isn't it too bad about George,' like I had died." Taiwan's defender went on to spend sixteen months as Special Envoy in Peking; Ford summoned him home in January 1976 to be Director of the CIA. This, by all accounts, was the job he enjoyed most. He helped Ford draft an executive order which placated the Agency's congressional critics; he resisted White House pressure to soft-pedal evidence that the Soviets had violated SALT I; and he approved the formation of the B team—a panel of outside experts picked to check the Agency's estimates of Soviet power—though he did not endorse their (critical) conclusions.

This various record helped him in his long years of obscure busyness: Bush knew everybody in the party; he was, in one way or another, *like* everybody in the party. But as soon as the light of attention was turned on him, it became a drawback: what was Bush like? Politically, he was the most conservative candidate in the field, apart from Reagan and Crane; several veterans of Reagan's 1976 effort were on his 1980 payroll. Yet Bush ran "left," because that's where the running room was. Slightly left, and more as a matter of atmospherics than anything else—Bush, one heard over and over again, was "reasonable," "responsible," "moderate," and so forth and so on. This, in addition to his dark-horse hard work, gave him a good national press even before Iowa ("George Bush," wrote *National Review*'s Washington correspondent in December 1979, "is the media Playmate of the Month"). But when a genuine liberal, John Anderson, came along, Bush became just another old pinup. The conservative movement, which was the party's largest faction in any case, had meanwhile singled him out for hostile examination.

One of the more bizarre forms this hostility took was a campaign against the Trilateral Commission. Bush had belonged for seventeen months to the commission, an internationalist talk shop for academics, businessmen, and government types, the brainchild of Zbigniew Brzezinski and

David Rockefeller. It had come to general notice when it turned out that Jimmy Carter, along with Walter Mondale and a dozen other members of his administration, had all been members. The Manchester *Union-Leader* soon included Bush's membership in it in the catalogue of Bush's sins, while the purer in spirit printed sinister charts showing David Rockefeller at the center of a web of dupes, one of them George Bush. It was a typical failure of concrete thinking. Clubs do not admit people to boost their careers or form their opinions; they admit those whose careers are already well advanced and with whose opinions they are already comfortable. A deeper, and valid, question remained: what, in Bush's career, showed imagination and toughness of mind?

Reagan, finally roused by his Iowa loss, had fired Sears, the failed strategist, and hired new ones. It wasn't important; the difference was in Reagan. He rolled over Bush in New Hampshire and the South and, in a Chicago debate before the Illinois primary, over the age issue as well. Wage and price controls, he said, had failed even when Diocletian used the death penalty to enforce them. "And I'm one of the few persons old enough to remember that" (sure looks good for seventy, doesn't he?). Reagan won Illinois, and the ball game.

The next four months gave Bush the chance to display some toughness. Alone now in the field, running out of money, the media's attention focused firmly on Anderson's stroll to a third party, he kept fighting long after he must have known it was hopeless (he managed to win three late primaries, largely because all Republicans except his die-hard supporters had lost interest). His greatest annoyances during the endgame came from Gerald Ford. At the time of the southern primaries, the former President began making presidential noises. It was a pure distraction. Ford was not willing to spend sufficient time away from the golf course to make a serious effort. The Trilateral Commission and the Anderson surge were already on Bush's mind. He gritted his teeth. "Let's wait and see what the voters will do," he

said in St. Petersburg. "Come on in. The water's fine."
When the Republicans gathered in Detroit, Ford came up
again, in an even more improbable context. The notion was
put about that Ford would be Reagan's ideal choice as running mate. Reagan, who had come to like his old opponent,
was willing to give it a hearing. A ragtag of cronies and Ford
administration leftovers worked vigorously on the scheme.
Conservatives who disliked Bush viewed it, fantastically, as
an acceptable alternative. Ford himself, in an interview
with Walter Cronkite, allowed as how he might like to be a
kind of co-President. Reagan was not pleased. Once again,
at the last minute, he saved himself, not this time from
losing, but from looking like a fool. He did what the logic of
the situation had called for, and placed a call to George
Bush.

Come November, the twenty renegade "Wallace" votes
came back to the GOP, as did nearly everything else. The
favorite explanation of those who were unwilling to accord
Reagan's victory any significance—Walter Mondale, say—
was that it was due to the force of his personality. There was
an obvious weakness with this explanation. Ronald Reagan
was no more personable in 1980 than he had been in 1976
or 1968—or 1964. He had not won then; why now?

Reagan had come, in mid-life, to a position which was
new, inchoate, and despised. He supported its standard-
bearer when it took a major party to one of the worst
defeats in American history. Two years later, still wedded to
the position, he himself became governor of the nation's
most populous state. Another two years after that, he made
a run for his party's nomination which barely got off the
ground. His second run narrowly failed to unseat a sitting
President. On his third try, at the age of sixty-nine, he beat a
field of six challengers, almost all of whom had been
touched in some degree by the positions of the movement
he spoke for, and gave the incumbent a worse defeat than
Goldwater's. Since Ronald Reagan hadn't changed for
thirty years, there was at least a prima facie case that the
country had.

7
Funny Hats: Dallas

The Republicans who gathered in Dallas to renominate Ronald Reagan were greeted, like the Democratic delegates in San Francisco a month earlier, with unusually warm weather; only, "unusually warm" for eastern Texas in August meant 106 degrees, which was what the thermometers hit the Sunday before the convention opened. By Monday, what the Weather Service was pleased to call a "very weak cold front" had moved in, cooling things off to 101.

Neither temperature mattered to the delegates for longer than it took to dash from one pleasure-dome lobby to the cab or bus waiting to deposit them at the next. But they wiped out the protesters. Dallas was uncongenial territory to begin with. Protesters didn't have to come to San Francisco; they grow there, as in a petri dish. The hardy sorts who made the trip nonetheless were offered tent sites by the Trinity River, a low, airless stretch of bottomland that made the pavements chill by comparison. The city put in outhouses and sprayed for chiggers; the police, unlike the San Francisco force, were super-polite (moral: "liberal" cops, when put on the spot, have to knock heads; "right-wing" cops can afford to eat a little quiche). It was not enough. The left melted down and went away. The protesters who showed up at the Convention Center were a miscellaneous lot: Sikhs; pro-Shah Iranians; followers of a Taiwanese messiah; and a Christian whose study of the relevant texts had persuaded him that Reagan was the Beast of the Apocalypse: ADULTERY IS SIN, RON. HIS WOUND WAS HEALED. REAGAN & 666 & ANTICHRIST ARE ONE. The usual.

The delegates had the chance to take a variety of tours to points of interest; five times as many, according to the New York *Times*, went to Southfork, J. R. Ewing's ranch, as went to Dealy Plaza and the Texas Book Depository. So all traumas fade. Kennedy's death had been traumatic because he was young and energetic; because those to whom it falls to express public grief, the higher press and the lower intellectuals, were precisely those who had been most entranced by his administration, and by their role in it; because there had not been a presidential murder in sixty-two years (whereas any sixty-two-year-old alive in 1901, the year of William McKinley's death, remembered two other assassinations—Garfield's, Lincoln's). Other shocks had occurred since then. The diminished interest in Kennedy's death was accompanied, among many Republicans, by a renewed interest in some of the things he had done during his life.

The important pre-convention exercise in Dallas was not a parade but the pasting-up of the party platform. The convention itself was going to be a little like a parade; the renomination of Reagan and Bush was as certain as crocuses, and as choreographed as the Rockettes. But politicians are infinitely inventive, and those with ideas to push took them before the platform committee hearings.

The most successful pushers, not surprisingly, were the right, particularly the supply-siders. Jude Wanniski was staying at the Hotel Anatole. He had first made his name, and his point, with *The Way the World Works*, a best-seller in 1978. It was a history of the world seen through the prism of tax rates. Like most single-prism views, it had blind spots: everything between Commodus and Napoleon was dismissed as a sump of burdensome taxation (sorry, Sir Isaac; sorry, Wolfgang). But as it closed in on the twentieth century and America, it made a persuasive case for the supply-side approach. Wanniski had been a reporter once, for *The Wall Street Journal,* but since *The Way the World Works* he only saw reporters on the far side of pencils and pads. In one of the Hotel Anatole's atriums, the Republicans had been busy preparing for Reagan's arrival later in the week, and the balconies were hung with greetings painted on sheets, like parents' day at summer camp. Wanniski held forth over breakfast in the Mirage Kiosk.

The supply-siders had been revising reputations a lot less remote than Commodus's. Kennedy's, for instance. It had gone badly for Kennedy in recent years. The unsentimental left had turned on him, because he had gotten America into Vietnam. Moralists jeered, and immoralists leered, at his private life. About his last defenders were the supply-siders, who approved of the tax-rate cuts inaugurated by him in 1962, which lowered top rates from 91 to 70 percent and bottom rates from 20 to 14 percent, and which they held up as forerunners of Kemp-Roth. The Kennedy administration did not, of course, conceive itself to be acting on supply-side principles, but the supply-siders were generous. "The amazing thing about this one variation of the Keynesian model," wrote Wanniski, "is that it works! And it works not for the reasons given by Keynes" but because it "happens to coincide with . . . the Laffer Curve."

Wanniski spoke distractedly, looking elsewhere, fiddling with the butter knives. His talk was full of conversions, infiltrations, maneuverings—as appropriate to the spread of a secret brotherhood as of an idea. He looked pale and drained, and obviously wanted nothing more than to go back and do it all over again.

The first item the new economic right had fought for at the platform hearings was a flat tax. (Older free-market economists, going right back to Hayek, had been soldiering on this issue for decades.) The flattish tax sponsored by a pair of Democrats, Bill Bradley and Richard Gephardt, had thrown the supply-siders into a quandary. Wanniski recounted a powwow at Jack Kemp's home in August 1983 to debate the question: what should they do? Irving Kristol suggested that they co-opt the existing bill; Lew Lehrman, the man who nearly beat Mario Cuomo, argued that, to keep Kemp's name synonymous with tax reform, it had to be attached to a new proposal. There were, besides, problems with Bradley-Gephardt: for one thing, it abolished tax indexing. The chiefs agreed with Lehrman, and so the Kemp-Kasten bill was born. (Technically, the Kasten-Kemp bill, since senators' names by custom go first on all co-sponsored legislation. Not on bills co-sponsored by Kemp.)

The second issue had been what Wanniski called a four-letter word: gold. The United States had gone off the gold standard in 1933, but had not severed all connections between its currency and the metal until 1970. The supply-siders blamed the ensuing worldwide inflation on gold's abandonment and wanted a gold standard reinstated. Here most economists, almost all politicians, and all pundits, reporters, and TV anchormen parted company. No issue, except perhaps creationism, had a greater appearance of being the nostrum of cranks and madmen. Most of the scoffing was ignorant: it was frequently said, for instance, that a gold standard would put the United States at the mercy of the world's leading producers, South Africa and the Soviet Union; in fact, their percentage of the world gold supply was negligible. The supply-siders had embraced it with fervor. In 1982, Jack Kemp gave a Cross of Paper speech to the Federal Reserve Bank of Atlanta. "Whether we like it or not, money and credit have a moral dimension. People trade with each other because they believe they will not be defrauded by a change in the currency. . . . If you are wealthy, you can protect yourself against the risk of bad money" by going into real estate, futures, or tax dodges. "But the less savings you have, the more certain they are to be tied up in currency. . . . Honest money is a populist, bread-and-butter concern." Wanniski recalled another Kemp summit, this one designed to woo Kasten to the gold standard. All Kasten wanted to talk about was the deficit, until Congressman Newt Gingrich, another young Turk, got up and testified. "I want to say, Jack, I always thought you were fooling, but now I'm convinced." It sounded just like Alcoholics Anonymous. *That* was the way the world worked.

Newt Gingrich had also taken a role in the platform fighting. Next to him, Wanniski looked hidebound and stodgy. Gingrich had been the wrap-up speaker at the Moral Majority's Family Forum in San Francisco. For Dallas, he was camped in the Grenada Royale, a Moorish creation with a distant kinship to the Fox Theater. Gingrich was, along with Gary Hart, an adherent of the military reform school. He had recently gained notoriety by using the tag ends of congressional sessions to give speeches which, though they were delivered to empty chambers, went out over C-SPAN. One address, reading into the record a chummy letter from ten Democratic congressmen to the Nicaraguan junta, provoked the wrath of Tip O'Neill (the excessive wrath—the House rebuked O'Neill for his outburst). Gingrich's first career had been as a college professor; he had now written a book, *The Window of Opportunity*, which he could talk through at a moment's notice. He represented an Atlanta suburb—the Atlanta airport, he liked to say—and he had one of those New South accents, really Sun Belt, that would fit in anywhere from Cape Kennedy to Silicon Valley.

"What is our positive alternative?" he had asked the Moral Majoritarians in San Francisco. "In the Hegelian sense, what is our antithesis?" "Our goal in life," he answered himself in Dallas, was "to make Bangladesh resemble Dallas." In Gingrich's view, history consisted of a series of S-shaped curves, each describing a dramatic spurt in the quality of life: the agricultural revolution, the industrial revolution, and the (present-day) information revolution. Traditional economists were "gerontologists of the mature state," still reposing on the top of the second S. "What we need are pediatricians."

Pressed for specifics, he cited the fact that in 1984 one dollar bought four million times more computer power than it had in 1962; also, that a farmer in south Georgia who

had been superovulating cows, and transplanting the em-
bryo calves into Holstein mothers, had managed to raise
twenty-five a year. "There is not an economic model in the
world that would show you that kind of meat production."

The means of unlocking this bounty were free enterprise
and (perhaps surprisingly—futurists tend not to be believers in the Decalogue) traditional values. "Learning is hard.
There is no substitute for work. The longer we tell poor
people there's an easy way, the more we trap them." A
country pulsing with opportunity—Gingrich, Kemp, and
other like-minded House members had formed a caucus
named the Conservative Opportunity Society—would have
no serious foreign-policy problems. "Foreign policy should
be at least half economics," Wanniski had said. Gingrich
agreed. A humming America would simply leave the Soviets in the star dust. We "have the potential to knit together,
from Seoul and Tokyo to Berlin, 90 percent of the scientists
in the world—an incredible base of economic growth and
productivity. . . . The voters of Bavaria and Kyoto matter
as much as those of Atlanta. . . . As long as we contain the
Soviet Union militarily, it's of little importance to us how
long it remains a bizarre and deviant culture." The "long-
term goal" of foreign policy should be to "turn the Soviets
into the equivalent of the Ottoman Empire."

The military planks of the platform, like the policy of the
Reagan administration, were securely in the hands of the
Pentagon, which was uninterested in S curves. On economics, though, the supply-siders and Conservative Opportun-
ists enjoyed a total victory. The platform called for "a fair
and simple tax system," to which a "modified flat tax" might
be "a most promising approach." Over bitter opposition—
the White House, Wanniski claimed, had been "horrified"—
the platform also urged "an end to the uncertainties" of
money and credit. "The gold standard may be a useful
mechanism . . . to sustain price stability."

The bitterness of the opposition was an unlooked-for result of the intraparty struggles of the sixties and seventies.
The conservative forerunners of the young right had deter-

mined to break the power of the party's liberal wing, and they had. They had not reckoned, however, on a third thing —not, strictly speaking, a force; more a disposition. The third Republican faction called themselves, when forced by pushy rebels to adopt a name, "moderates." They might best have been called, simply, Republicans.

"Republican" had been taken up as a fighting word by Congressman Jim Leach, who represented a mixed corner —some farms, some factories, some sleek suburbs—of southeastern Iowa. Two months before the convention, Leach had announced the formation of a group called the Republican Mainstream Committee. Though the committee, by the look of its letterhead, could have caucused in a largish phone booth, they claimed to represent the entire stream of Republican history; Lincoln, Roosevelt (the good one), Willkie, Eisenhower, Robert Taft, and Goldwater. Their presumed constituency today, as outlined by Leach— the North and the "comfortable middle class," as opposed to the South and the "somewhat less comfortable" middle— was in fact a fair description of the party's historical core, as well as the antithesis of the groups pursued by Clifton White (Leach also mentioned "internationalists" and members of mainline churches). "We Republicans," Leach wrote in his manifesto, should "emphasiz[e] older approaches to new problems. We cripple ourselves by experimenting with social theories which jeopardize our philosophical underpinnings."

On closer inspection, a number of Leach's underpinnings looked as if they had been borrowed from the Democratic wardrobe. There was an old tradition in the Republican party of liberals stealing rhetorical bases as "moderates"; Nelson Rockefeller was a "moderate" when he chose; so was Jacob Javits. A fair amount of the same thing was going on in the Republican Mainstream. Its self-chosen enemy was the New Right; its manifesto called on Republicans to put their shoulders to arms control and the UN; it called school prayer "the ultimate in state welfarism"; and, in words that might have been uttered by Gary Hart, called for a Latin American policy of "transferring food," not "selling bullets."

Leach's major point of contact with party orthodoxy was budgets. "I'm not a big spender," he liked to say, in contrast to Rockefeller; "the sum total of my votes [would have been] a smaller federal budget than Ronald Reagan's." But the Republican point man on that issue, for the last two years, had been Bob Dole.

The Reagan landslide of 1980 was not merely personal; it also netted a gain of twelve Republican senators, enough for a majority—the first Republican Senate majority in twenty-six years. Dole became chairman of the Finance Committee; the tax increase of 1982 (officially known as the Tax Equity and Fiscal Responsibility Act) was largely his doing.

Never was a politician's reputation as transformed as Dole's was by TEFRA. Dole had preceded George Bush as Republican national chairman ("Thank goodness," he said of the Watergate tapes, "whenever I was in the Oval Office I only nodded") and ran as Gerald Ford's vice-presidential candidate in 1976. In both roles, he was a mordant partisan, and fastidious people did not like it, not at all. The old Dole was "dark-visaged, sardonic," a "fiery jack-in-the-box" (New York *Times*). His debating style showed "smiling amorality" and "cruel skill" (Garry Wills). A White House spokesman—from his own party yet—compared him to a "hungry Doberman pinscher," while another Republican said he "couldn't sell beer on a troopship." Suddenly, post-TEFRA, all that changed. Dole was "sound[ing] an independent voice" (New York *Times*). His colleagues were inclined to "take him more seriously" *(Time)*. He was "our kind of guy" *(The Village Voice)*, someone who had "grown" (George McGovern), "grown more than anybody in this town" (Robert Strauss). TEFRA, the agent of this change, was a hodgepodge of provisions. The direct political effect of the law was slight: a rise in the tobacco excise cost the Republicans half a dozen House seats in Virginia and the Carolinas in the 1982 off-year election. But the broad impact of an attempt, supported by a Republican Senate, to raise $98.4

billion in taxes over three years was enormous. It was nothing less than a repudiation (the White House called it a "mid-course correction") of supply-side economics. That was why liberals and Democrats lionized the repudiator. But Dole's reasons for acting more different; he had never bought supply-side economics in the first place.

Dole's last place had almost been the Po Valley. In April 1945, Second Lieutenant Dole was leading a platoon of the 10th Mountain Division near the town of Castel d'Ianno when a German shell caught him in the spine and the right arm and shoulder. It took Lieutenant Dole thirty-nine months to recover the use of his legs; his arm never recovered.

He took his dark visage into politics in 1950, in the Kansas House. One unbroken thread of the next three decades was farm-belt politics. Price supports, beef import limits, Meals on Wheels, gasohol, food stamps, Soviet grain sales—he backed them all. (The Ford-Dole ticket, James Reston remarked, would play all the way from Grand Rapids to Topeka.) But apart from the pocketbooks of his constituents, he was firmly on the Republican right. He backed the ABM system, tax indexing, and "the ultimate in state welfarism"; opposed the Panama Canal treaties, busing, abortion (right-to-lifers saved Dole's neck in the Watergate election, when he was running a tight race against an obstetrician who had performed abortions, and Dole never forgot it). He also consistently believed that a penny spent had to be a penny taxed. During the seventies, he came up with an almost-balanced amendment, which would have required a balance five years out of every nine. When the great deficit trauma took hold in Reagan's term, Dole was ready. Spending cuts, the new Dole told me at the time, have "got to be the highest priority"; to cut taxes without cutting spending was the "highest folly." He gave the administration some credit ("The Reagan people," he told *The Village Voice*, "came along and tightened things up") but spoke of supply-side economics as a historical whimsy, already quaint, like world government or Free Silver. "It might have worked.

We'll never know." And if his old positions made him new friends, what veteran pol would complain?

It was ultimately a sad and rather lonely thing, Republicanism. To its credit, it could be said that, for all those years when Irish Catholics were electing James Michael Curley and Southerners were electing Theodore Bilbo, and both were voting for Franklin Roosevelt, the Republicans fought the losing fight of those who suspected that full-throttle, New Deal liberalism really wasn't the way to run the country. It was to their discredit that they fought so ineptly, and that they finally forgot what they were fighting about. The same again, please—a little more prudently, a little more honestly: that finally became the Republican message. The trouble with it was that they didn't expect anyone to believe it, and they hardly believed it themselves. In their hearts, they knew they were wrong.

Among the keenest diagnosticians of the Republican syndrome were the powers behind Leach's bugaboo, the New Right; and the keenest of these was Paul Weyrich. Weyrich had MC'd and co-sponsored the Family Forum in San Francisco to which Gingrich spoke about Hegel, as well as a second, similar meeting at the Dallas Hilton the week before the Republican convention.

Weyrich, of all the New Right, had the most practical political intelligence. At one time or another, nearly every one of his peers had entered into some bizarre and quixotic disaster. Howard Phillips, founder of the Conservative Caucus, had decided to enter the 1978 Massachusetts Democratic Senate primary. There is a respectable argument that hidden pockets of conservatism lie just beneath the surface of Massachusetts politics, waiting to be tapped. Phillips didn't find them; he finished fifth, behind a lesbian. Richard Viguerie, the New Right's premier technician of direct mail, leapt aboard the Connally campaign in 1980, just one month before it collapsed. Four years earlier, he and William Rusher had had a fling with a third party. The success of the scheme depended on convincing Reagan that the GOP was hopeless; Reagan was not convinced, and the

fledgling organization was hijacked by Lester Maddox.
Weyrich had a steadier hand. His specialty, in the purely
political arena, was Congress; half a dozen of the Republican senators elected in 1980 had been, in large part,
groomed and assisted by his Free Congress Foundation.

Mao Tse-tung, said Weyrich (shades of Mondale!), believed in making college professors become peasants after a
few years. "While I have no sympathy with Mao," he rather
liked that. The problem was Washington. "Legislators were
intended to live among the people for whom they'd passed
the laws." But being a congressman was now a "full-time
job." The result was a view of the world, common to Republicans and Democrats alike, which in turn defined the problems and provided the range of acceptable solutions.
"There is a difference," thought Weyrich, "between governing and holding office." The struggle in the party "isn't
so much ideological" as a contest between those who
wanted to "create a vision of government" on their own
and those willing to "accept the current status quo and live
within it."

Dole and Leach agreed. When Republicans were a minority, said Dole, it was easier to "sit back and carp." But
Senate Republicans had shown "we could behave like a
majority." "The real divisions in the Republican party today," wrote Leach, "are not between liberals, moderates,
and conservatives; they are between pragmatists and ideologues. The ideologues discuss issues abstractly; the pragmatists worry about making government work." Just so. But
work for whom?

Weyrich had warned Reagan it would be tough; he remembered telling him back in 1975 that if he wanted to
achieve what he had been preaching, he would have to
confront the Washington establishment. "That's not my
style," Reagan had answered. "I've always worn a white
hat."

All the factions and and proto-factions sheltering under
that big white hat were not perfectly happy. The Republicans resented their party's newfangled agenda; while from

supply-siders and the New Right alike, one often heard
Reagan tolerantly described as a "transitional President"—
a political pithecanthropus, primitive himself, but useful as
a link to the higher life forms of the future (say, President
Gingrich). In Dallas, and for at least the next three months,
the factions were still. No politician abandons a winner. But
no politician looks no further than the next election: 1988
was only fifty-one months away.

The Dallas Convention Center, as characterless as the
Moscone Center, was at least aboveground. One flank shel-
tered, incongruously, a small, tumbled graveyard. Some
nights, stranger still, the graves and the parking lots were
littered with grasshoppers, live and mashed (a foreshad-
owing, at least to the Antichrist man, of the seventh plague).
A few plagues on most of the speechmakers would have
been welcome. Some struggled against high expectations.
Congressman Guy Vander Jagt, of Michigan, who gave the
keynote at the 1980 convention in Detroit, had suffered on
that occasion from a week-long buildup as a great orator.
What impressed the networks so was the fact that Vander
Jagt spoke from memory. There were sidebars showing him
rehearsing in the woods, gosh-shucks interviews in which
he deprecated his talent. The speech, alas, might better
have stayed in the woods. This time around, he said (on
Monday night) that "Ronald Reagan has brought forth on
this continent a new conception, dedicated to the proposition that government should do a little less, so people can do
a little more." Lincoln wouldn't have worried; neither
would Edward Everett.
The 1984 keynoter was to face the highest expectations—
comparison to Mario Cuomo. The task fell to Katherine
Ortega, thirty-six-year-old Treasurer of the United States
(her signature is in your wallet). Under the circumstances,
she did as well as it was possible to do. "I believe in President Reagan and in what he stands for," she opened, ". . .
not because I am a woman, not because I am of Hispanic
heritage, but above all because I am an American." This was

good; this cut through the lard of ethnic and sexual politics like a whip. The only difficulty with it was a suspicion that it might not be entirely true. The clever Republicans *(we know we're wrong)* who managed the convention did not seem to quite believe their keynoter's principles. They had assembled a speakers' list that looked like a GOP Rainbow Coalition, a cry for approval of the party's pluralism. The good thing about such exercises is that they show a kind of democratic courtesy: Whitman for everyday use ("Kanuck, Tuckahoe, Congressman, Cuff"). The problem, as with all affirmative actions, is that they leave you not knowing who was genuinely wanted. For the rest, Ortega managed six times to put Mondale and Carter in the same sentence.

Ortega ended the evening, but the emotional keynoter of the convention had gone first. There had been some talk of UN ambassador Jeane Kirkpatrick giving the keynote herself. The clever Republicans successfully opposed the choice. They had personal considerations—she had been at loggerheads with temporizers of all varieties, Republican and State Department, throughout her tenure with the Reagan administration. But the stylistic calculus also came into play. A woman was needed for the keynote. Biologically, of course, Kirkpatrick was one. But she was also, in all matters relevant to her job, a conservative. Since feminism is a liberal issue, Kirkpatrick did not qualify as a woman ideologically. (Neither, for the same reasons, does Margaret Thatcher.) Kirkpatrick was also a registered Democrat, and hence stood outside the tradition of Wendell Willkie.

The delegates didn't care; they loved her. The hall filled with signs, which looked hand-lettered; in fact, they had been run off and passed out by Lew Lehrman, but (success being attention to detail) were made to look homemade. The delegates waved them with real enthusiasm. Kirkpatrick wore glasses to read her text, and a green dress and jacket with high, peaked shoulders and knobbly little tufts of material, which had the look of being cut to an old pattern, perhaps as old as when Mondale was an anti-Communist.

Kirkpatrick had grown up in the same cold war Democratic milieu as Mondale had. Born in Oklahoma, she had gone from Barnard to the State Department. She married an academic, Evron Kirkpatrick, and became one herself, joining the faculty of Georgetown in 1968. Her husband was a longtime adviser to Hubert Humphrey; she helped found the Coalition for a Democratic Majority, an incubator of Humphrey and Henry Jackson campaigns during the early seventies. Her introduction to Republican politics came through neoconservatism. In November 1979, *Commentary* published "Dictatorships and Double Standards." The double standards she anatomized were those of the Carter State Department, which saw the world as a perpetual becoming, an irresistible progress toward "rational humanism." In accordance with this vision, reactionary despots, like the Shah and Somoza, destined for history's ash heap, could only be let go; America was obliged to deal instead with the future, which was Khomeini and the Sandinistas. Kirkpatrick took the distinction and stood it on its head: "authoritarian" regimes of the right were more acceptable as American allies, because less oppressive in themselves and more inclined to evolve along democratic paths. In the "totalitarian" states of the left, tyranny was forever. Reagan, impressed, asked her aboard the campaign and, in due course, his administration.

Kirkpatrick's speech was received as warmly as her appearance at the podium. It was a triumph of substance over style. She stepped on all her applause lines, reading in a dry, arrhythmic lecturer's tone that seemed to say, "As I wrote in my last monograph on the subject . . ."

After an opening flourish, comparing the Democrats of today—"San Francisco Democrats"—with the kind she had admired and worked with—"they were not afraid to be resolute, nor ashamed to speak of America as a great nation"—she presented the three-part core of her speech: a thumbnail argument for the necessity of an assertive American foreign policy; a catalogue of recent Democratic shortfalls; and a rundown of Reagan's successes.

"The United States cannot remain an open, democratic society if we are . . . a garrison state in a hostile world. We need independent nations with which to trade, to consult and cooperate. We need friends and allies with whom to share the pleasures and protection of our civilization. We cannot therefore be indifferent to the subversion of others' independence, or to the development of . . . new vulnerabilities by our friends.

"The last Democratic administration did not seem to notice much, care much, or do much about these matters." There followed a list of unmet challenges: the SS-20s aimed at Western Europe; bases aimed at us in Cuba; fifteen countries—"Laos, Cambodia, Afghanistan, Angola, Ethiopia, Mozambique, Northern Yemen, Libya, Syria, Aden, Congo, Madagascar, Seychelles, Nicaragua, and Grenada"—into which Soviet influence expanded. Carter had "looked for an explanation for all these problems and thought he found it in the American people." But "it wasn't malaise we suffered from, it was Jimmy Carter" (applause) "and Walter Mondale" *(yay!)*.

Ronald Reagan was a "very different kind of President" (assent). The source of the difference was confidence—in "the American experience," "the legitimacy of American institutions," "the decency of the American people," and "the relevance of our experience to the rest of the world." The results of Reagan's confidence formed another list: a healthy economy, a refurbished military, Pershing missiles in Europe, Communists out of Grenada.

"And at each step of the way, the same people who were responsible for America's decline have insisted that the President's policies would fail." So for her peroration, she circled back for another round at her opening targets, the San Francisco Democrats, and along the way put the phrase "America First" to a new use. "They said that saving Grenada from totalitarianism and terror was the wrong thing to do. They didn't blame Cuba or the Communists for threatening American students and murdering Grenadans. They blamed the United States instead. But then, somehow, they always blame America first.

"When our marines, sent to Lebanon . . . were murdered in their sleep, the blame-America-first crowd did not blame the terrorists who murdered them, they blamed the United States. But then, they always blame America first.

"When the Soviet Union walked out of the arms-control negotiations . . ." By now, the audience was ready. "When Marxist dictators shoot their way to power in Central America, the San Francisco Democrats . . . blamed United States policies of one hundred years ago." *But then, they always blame America first.* The band played the title song of *Oklahoma!*

Kirkpatrick was the star of a New Right reception at the Sheraton Center after adjournment. Richard Viguerie, the host, made a reference to a "woman President of the United States." The crowd cheered; they were ready to nominate her then and there. Host and guest were conscious of the ironies. "Who would think," Viguerie said, "we'd be here tonight in Dallas to honor a former adviser to Hubert Humphrey?" "Stranger things may have happened," Kirkpatrick agreed, "but they escape me." Maybe not so strange. The trait she had singled out in Reagan's personality, confidence, was also the distinguishing feature of Hubert Humphrey. Indeed, in Humphrey it was so effervescent that it often seemed unballasted by anything else. Problems? Problems! We'll fix 'em! Fix 'em right up! Anything at all! But among the infinity of things Humphrey had confidence in was that America was good, and good for the world. It was this, as much as any subservience to Lyndon Johnson, which made the left wing of his party loathe him. Dr. Kirkpatrick left her audience with a reading assignment: an article in the latest issue of *Commentary.*

The second emotional favorite of the convention spoke on Tuesday, though for Jack Kemp enthusiasm was tempered by partisanship. He was one of the top two candidates on everybody's list for 1988, and the supporters of other would-be heirs were restrained in their applause. Kemp's advance people had been busy, and the crowd was sown with his placards.

He shared the podium with two prominent Republicans, three if one stretched the designation to cover Secretary of Transportation Elizabeth Dole. That was probably stretching it too far. Mrs. Dole's Republicanism was a matter of matrimonial accident. She had acquired the GOP as one of her in-laws. Robert Dole's first marriage, to his physical therapist, had broken up after a quarter of a century; three years afterward, he married a liberal Democrat. Elizabeth Dole switched parties, but not opinions; her rise was a function of his growth. She was introduced by her husband, who was greeted by a few androgynous DOLE 1988 signs. His remarks were brief, almost curt, as if some smiling amorality were occurring to him, but he was restraining himself.

Kemp was followed by Gerald Ford. It is in irony of image-making that one of the most athletic men ever to occupy the Oval Office came to be seen as a head-banging spaz. Ford's speaking style surely had something to do with it. In Dallas, he managed to call the President of the United States "Robnald Reagan," and he dropped full stops in the middle of his sentences like a lone, out-of-town traveler struggling with four suitcases in the main hall of Grand Central Station. "Vice-President Mondale wants this election to be a 'referendum on the future.' I can't blame him. For wanting to forget the past, the four years of Carter-Mondale from 1977 through 1980. Who wants to remember? Four years of roaring inflation, skyrocketing interest rates, and so-called 'malaise.' " But the delegates seemed genuinely to like and admire him—with some reason. Thrust into a position he would never, in the normal course of things, have sought or reached, he had done an earnest job. His worst judgment was to try to perpetuate the anomaly by seeking re-election; his best, curiously, was probably the act that most damaged his chances, the pardon of Nixon —not that Nixon deserved it, but the country deserved to be spared two and a half years of partisan carnival. His text flayed Mondale's record as a Vice-President and senator, and included this Republican credo: "The fairness issue belongs to leadership which promises the American people no more than it can deliver, and then delivers what it promised."

Jack Kemp's national career had been an attempt to create a leadership which promised the American people what they could deliver for themselves, and then encouraged them to deliver it. Such slight mental shifts, he hoped, would set the tectonic plates of politics grinding.

Kemp had reversed the national pattern, born in Los Angeles and ending in upstate New York. As a boy his passion was sports: he did a high school assignment on great inventions by writing about the forward pass. He played football in college (Occidental) and went to the pros in 1957. The new American Football League gave him his chance at first-string play; Kemp continues to wear the ring that is a token of his playing in the 1965 AFL championship game. The AFL also gave him his first taste of politicking. Like Reagan, Kemp served as president of his union, in which office he helped negotiate a pension plan.

For seven years, Kemp quarterbacked the Buffalo Bills. The cities of upstate New York are inward-looking and self-absorbed, and at the same time sensitive to slights—none more so than Buffalo, which is the most slighted (an infamous *Sports Illustrated* article, which depicted Buffalo as a kind of forties time capsule, where all the men wore double-breasted suits—this was before SoHo boutiques began snapping them up—is still resentfully remembered). Buffalo's drabness was due to economic stagnation; Kemp's thoughts turned to the problem when he was approached by local Republicans to run for Congress.

He won his first race in 1970, narrowly. His only hands-on experience of government had been an off-season interning on the staff of freshman Governor Reagan; his heavy reading had consisted of the Durants' *History of Civilization*. In the mid-seventies, he began to make up for lost time. He encountered "supply-side economics" in an article by Jude

Wanniski in *The Wall Street Journal* and got to know both
Wanniski and Irving Kristol. (The first time they met, Kristol suggested that the congressman read some pieces in *The
Public Interest;* by their next meeting, Kemp had read every one and had questions.)

Withal, he kept an uncomplicated, down-home manner.
The following story is attested by a liberal of good repute.
Kemp was a guest at a Republican bash in the Washington
suburbs early in the Reagan administration. He was by no
means the biggest shot in attendance: senators pulled up in
their limousines; so did Richard Nixon. Kemp came in his
car, debarked, but, alone of the guests, instead of going
directly inside, walked across the street and chatted with
the party of DC policemen on duty, as it might be about
football. "Oh, my God," thought the liberal, "another Republican with the common touch." "Jack," mused Newt
Gingrich, "showered with guys that most Republicans
never meet."

Kemp looks like a graying Dick Clark (but then, so does
Dick Clark). He speaks choppily and impetuously and
above all enthusiastically. Listening to him is like riding a
jeep full speed cross-country; he can make Reagan seem
solemn and long-faced.

His subject, in a deliberate attempt to expand his range of
issues, was foreign policy, though, as with Gingrich and
Wanniski, it came out half economics. "The ultimate containment," he had said earlier in an interview at his hotel,
"is not only to be a reliable partner, but to be a reliable
model." Kemp was camped in the Wyndham, not the largest of Dallas's hotels, but one of the more startling, with a
helix staircase of gold plates and white tube lights and a
carved, half-size Indian elephant in the lobby. Kempery
was inescapable; it floated over the very breakfast tables:
". . . economic growth . . ." one heard Republican delegates murmuring to interviewers from the hometown papers. "Democratic capitalism," Kemp insisted, was not
anachronistic, but "the wave of the future." Similarly, in his
speech to the convention, he asserted that the "leaders of

the Democratic party" were "not soft on Communism. They're just soft on democracy." America had to "share the American idea with the rest of the world" (Kemp singled out particularly "our sister democracy Israel"). This involved two steps: "liberaliz[ing] the trade of the world," through free markets and a "dollar as good as gold"; and expanding the principles of human rights that underlay the American system—rights relevant to "the Polish steelworker, the South African black, the Soviet Jew. . . . The world is full of democracies yet unfounded; [to] bring . . . this dream to all people everywhere [was to] fulfill . . . the American Revolution." He was rousingly cheered, and the Texas delegation gave the responsive chant of *"Viva—Olé!"* which had been its slogan at GOP conventions since 1964.

The main business of the Wednesday session was formally to set the diadem on Ronald Reagan's brow. But before that, it heard from the man the party had followed to defeat twenty years earlier.

On Tuesday afternoon, there had been a cocktail party at the Ambassador Park for the "Old Friends." Old Friends was a code phrase for "Hard Core," the nickname of those who had been tapped by Clifton White, William Rusher, and John Ashbrook to lead the revolution twenty-three years ago. The former hellions, fortyish then, were pushing Social Security age. Some would never reach it (Ashbrook had died in 1982, in the midst of a last campaign). Ray Donovan, still the Secretary of Labor, told the function of his own political origins and subsequent migrations: the only two pictures hanging on the walls of his home when he was growing up had been of Pius XII and FDR. But only two Old Friends came to their own party, White and Rusher, and they missed each other. The final success of a faction is when it disappears.

Goldwater was introduced Wednesday night by the man who had seconded his nomination at that other San Francisco convention two decades ago, John Tower. "The incomparable, unstoppable Barry Goldwater," Tower concluded, and while the wide screens over the podium displayed old black-and-white clips of that imperious demeanor, Goldwater came to the lectern, looking all too stoppable. He was old and sagged, and when the ghostly film stopped, he paced slowly and steadily through his text while people milled and reporters flipped through papers. "Tonight," he said, "I want to speak about freedom. And let me remind you: extremism in defense of liberty is no vice." This elicited a wistful cheer. (In 1964, the liberals had treated it like the last days of Weimar.)

Goldwater's relations with the conservatives who had followed in his path had not always been good. He had opposed his most effective speechmaker in 1968 and 1976. Most spectacularly, he had denounced the New Right, partly from personality clashes—no one in that feud was notable for deference or reticence—but mainly from differences on issues, the most important being abortion. Folks who hadn't given Goldwater an inch of ink since Johnson hammered the stake through his heart played the story big; overnight, he had become a sage, a case of late growth. But tonight, he confined himself to more familiar themes.

The main theme was defense. "What, may I ask, was more extreme than our revolutionary war? . . . As Tom Paine said in that day, tyranny, like hell, is not easily conquered" (light applause). "It has been the foreign-policy and defense weakness of Democrat administrations that have led us to war in the past. . . . Every war in this century began and was fought under Democrat administrations." Here the rhetoric of nationalism and isolationism joined hands: if we stay strong, we'll stay out of trouble. Goldwater ended with the umpteenth reference of the convention to the summer Olympics, and perhaps the only interesting one. "Let me warn [the] Democrats. . . . Remember the millions of Americans who cheered, waved flags, and felt joy in their hearts and tears in their eyes . . ." Over the next few weeks, the Democrats, stung by the GOP's Olympic flag waving, would insist that they loved Mary Lou Retton as much as anyone. No doubt about it. But cheering and flags had not been universally loved at the time of the Games. Poor Jim McKay and the other ABC announcers had been twitted for bubbling over America's medal totals. It was bad taste; it was not the way UNESCO or the Contadora group would have reported it. ABC Sports, chastened, dutifully tried to give greater prominence to athletes from other countries (they had always given them prominence: any satisfying athletic contest depends on having strong and respected opponents). But it was a clash portending a misunderstanding of the national mood. "Don't you Democrat leaders," Goldwater warned, "try to tell me that Americans don't love and honor America." Goldwater hailed Reagan—"in your hearts, you know he's right"—and got his biggest hand. "My friends, *vaya con Dios,* till we meet again."

At last the crown was ready. The states at the front end of the roll call made the necessary yieldings to bring to the podium Senator Paul Laxalt of Nevada, who had nominated Ronald Reagan twice before. The tradition of not mentioning the nominee's name until the last sentence had been dying for years; its vitality depended on the existence of speakers who could hold unbroken attention over twenty or forty minutes. Laxalt was its death. At Kansas City, he had simply begun, "I nominate Ronald Reagan." Eight years later, he managed to withhold the name till the second sentence. When he finished, the delegates were allowed to whoop.

A high school band took its place behind the Massachusetts delegation at the extreme right front corner of the hall, where its director, a youngish man in a light linen suit, kept it in order with vigorous strokes. Not easily, for his charges were drowned out by half a hundred young kids, marshaled in to give insane Texas yells, who were in turn overwhelmed by the main orchestra, located, as at San Francisco, at the back of the hall center, blaring over the sound system. Over them all, like a bunting overcast, hung two dozen slings of red, white, and blue balloons. The bandleader kept up manfully, one ear cocked to the PA thunder,

but after one, two, three numbers, broke away from the
main musical body, they doing "It's a Grand Old Flag," he
leading "The Stars and Stripes Forever," not quite audibly,
though he made for an Ivesian undertow. An Uncle Sam
paraded on stilts, girls in short skirts waved flags to one of
the competing rhythms, the slings opened or failed to, balloons tumbled and shattered. And yes, there was a red,
white, and blue boater supporting a toy elephant spraying
silver needles out of its upturned trunk. Dull would he be of
soul who could pass by a sight so touching. They kept it up
for twenty-two minutes.

The Republican contribution to the art of the convention
film was less satisfying. It ran Thursday, the last night, and
would be used to warm up campaign rallies throughout the
fall; bits of it had already appeared as short TV spots. Its
theme, and the theme of all Republican advertising, was
that America was feeling good; you feel good; so vote for
Reagan. (Richard Viguerie would argue, post-election, that
one unintended effect was to make viewers feel good about
all incumbents, Democrats included.) There was a country-
and-westernish theme song, with the refrain "I'm proud to
be an Americaan" and "God bless the U.S.A." That was for
the climax; the background music ran back and forth from
atmospheric, "nature" passages to department-store pop, as
if "Appalachian Spring" had been put in a blender with the
theme from *Chariots of Fire*. Morning papers slapped on
porches, flowers pushed up in fields, citizens testified to
Reagan's abilities. "It's remarkable," chirped a youngish
woman in praise of his communication skills, "he's been on
television, what—twenty-six times?" (Careless writing.
What real person would know how many times he'd been
on TV?) There was a long tribute to the late Cardinal Cooke,
a piece of tokenism endurable only because Reagan had
been moved by Cooke's attentions during his recuperation
from the attempted murder and had reciprocated during
Cooke's fatal illness. A clip of the People's Republic of
China: "tremendously capable people." And one vignette,

genuinely affecting, of the fortieth anniversary ceremonies at Normandy (the Democrats should have insisted that they, too, hated Hitler).

The film, falling between Bush's and Reagan's acceptance speeches, acted as a seventh-inning stretch between junior and big-league oratory. Bush's effectiveness on the podium depended heavily on his mood. He was at his best when depressed, or in a tight spot, or slightly under the weather. Then—as in the months after his New Hampshire loss, or the hours during which Reagan was in surgery—he seemed what he most was: earnest, conscientious, dutiful. When he was exhilarated, all sober impressiveness vanished, as he took off on improvised syntactic loop-the-loops, only to find, in mid-flight, that he'd brought no verb along, and had no hope of finding one. Bush had carried on the Carter administration's most enduring legacy, the firm integration of the Vice-President into the administration. Like Mondale before him, he had defended the record, done the chores, and given his counsel. His acceptance speech was a verbal expression of this relationship. "As Vice-President . . . I've seen a real leader in action. No longer do we read and hear stories about the job of President being too big for any one person. Gone are the days of blaming the American people for what was really a failure not of" them "but of our national leadership. . . . I am proud to serve with a President who doesn't go around apologizing for the United States of America. . . . And I don't care what Walter Mondale says about it or what Tip O'Neill says about it"—not surprising—"Grenada was a proud moment in the history of the United States of America" (applause). His doughtiest strokes were given in defense of Reaganomics. "This President—this President has turned this country's economy around. . . . For over half a century, the liberal Democrats have pursued this philosophy of tax and spend, tax and spend. And sure enough, out of that Moscone Center in San Francisco, that temple of doom, came Mr. Mondale's first promise—a solemn promise to raise everyone's taxes. . . . The American people have a message for the tax raisers, the free spenders, the excess regulators, the government-knows-best hand-wringers, those who would promise every special-interest group everything, and that message is, Your time has passed" (cheers). "Your time has passed."

In the time that had passed between San Francisco and Dallas, the issue Bush touched on had excited the season's intensest speculation. The internal maneuverings within the Republican party had, ultimately, more importance for the future. But there were concrete political challenges to be addressed now. The Democrats had made an effort to redefine the rhetoric clustered around the word "family," and they had done their own share of flag waving. Any party of the right (even one as marginally and shamefacedly to the right as the traditional GOP) would have no trouble holding its own on such matters. The most problematic challenge was taxes. Mondale's frank promise to raise them was, by any conventional wisdom, suicide and insanity. Liberalism had succeeded for fifty years by either ignoring the fact that revenue would have to be raised or pretending that it would all be raised at the expense of other people. "The trick of liberalism," Wanniski pointed out, "was to never give the same speech in different parts of the country." Mondale's avowal was at least momentarily impressive, because it had finally become clear that raising taxes was exactly what he would want to do, and candor was refreshing. It made tactical sense, to the extent that the Republicans—the old-time, true-believing Republicans— wanted to raise them too, and would feel compelled to admit it. And of course, they did want to raise them, or saw no alternative to doing so. Republicanism was not a phenomenon solely of the Congress; Robert Dole had not passed TEFRA single-handed. It percolated up to the highest levels of the administration. Bush talked now like one who had seen the light, but only four years earlier he had called supply-sideism "voodoo economics," a phrase which enriched four years of Democratic speeches and filled editorial cartoons with witch doctors and bubbling sacrificial kettles. Reagan's White House staff were early converts to

TEFRA, and Reagan himself had finally gone along, and brought all of the party except for the House supply-side core into line behind it. (He was perhaps the only person in Washington who sincerely believed that it was only a "mid-course correction." He may also have been right.) The deficit continued to yawn: all the revenue raised by TEFRA vanished in its depths without a ripple (strange), and the clever Republicans were gritting their teeth against the day when they would raise taxes yet again. And unexpectedly Mondale had spoken their most secret thoughts. White House aides (unnamed, *bien sûr)* spent the next week or so anxiously telling the press what a great move it had been.

Such were the considerations that kept Reagan, when his time came, from making the absolute, flat-out, Shermanesque pledge "I will never raise taxes." But the supply-siders had done their work too well; the GOP said everything but. "President Reagan," said Bush, "cut tax rates across the board for every single American, and he will keep those tax rates cut." Reagan's own acceptance speech was sown with similar promises. "Our opponents are openly committed to increasing your tax burden." *Boo.* "We are committed to stopping them, and we will. . . . Our tax policies are and will remain pro-work, pro-growth, and pro-family. We intend to simplify the entire tax system, to make new taxes more fair, easier to understand, and most important, to bring the tax rates of every American further down, not up." *Yay.* "If we bring them down far enough, growth will continue strong; the underground economy will shrink; the world will beat a path to our door; no one will be able to hold America back, and the future will be ours."

The cheer that followed that paragraph coalesced into a repeated chant of "U.S.A., U.S.A." Reagan was interrupted by these and other forms of applause ninety-four times, not counting laughter, hisses, cries of "Yes!" and "No!" and other forms of audience reaction. (There were even chants of "Four More Years," which one would have thought the Republicans would have retired after Watergate, but after all, they were trying to be the party of hope.) He looked out at a hallful of flags (156 of them for the posting of the colors, give or take), signs (PROTECT BABY DOE; GO FOR THE GOLD; JESUIT FOR REAGAN—he must have been the only one), and all the traditional state paraphernalia—Hawaiian shirts, Kansas sunflowers. It was, like many a Reagan speech, surprisingly (surprising because what gets remembered from speech to speech is their net effect, which is always emotional) full of facts and figures: their failures, our achievements. There was one break in that simple binary pattern. "I began political life as a Democrat, casting my first vote in 1932 for Franklin Delano Roosevelt. That year the Democrats called for a 25 percent reduction in the cost of government by abolishing useless commissions and offices and consolidating departments and bureaus, and giving more authority to state governments. As the years went by and those promises were forgotten, did I leave the Democratic party, or did the leadership of that party leave not just me but millions of patriotic Democrats? . . . As Democratic leaders have taken their party further and further away from its first principles, it's no surprise that so many responsible Democrats feel that our platform is closer to their views, and we welcome them to our side."

He ended with a cornball catalogue, tracing the path taken by the Olympic torch on its way to Los Angeles, which gave almost every hamlet and roadside diner in America a chance to be cheered, and gave as well a generous dollop from the melting pot. "And then, in San Francisco, a Vietnamese immigrant, his little son held on his shoulders, dodged photographers and policemen to cheer a nineteen-year-old black man pushing an eighty-eight-year-old white woman in a wheelchair as she carried the torch." No Hispanics? "My friends, that's America." *Yay.*

The passage about Franklin Roosevelt was not corn. Reagan's point about Democrats disappointed by the platform was disingenuous. The Democrats had claimed in 1932 that they were willing to cut government; but they, and particularly Roosevelt, had been willing to try almost anything— free trade, protection, balanced budgets, deficit spending, a dash of fascism, a pinch of Five-Year Plan. Their unprejudiced enthusiasm was a key to their success. And one remedy Roosevelt never abandoned, at least as rhetoric, was soaking the rich. As a broad sociological observation, however, Reagan's remark was perfectly true. Large categories of conduct and feeling which the Democrats had once ignored, or casually accepted, or fervently believed in, were simply no longer acceptable in the party. Many Democrats had left on that account; some of them had come to provide the GOP's freshest brains.

The convention ended with a languorous Ray Charles' "America," the beat always in the next county, but soothing as surf; a hold-hands rendition of "God Bless America"; a benediction; then out, among the grasshoppers and the dead.

8
The Mob,
the Doldrums,
Church and State

While the Republicans celebrated and orated and schemed for the future, the hottest political story of the month was being played out, not in Dallas, but at New York's Kennedy Airport, where Geraldine Ferraro had called a press conference at which, she promised, she would tell all about her finances. It was, after "Hymietown" and Hartpence, the press's third "story" of the campaign: something surprising or significant added, by the press's efforts, to the public record. In this case, incompletely added. Unlike Jackson's slurs or Hart's names, the trail of misdeeds and omissions winding in and out of Ferraro's life was not simple. The press went at the details spasmodically; most reporters and editors gave up halfway, berating those who pushed on.

From the first, Ferraro's problems had to do with her husband, John Zaccaro, and his business affairs. Walter Mondale, as we have seen, sidestepped the limits on individual campaign contributions by spinning off a multiplicity of delegate PACs. When Ferraro made her maiden run for Congress in 1978, she tried spending $110,000 in loans from her husband as her own money. The Federal Election Commission frowned on the transaction and ultimately exacted a small fine. Meanwhile, though, the candidate was directed to return the loan. This she managed to do by selling a half share in a building to a partner of her husband's who paid precisely the required sum, and who sold it, in turn, to Zaccaro, at no profit to himself three months later. As the Keynesians used to say, we owe it to ourselves.

The couple's finances continued to be linked over the next six years. Nothing wrong with that—except that Ferraro had omitted Zaccaro's activities from the financial-disclosure forms she was obliged, as a congresswoman, to fill out, on the grounds that she derived no benefit from them and had no knowledge of them. Yet, as her style of life was scrutinized, the benefits seemed palpable—kids in good private schools; the home in Forest Hills; vacation houses on Fire Island and St. Croix (Archie Bunker's district, indeed). The plea of ignorance had to contend with the fact that Ferraro was a shareholder in her husband's main real estate business, as well as its vice-president and secretary-treasurer. Her non-disclosures were improper, possibly criminal. (George Hansen, an Idaho Republican who left portions of his wife's business off his forms, was looking at a five- to fifteen-month jail sentence.) Things did not get really ripe, though, until investigators directed their attention to what, exactly, in John Zaccaro's business was undisclosed.

The husband of the would-be heartbeat away turned out to have a more than random number of dubious associates. Sometimes, in their zeal, reporters pushed past the bounds of relevance, even decency. Zaccaro's father, and founder of the family business, it was duly noted, had been a character witness on a mobster's pistol permit in 1946; Ferraro's own father, the Newburgh restaurant owner, had been indicted for gambling a month before he died (whereupon the charge was dropped). But several other connections appeared to be considerably more fresh.

One Zaccaro property in Manhattan's Chinatown housed a gambling den. Another—half a block away from Zaccaro's office—had a porn operation for a tenant; packages of its wares—*Whips and Chains, Smut*—were regularly loaded and unloaded on the sidewalk. Around the corner, in the last sliver of the shrinking Little Italy neighborhood, a reputed capo of the Gambino family maintained a residence in a building owned by the Zaccaros from 1963 till 1971. ("Not just anyone could be [his] landlord," one magazine reported, quoting an anonymous "law enforcement specialist." "The family . . . trusted the Zaccaros."[1]) Another gentleman, convicted as a labor racketeer, took loans for real estate deals from the Zaccaros throughout the sixties, and later made contributions to Ferraro's campaigns, the last only three months before the San Francisco convention. Indeed, her first campaign manager—the one who decided that the name Ferraro "flowed better" than Zaccaro—was an associate of yet another mobster, whose kept union local also gave her campaign money.

Not all the guilt was by association. In 1983, Zaccaro had been the broker for a real estate deal financed by an improper loan from a credit union. Acting on another deal for the same client, Zaccaro submitted bogus statements to potential creditors, and offered, as his own contribution to the financing, $80,000 borrowed from the estate of an eighty-four-year-old widow for whom he was acting as conservator.

These were not exactly the family issues the Democrats hoped to reclaim. Here was their star candidate, their historic breakthrough, fudging on government forms, repaying illegal loans with sweetheart deals, her husband's business life turning up crooks like earwigs. Ferraro's first response to cries for full disclosure was reticence. She would reveal her tax returns for the last six years, but not her husband's. " 'Gerry,' " she reported him as saying, " 'I'm not going to tell you how to run the country. Don't tell me how to run my business.' You people married to Italian men," she added, "you know what it's like." Three

days later, the paterfamilias announced that he was "recon-
sidering." When Ferraro and her accountants appeared at
an airport hotel for her August 21 press conference, they
and the press came armed with copies of her and her husband's tax returns, which had been distributed the day before.

What followed was a masterly performance—cool, dogged, unflapped, applauded at its end by the reporters themselves. It was the more impressive because the returns in
fact did not tell all. Only Zaccaro's main business had been
revealed; not his subsidiary deals or partnerships. The income of the family firm was all there, duly taxed—in some
cases, under- and overtaxed—but not all the sources from
whence it came. Itemized elaborations, which Zaccaro had
submitted to the IRS, were not given to the press. Ferraro's
accountants had made a digest and called it a release.

But the press, for the most part, had had enough. With a
few exceptions—in October, Zaccaro told *Redbook* he
would "insist" on attending cabinet meetings—Ferraro's
husband was forgotten, and her own dereliction was treated
as a peccadillo. (That was more or less the verdict of the
House Ethics Committee, which reported in December
that she had "improperly . . . fail[ed] to disclose her husband's financial interests" through "error, oversight, and
misinterpretation.") A few "serious" papers—*The Wall
Street Journal*, and the Philadelphia *Inquirer*—kept up the
chase, in which they were assisted by the New York *Post*,
the New York *Tribune*, and the Washington *Times*, though
since the first was owned by Rupert Murdoch and the last
two by the Unification Church, they could never merit the
attention of sober folk. The quiescent main body of the
media resented even these few renegades. "Has Ferraro
been the victim of a hit job?" asked *Newsweek* after one
Wall Street Journal piece.

Why did the press call itself off? The Kennedy Airport
press conference, as one reporter who attended it pointed
out,[2] disrupted press assignments and responsibilities. The
lead treatments of the event were written, not by the

grunts who had been chasing down old bills of sale and the addresses of Mafia capi, but by the Ferraro press corps traveling in her campaign plane. This corps had had little chance to sift the relevant dirt and took her performance at face value. Most of the dirt, indeed, had nothing to do with Ferraro: a point only partly relevant, since business friends may gain entree to government circles through spouses as well as officeholders (and will increasingly do so as more politicians' wives pursue careers and more married women hold office). Finally, though, the death of the Ferraro story was hastened by the same thing which had delayed the emergence of "Hymietown": social studies. The press was not there to verify, instruct itself, or carry report. Instead, it was conscious of dealing with firsts: the first black, the first woman. One columnist wondered swoonily if twenty-first-century schoolchildren would have to memorize the date Mondale tapped her. There was a duty to the textbook, as there was a duty to the late city edition—where the story would certainly be long, probably inconclusive, and possibly irrelevant. The textbook won.

With the Dallas convention and the Ferraro non-scandal concluded, the election entered a halcyon calm. This was acceptable to Reagan, who found himself, according to all polls—friendly and hostile, Republican and Democrat—sitting atop an enormous and undwindling lead, as great in some surveys as 27 percentage points. It was particularly acceptable to the clever Republicans who, convinced of their own innate hatefulness, have no recipe for victory in presidential elections apart from the appearance of sudden and inexplicable spells of good fortune, at which they cross their fingers and hope it will last forever. It was not acceptable to Walter Mondale, who lay at the base of those tall 27 points.

Yet he could do nothing. He slid from nadir to nadir. At the end of August, he was endorsed by John Anderson. Six days later, he marched in the New York City Labor Day parade. The advance men failed utterly. No crowds gathered, Mayor Koch was elsewhere, Mondale's progress down Fifth Avenue generated all the excitement of a street sweeper. Two weeks later, addressing a rally at the campus of USC, he was booed by hundreds of students. It soon appeared that the Republicans had encouraged this naughtiness, though Mondale's whingeing, pasty presence, out in the California sun, must have made heckling him all but irresistible.

There were numerous explanations of this torpor. Mondale's was that Reagan had contrived it, by not addressing the issues. That might explain Reagan's performance; it could not excuse Mondale's. It takes two not to talk. If Mondale had such burning issues, why wasn't he catching fire? "Not addressing the issues" is anyway politicians' code for "not addressing *my* issues," and of course no one's opponent ever does that unless forced to it. A favorite Mondale example was toxic waste dumps, which he saw as a festering problem, bred by indifference, corruption, and greed (Gary Hart had spoken of "Reagan and his greedy gang of polluters"). Naturally, Mondale addressed it continually. Reagan, who saw it—to the extent he focused on it at all—as an administrative bungle which would be cleared up by new personnel, just as naturally did not address it. For similar reasons, Mondale never addressed tax rates and their relation to productivity.

There was a seasonal aspect to the electorate's sloth. The willingness of citizens to pay attention to politics runs in cycles. Politicians and political reporters, of course, never leave off. The average partisan voter rouses himself about January of election year and stays tuned in to his party, and perhaps also to the other, until the primaries have been decided. He and the less dedicated voter will glance at the conventions, and not come back until—when? The traditional date for the riveting of national attention on presidential politics used to be in October, at the end of the World Series. These days, one talks of Labor Day, but that may be early. The real day of awakening probably falls in between, and closer to the World Series—in which case the September slump was not at all out of the ordinary.

A third explanation was that the voters had already made up their minds, and the polls simply reflected their settled convictions. Neither man was new goods. Mondale had been in the nation's eye, as Vice-President and campaigner, for most of eight years; Reagan, on and off since his Goldwater speech, for twenty. Perhaps the public felt it already had a pretty good idea of where the two men stood, and what they represented, and had made up its mind accordingly.

The vacuum did not stay unfilled. Over the early autumn hush, there arose a discussion of an issue of long-term, even philosophic importance: the relation of religion and politics.

Religion had permeated the Democratic primary campaign. Jackson was a minister. Mondale was a minister's son, and Hart a former divinity student; McGovern was both. Askew was a church elder. All the Democrats used religious figures of speech and justifications continually. McGovern invoked the Creator's perspective on the arms race. Mondale called nuclear weapons "god-awful" and said that social injustice was a "sin." Ferraro testified that she had been shaped by her faith.

Some of this was boilerplate. All politicians invoke God. Nelson Rockefeller's stenotypist developed an acronym, BOMFOG—for "the brotherhood of man, under the fatherhood of God"—because the phrase appeared so often in his speeches. Americans expect such invocations as a matter of course (the three "taboo themes" of the American book industry, said Vladimir Nabokov, were pedophilia, miscegenation, and "the total atheist who lives a happy and useful life and dies in his sleep at the age of 106"). Perhaps Americans also discount them. But the Democrats' God talk was not mere ritual; it reflected an understanding of ethics and public policy. Some codes of human behavior, the Democrats believed and argued, flowed from the order of the universe; others didn't; they upheld the ones that did. Ronald Reagan, said Mario Cuomo, practiced the ethics of Darwin; Democrats practiced the ethics of St. Francis of Assisi (the "most sincere Democrat"). It might be going too far to say that God was on the Democratic party's side. But He was on the side of their beliefs; in the political realm, they were on His side.

Republicans, meanwhile, did their own invoking. One of their most controversial religious allies was the Reverend Jerry Falwell.

Falwell was born in Lynchburg, Virginia, a city on the border between Appalachia and the world, of a mixed family—a violent, alcoholic father (he killed his own brother in a duel); a religious mother. Falwell became a Christian in his twenties. He went to a Bible college in Missouri, then returned to Lynchburg in 1956 to open a church in an old bottling plant. A dozen years and two thousand members later, it had become the ninth-largest church in the country.

As far as the country was concerned, his church might as well have been on the moon. About the last America had heard of fundamentalism was Mencken's account of the Scopes trial and such feeble retellings as *Inherit the Wind.* Since their defeat in Dayton, fundamentalists had been relegated to the category of invisible facts—things which perhaps exist but, since no one thinks or talks about them, have no importance. Fundamentalism took its name from *The Fundamentals: A Testimony to the Truth,* a set of biblical commentaries published in Los Angeles in the 1910s. As the tone of the title suggests, the movement was from the beginning in retreat. Other theologies had taken over the Protestant churches. Soon after their defeat in the Scopes trial, fundamentalists retired from the public realm as well. "We have a message of redeeming grace through a crucified and risen Lord," preached Falwell in 1965, expressing the consensus fundamentalist view. "Preachers are not called to be politicians but soul-winners." The soul-winning message consisted of mysteries believed by orthodox Christians of all denominations—the Incarnation, the Resurrection, the virgin birth—as well as the arcana of Revelations, including graphic images of last things. "When the trumpet sounds," said Falwell in another sermon, "stark pandemonium will occur on . . . every highway in the world where Christians are caught away from the driver's wheel."

But what about the interval before the trumpet's blast? Falwell's 1965 sermon had been directed against liberal churchmen active in the civil rights movement (Falwell at that time accepted segregation as biblically sanctioned and acknowledged later that it took a considerable mental wrench to overcome the mistake). By the seventies, he had found issues of his own that he felt could not simply be left until the millennium. Falwell's interest in next-to-last things was specifically triggered by the Court's abortion decision, *Roe* v. *Wade*. By 1976, he was declaring that "the idea that religion and politics don't mix was invented by the Devil to keep Christians from running their own country."

Falwell's formal political debut was arranged by the New Right. In 1979, a common acquaintance set up a meeting with Weyrich, Viguerie, and Phillips. Weyrich first spoke the phrase "moral majority" in passing, and thought it was too off-putting to be an effective title. But the others liked it. The Moral Majority, chartered that June, made a generalized, unsectarian pitch (no talk about Christians running their own country): against abortion, ERA, the gay rights movement, drugs, and pornography, and for a strong defense; in its own terms, pro-life, pro-family, pro-moral, and pro-American.

The phenomenon of the religious right went far beyond Falwell, who was not the only preacher who had gotten into politics. (He and his fellows, curiously, had built their national audiences through television—the supposed homogenizer instead defining and distinguishing.) But the Moral Majority was the lightning rod. During the 1980 election, Falwell was routinely lumped with neo-Nazis and the Klan, and compared to Khomeini and Jim Jones.* On his fundamentalist flank, meanwhile, he was condemned for "subtle ecumenicity." Many Republicans did not appreciate his

---

* Jones was in fact an atheist; the ideology of the People's Temple cult, to the extent it had any, was a kind of comic-book Leninism.

help—moderates, as a matter of course, as well as at least one conservative in whom the libertarian tradition was preeminent. Barry Goldwater, in the course of his post-election squabble with the New Right, remarked that Falwell deserved a "kick in the ass." But Reagan took the religious right seriously. "I know that you can't endorse me," he told a rally of evangelicals in Dallas in August 1980, "but . . . I want you to know that I endorse you." Many of that election's losers took it seriously too. "They beat my brains out," said one defeated pol, "with Christian love."

Four years later, the new religious right shared the spotlight with that very old religious right, the Roman Catholic Church. Its right-wing days, many observers hoped (or feared), were long past. The Catholic Church's major political initiative during the Reagan administration had been the American bishops' pastoral letter on nuclear war. The bishops' letter had a textual history as complicated as *Hamlet:* three drafts, the third at the behest of the Vatican, John Paul II having been widely said to have been displeased with the tendency of the first two. Whatever its final meaning, it was taken, particularly in the early stages, as an ecclesiastical addendum to the freeze movement, with which it coincided. Many bishops, on their own, embraced pacifism explicitly; George McGovern and Helen Caldicott had appeared in the Des Moines cathedral with no sense of anomaly.

But the Catholic Church had also taken a political stand, for the last dozen years, against the legalization of abortion (a third of the Moral Majority's members, interestingly, were Catholics)—a continuity with its old right days, never abandoned. There was, moreover, an intrinsic asymmetry between the two positions. The pastoral letter on nuclear weapons, in all its incarnations, was long and complicated, and afflicted with the turgidity that darkens all Catholic official prose. It left to politicians the responsibility for deciding how best to achieve the ends it marked out as moral. The position on abortion, by contrast, was plain. The Catholic bishops stressed repeatedly that the two positions had equal weight, that they were both authoritative expressions of Catholic teaching. But in practical political terms, any American politician who was not an explicit warmonger—which is to say any American politician—could find some way of putting himself on the right side of the pastoral letter. The abortion issue required other shifts.

The question arose in a particularly acute form with the selection of Mondale's running mate. Ferraro's congressional record was down-the-line pro-choice; she also was (and much was made of the fact) a Catholic: "very religious," said the governor of New Mexico in San Francisco; shaped by her faith, she had said when she appeared with Mondale in Elmore.

It was in Elmore that Ferraro tried out her first response. The right-to-lifers—who had been showing up for nearly everything since the Dartmouth debate—brought their chilblains and their signs to Minnesota, where a few of the latter now had a personal angle. HEY, FERRARO, WHAT KIND OF CATHOLIC ARE YOU? Questioned about the protesters, Ferraro responded by questioning Reagan's religion. "The President walks around calling himself a good Christian and I don't for one minute believe it because the policies are so terribly unfair and they are discriminatory and they have hurt a lot of people."

Three days later, Mondale took up the attack. "My faith," he told an interviewer in Lake Tahoe, where he was resting up for the convention, "unmistakably has taught me that social justice is part of a Christian's responsibility. My upbringing taught me a sense of community." Reagan, who had had a similar small-town background, "would have to explain how he came to a different conclusion."

These arguments were essentially the same as the one Mario Cuomo would advance in his keynote speech. Cuomo, it is true, would not spell out the conclusion, though it followed logically from what he said. If the Democrats embodied the principles of St. Francis—of Christianity—while the Republicans, who disagreed, embodied instead the principles of Darwin, then any Republican who professed to be a good Christian must be false, or, as Ferraro said, unbelievable. QED. The resemblance between her assault and Cuomo's credo was not accidental, for it came out later that he had encouraged her to make it.

Attacking Reagan was all very well. But that still begged the question of a Catholic politician's responsibilities on the abortion issue. Cuomo took it up next, directly.

He did so by taking on Archbishop (not yet Cardinal) John O'Connor of New York. Any Catholic, Cuomo said in an interview published in early August, who took O'Connor "literally . . . can only vote for a right-to-lifer." O'Connor had indeed said as much, or nearly as much, in a news conference back in June: "I don't see how a Catholic in good conscience can vote for a candidate who explicitly supports abortion." But this was before a Catholic who explicitly supported abortion had been put on a national ticket. O'Connor answered Cuomo's interview the day it was published with a demurral. "My sole responsibility is to present . . . the formal official teaching of the Catholic Church. I leave to those interested in such teachings" to judge how "the public statements of officeholders and candidates" match up. Cuomo professed himself "delighted" with O'Connor's clarification.

In Archbishop O'Connor, Cuomo had found an opponent worthy of his mettle. O'Connor had succeeded to Cardinal Cooke's place after a career as a Navy chaplain, in which he rose to the rank of rear admiral. He was personally unprepossessing: bespectacled, almost squirrelish in appearance; fussy in his enunciation, as if he had once overcome a slur. As with Cuomo, the appearance deceived. O'Connor was John Paul II's point man in the drafting of the nuclear-arms pastoral letter and in the American church generally. An intelligent Pope trusted his intelligence and his orthodoxy. He was not going to be caught in any overt political interventions; he was also not about to let the faith be defined by random faithful.

Early in September, O'Connor bore in more directly. He criticized Ferraro by name for the first time, on doctrinal grounds, for having said "things about abortion relative to Catholic teaching which are not true. . . . I have absolutely nothing against Geraldine Ferraro; I will not tell anybody in the United States you should vote for or against" her "or anybody else." But "she has given the world to understand that Catholic teaching is divided on the subject of abortion" when in fact there was "no variance," "no flexibility," and "no leeway."

Ferraro denied on September 10 that she had ever misrepresented her church, whereupon the archbishop produced evidence—a two-year-old letter, signed by her, inviting Catholic congressmen to a briefing by Catholics for Choice, a group of pro-abortion Catholics, who would "show . . . that the Catholic position on abortion is not monolithic and that there can be a range of personal and political responses to the issue."

Ferraro took cover in the ambiguity of the word "Catholic." The Church's position on abortion, she conceded, after O'Connor produced her letter, was "monolithic." "But I do believe that there are a lot of Catholics who do not share the view of the Catholic Church." The Catholic position, in other words, equaled the position of Catholics; when in doubt, take a poll. She and O'Connor, she said on the eleventh, had simply "agreed to disagree." "Religion," she added later, "has been injected into a presidential campaign. I have not welcomed it [certainly not since Elmore] and I do not want it to be an issue in this race."

The fact was, Ferraro had been too out-front, both in her advocacy of abortion and in her appeals to piety, simply to fudge the question, and she was not subtle enough to craft a convincing synthesis. But help was on the way. On September 13, Mario Cuomo was scheduled to deliver a talk to the Theology Department at Notre Dame. The very man who had sponsored St. Francis for membership in the Democratic party would set things right.

Cuomo presented himself to his audience as "an old-fashioned Catholic who sins, regrets, struggles, worries, gets confused, and most of the time feels better after confession"; also as a lawyer and a politician. What was the right relation between his faith and his career? Cuomo suggested criteria in the form of questions. Was his belief "helpful? . . . essential to human dignity? Does it promote harmony? . . . Or does it divide us so fundamentally that it threatens our ability to function as a pluralistic society?"

Pluralism was the key; because of it, "public morality" in America "depend[ed] on a consensus view of right and wrong." Gauging the state of the consensus was "a matter of prudential political judgment." The way to the synthesis was now all clear.

"My wife and I," Cuomo stressed, "were enjoined never to use abortion to destroy the life we created, and we never have. . . . For me life or fetal life in the womb should be protected, even if five of nine justices of the Supreme Court disagree with me. . . . But not everyone in our society," he went on disarmingly, "agrees with me and Matilda." Cuomo the politician gave his readout of the consensus: anti-abortion laws were "not a plausible possibility" and "wouldn't work" anyway. "Given present attitudes, it would be Prohibition revisited, legislating what couldn't be enforced and in the process creating a disrespect for law in general." *Vox populi* was not *vox dei;* it might be the opposite. But in a democracy, it was the voice of necessity. Cuomo the politician bowed his head to it.

It was an attractive statement, far more so than any of Ferraro's. He hadn't entangled himself in disputes over the "Catholic position," and he had avoided the inconsistency of disdaining Reagan's Christianity in July and complaining about religion in politics in September. There was only one weak spot. Consensus was the glue that held his position together. Who provided the consensus on abortion? Two hundred million Americans, ultimately. But wasn't Governor Mario Cuomo a prominent and respected one of them? When, before Notre Dame, had he made a resonant statement of his personal opinion of abortion? Whatever his pledges to God and Matilda, Cuomo, in his public life, had been "for" abortion, every bit as much as Ferraro. His poli-

tics and his judgment of the consensus coincided to a remarkable degree. Cuomo had found, in consensus and prudence, a way of having religion when he wanted it and not
having it when he didn't.

O'Connor answered him—not by name, though the sense
of slow-motion debate was palpable—in an address to a
Catholic medical group on October 18. It was a speech
scored, in publicity terms, for full orchestra and brass band;
Mother Teresa of Calcutta sat by the lectern as he spoke. He
fingered the weak spot directly. "You have to uphold the
law, the Constitution says. It does not say that you must
agree with the law, or that you cannot work to change the
law. . . .

"There are those who argue that we cannot legislate morality. The reality is that we do legislate behavior every day.
. . . It is obvious that law is not the entire answer to abortion. Nor is it the entire answer to theft, arson, child abuse,
or shooting police officers. Everybody knows that. But who
would suggest that we repeal the laws against such crimes
because the law is so often broken?"

He left the debate where he had first entered it. "I have
the responsibility of spelling out . . . with accuracy and
clarity what the Church officially teaches. . . . I have simultaneously the obligation to try to dispel confusion about
such teaching wherever it exists, however it has been generated, regardless of who may have generated it. . . . I
recognize the dilemma confronted by some Catholics in
political life. I cannot resolve that dilemma for them. As I
see it, their disagreement, if they do disagree, is not simply
with me" but "with the teaching of the Catholic Church."

While the Catholics curvetted, Protestants and Jews were
not still. On August 24, the morning after his nomination,
Ronald Reagan addressed an ecumenical prayer breakfast
in Dallas. "I believe," he began, "that faith and religion play
a critical role in the political life of our nation and always has
[sic]." Reagan ran through mentions of God in American
founding documents—the Mayflower Compact, the Declaration of Independence, Washington's Farewell Address.

(He did not mention, though he might have, the Northwest Ordinances, which reserved land for schools on the grounds that "religion, morality and knowledge" were "necessary to the good and the happiness of mankind.") "The truth is," he concluded, "politics and morality are inseparable. And as morality's foundation is religion, religion and politics are necessarily related." That was a plausible description of American history; indeed, an incontrovertible description of the behavior of the politicians involved in the 1984 campaign.

But in the middle of his speech, Reagan made a slightly different point. Reviewing the Court's school prayer decision, Reagan noted that there were those "fighting to make sure voluntary prayer is not returned to the classrooms. And the frustrating thing for the great majority of Americans . . . is that those who are attacking religion claim they are doing it in the name of tolerance, freedom, and open-mindedness. Question: Isn't the real truth that they are intolerant of religion?"

Reagan had isolated an anomalous but significant strain in American political life: the aggressive secularist. "Secular humanism" had become such a favorite buzz word of Falwell types that most people naturally assume that they had coined it. It was, in fact, a self-description, devised by secular humanists. They represented a genuine, if marginal, American tradition: of Paine and Ingersoll; of the village atheist and the village crank. Their organs were gray magazines like *The Humanist* (Walter Mondale's brother Lester was on its editorial board), subsisting on anti-religious propaganda and exposés of ecclesiastical plots. ("Fundamentalists who collaborate with the Vatican are used by the Holy See to counter the best interests of the United States.") As an electoral force, they were nearly nil, but to the extent their ethos informed groups like the American Civil Liberties Union, they wielded disproportionate judicial clout. Of them it could reasonably be said that they were "intolerant of religion."

Your opponents' most vulnerable allies are always fair

game. But there were other elements, not recognized by Reagan, in the opposition to school prayer. By far the smallest group was the authentic civil libertarians. Most supporters of absolutist interpretations of the Bill of Rights have ulterior motives, but there are a handful who sincerely revere it, in the same way that cargo cultists honor the DC-3: they don't know what it was for, or how it got there, but they know it is holy. (So sincere was Nat Hentoff in his devotion that he had begun to question abortion and infanticide on civil libertarian grounds, and even appeared at the Family Forum in San Francisco.) The great majority of the prayer decision's supporters—the Walter, not the Lester, Mondales—simply saw it as a matter of pluralistic good housekeeping: The less we all try to believe together, the better we'll each believe by ourselves.

There were, finally, those concerned about school prayer and religion in politics generally who might be called aggressive theists: believers in one faith, suspicious of the encroachments of others. The line from *The Humanist,* quoted above, recalled good old-fashioned Protestant No Popery. It was kindred sentiments that Walter Mondale now tried to rouse.

He and Reagan both addressed a Washington convention of the B'nai B'rith service group on September 6. Mondale led off with a reply to the Dallas prayer breakfast. He denied that he was "intolerant of religion": "never before" had he "had to defend my religious faith in a political campaign." Right; and he hadn't attacked anyone else's since Lake Tahoe. But the bottom line of his speech was the threat of fundamentalism. Reagan's religious right supporters were a "determined band . . . reaching for government power to impose their own beliefs on others." Three days later, Senator Kennedy took up the same theme: the "intolerance which still flourishes at the extremist fringe of American politics . . . infects the very center of our national authority."

In his B'nai B'rith appearance, Reagan backed out of the fight he had picked; the clever Republicans, solicitous of his

September lead, would risk nothing that might disturb it.
Mondale, however, did not back off. Falwell replaced James
Watt as the demon of his and Ferraro's rhetoric all the way
till November. If it was not a conscious attempt to alarm
Jewish voters by waving fundamentalist hobgoblins, it gave
a good impression of one.

Falwell, it must be said, had given Jewish Americans reason to worry about him; not good reason maybe, but reason.
He had carefully expunged the Christian-country language
from his rhetoric. He was, moreover, a firm, not to say
zealous, supporter of Israel; Zionism was a precondition of
membership in the Moral Majority. Menachem Begin had
given him an award as a friend of the country. Nonetheless,
the talk had been there; and some of Falwell's fellow clerics
were capable of odd statements. "In all due respect," one
Reverend Bailey Smith had said in the midst of the 1980
campaign, "I do not believe that God hears the prayers of
Jews." For weeks, the quotation was routinely attributed to
Falwell, a fine example of unconscious editing: he *ought* to
have said it; therefore, he must have.

And what kind of a friend of Israel was he anyway?
Falwell's Zionism, like Begin's, was derived from biblical
exegesis. The existence of the State of Israel was a necessary
precondition of his chiliastic scenarios. Sophisticates didn't
like this at all ("mad," "bonkers," "rattle-brained tripe" ran
a typical judgment). On the deepest level, Falwell inadver-
tently called attention to splits within the Jewish community itself. His Jewish allies—and there were a fair number
—tended to be Orthodox, of deep hue. Falwell's "subtle
ecumenicity" competed with alliances that Jewish liberals
had made with entirely different parts of the Gentile culture.

Mondale needed Falwell, to undo the effects of his own
pusillanimity in the face of Louis Farrakhan. The implied
parallel was scurrilous. Falwell's social behavior was about
as much like Farrakhan's as it was like Jim Jones's. Falwell
had never made death threats or written off whole races as
devils. But his reputation was such that he might profitably

be used to cancel out the memory of the Muslim. At least, Mondale was willing to try.

So the September debate broke off in partisan jockeying. American politicians called in religion when it supported them; when it did not, they tended to talk about separation of church and state. They found their room to maneuver in the discontinuities of the American system. Some of these had been built in from the first; others were late alterations. Church and state had been separate at the national level since the First Amendment. Religion and state, however, had never been divided. The American government, and its leaders, had traditionally professed a reticent theism, which saw God as taking a special interest in America and as the source of proper American ethics (whatever the leaders in question believed them to be). The tradition was still alive: churches have kept their tax exemptions, Congress has kept its chaplains, pennies still declare that our trust is in God. Church and religion both, finally, played a lively role in American politics, limited by the restraints of decorum: it is okay to draft God for your side; less okay to point out His absence from the other side; not okay at all to call specific politicians Godless. The new tradition, that of the humanists—that religious forms and expressions must make no intrusion into the political realm whatsoever—could be called on by a politician who felt the heat of believers upon him; though to do so, one ran the risk of seeming to be a clumsy hypocrite, like Geraldine Ferraro.

Many questions had been left untouched. There was the strange theological genealogy of fundamentalism, whose roots went back to the radical Reformed left of Thomas Münzer. There was, for the philosophically inclined, the question: What kind of god might a consistent liberal be said to believe in? Jefferson believed in Nature's. But nature was now Becoming—the world through evolution, man through history. Was Walter Mondale's god finally god in history? And was that a fancy way of saying, with the Carter State Department, that history was god? (Maybe Walter was more like Lester than he knew.) To ask these questions was asking

too much of an election; Mondale and Reagan, Cuomo and
O'Connor, had already debated at a level of theoretical
complexity which politics seldom reaches.

Nadir to nadir. Reagan announced that, after years of
harsh words and silence, he would meet Andrei Gromyko at
the end of September. Mondale arranged to meet Gromyko
the day before in New York City. Politicking on both their
parts? Of course. But foreign maneuvers are a recognized
advantage of the incumbent, like white having the first
move in chess. As Reagan had learned four years earlier
after his Iowa defeat: Don't try a Rose Garden strategy
unless you have a Rose Garden. Mondale's ride, from the
Plaza Hotel to the Soviet mission, a distance of ten blocks,
took ten minutes, "largely," according to the press pool
report, "because New York motorists and pedestrians ignored the motorcade." Back at the Plaza, Mondale recounted what he had told the Foreign Minister: that Americans wanted arms control "under President Reagan" (N.B.
to the American people: *but you aren't going to get it,
unless you vote for me);* and that Afghanistan, Solidarity,
and Soviet Jews should have their yokes eased. What had
been the Russian's reaction to his human-rights appeal?
"Hard to characterize."

Then there was the Springsteen skirmish. This was no
trivial matter. Bruce Springsteen had sold more records
than Haydn, though not as many as Prince. Among his fans
was Ronald Reagan, or so Reagan suddenly said, adding that
Springsteen's music aptly expressed a new mood of pride
abroad in the land. Mondale couldn't let that one pass. At a
rally in New Brunswick, he deplored the attempt to "steal
one of New Jersey's greatest heroes. . . . Bruce Springsteen may have been born in the U.S.A., but he wasn't born
yesterday."

The New Brunswick rally had the energy of a spinning,
deflating balloon. A chilly rain had driven it indoors, into an
old ugly theater. Two folk singers—the Mondale campaign
had inherited them all—did the warming up, a fat bearded

man and a slight bony girl, both with long straight hair and regulation folk-song accents: "Ol' Hickry said we cud takem by surprise / if'e held are far till we lookem inna eyes." Porky representatives of the New Jersey Democracy filled the stage, dutifully flapping streamers in time. The crowd, though large, was nearly two-thirds kids from Rutgers, cutting Soc. 10, or perhaps attending for credit. A particularly gruesome politician, he must have been the mayor, poured scorn on the pundits who predicted defeat, praised Mondale's many virtues, then, dropping to a bedroom voice and getting really *close* to the mike, affirmed "[pause]— Fritz Mondale is a truly decent human being." The decent human being, when he arrived, had the bright cheeks and the caved-in smile of a jack-o'-lantern a week after Halloween. He looked as if he hadn't changed suits since the hostage crisis.

His speech had several pointed phrases, but they were all quotations: from Springsteen; from the surgeon who had operated on Reagan after the assassination attempt, and who had recently written to the Los Angeles *Times* to point out that he had gotten through med school on a low-cost federal loan (the students cheered from the heart). Most important was James Reston. Reagan, the Yoda of the Op-Ed page had written, was the "most passive, remotest President since Calvin Coolidge." This had become the September theme of the Mondale campaign. As with the election, so with the country: Reagan slid over reality and shirked his work; he neither faced the issues nor did his job. "We need a President who masters his government, who knows the essential facts, who is in touch and in charge . . . who stands up and takes responsibility."

One fact gave the indictment credence—a third bomb attack on American positions in Lebanon. Surely it was more than the typical American impatience with muddle and difficulty to feel that the entire Lebanese intervention had, from its start, been unduly muddled. It may have been true, as Jeane Kirkpatrick said, that there, as elsewhere, the Democrats blamed America first; but it was also true that there, in the areas of diplomatic and military competence at least, America, or the administration, had been blameworthy. Reagan had made matters worse with a trivializing metaphor, comparing the difficulties of fashioning a Lebanese policy with the problems of remodeling a kitchen. The incident gave Mondale his only good unborrowed lines. "The first time could have happened to anyone. The second time could have been prevented. . . . This third time was inexcusable." He quoted Truman on the buck stopping here; under Reagan, "the buck stops everywhere but here. . . . We need a tough President who can protect the American people."

But—nadir after nadir—was Mondale that man? Even if he was, why should the American people turn to him? The single blip of bad leadership that Mondale was able to point to in the whole month of September was a blunder in an endgame, a stumble on the way to the door. Reagan had tried something; it hadn't worked; he was pulling out: that was how it was being seen. If the blast which killed 241 marines had happened while Jimmy Carter was President, *The New Republic* wrote at the time, there would have been calls for impeachment. Just so; for it would have seemed like a final, grotesque summation of his presidency, the bang at the end of the whimpers. Reagan failed in a context of success.

The week before, Reagan had come on a mild, clear evening to Hoboken, New Jersey. As the young professionals, maddened by Manhattan rents, leap off the West Side and paddle across the Hudson, Hoboken is fast becoming gentrified; an article a few years ago in the New York *Times* recounted the scandal in a local bar when the owner added quiche to the menu; he would hold the line, though, he said, at ferns. Reagan was not coming for the gentry, but for a supper celebrating the 74th Annual Novena and Outdoor Fest of St. Anne's Church. Catholic functions had been high on his itinerary; while Ferraro had been going falls with Archbishop O'Connor earlier in the month, Reagan had paid a visit to a Catholic shrine in Doylestown, Pennsylvania, with Cardinal Krol, who praised him for his support of tuition tax credits. The St. Anne's Church supper was also intended to focus on the issue. The neighborhood was hung with American flags, with the slight sepia tint that old flags get, and almost as many Italian flags, also venerable (one still bore the arms of the House of Sardinia).

Reagan's supporters were massed on the front steps of the church. They faced a group of protesters (Manhattan had been papered with notices for a week), lined up behind police sawhorses, whose signs ran from allusion to blunt assertion: THIS IS NOT THE SHINING CITY and REAGAN IS A PIG. In that cohort of liberalism, two right-to-lifers kept the vigil: PRO-LIFE, PRO-REAGAN. When the unwelcoming committee started up a chant of "Reagan must go," they were drowned by lusty hoots. In the crowd of curious on the street, a drunk, exhilarated by warm air and fried brains, called, "Give him an Oscar!" Clowning high school boys hoisted themselves precariously on each other's shoulders for a look, shouting, "Yo, where's Reagan?"

Presumably, he was inside. Four helicopters had roared over the little streets, eliciting enthusiastic, futile waves and cheers; then nothing. A marine in dress uniform stood at the gate of the pocket-sized lawn, next to the statue of the Virgin's mother, exciting speculation that perhaps Reagan would emerge there. But the only signs of life or acknowledgment from the church was a white, unrecognizable hand that appeared occasionally at a second-story window, waving through the blinds. The kid on watch saw it. "C'mon out, we know you're in there!" The crowd gave eager, frustrated murmurs.

Away from the church, on the motorcade route, the homegrown signs were more congenial: 6TH STREET WELCOMES PRESIDENT REAGAN; GIVEAWAYS ARE CRUTCHES, REAGAN SAYS WALK; one protest from the right —UNBIND CUBAN HANDS (to do the Bay of Pigs properly). The out-of-towners, alerted to his route, hurried over, but got no more glimpse of him than the residents: in the midst of the motorcycles, the police cars, the convertible packed with Secret Service men, and the network station wagons, from a speeding black limousine flying the presidential flags from the fenders, out of one rolled-down, smoked-glass window, Reagan waved. Anyone who'd parked his deck chair on the wrong side of the street missed him. In a few minutes, over the row houses and the old commercial buildings, came a noise like thunder, a rush of wind, then the choppers, big as buses, faster than the motorcade, sweeping back to the Rose Garden.

REAGAN, one sign caught it, EAT AND RUN.

9
The Leadership Issue

We need a President, Mondale had said, *who masters his government, who knows the essential facts, who is in touch and in charge.* Reagan, Mondale added, was not that man—a charge Reagan and the aides who coached him for the first debate took seriously.

The charge was right or wrong, but it was not baseless; it referred to objective, observable realities. President Reagan may have known—presumably he thought he knew—all the facts that were "essential." But there was no denying that he kept track of fewer facts than certain of his predecessors—notably Jimmy Carter. "Senator Carter [of the Georgia State Senate] was hardworking. He had pledged . . . to read . . . every bill before he voted on it. To get through the 800 to 1,000 bills before the Senate each year, he took a speed-reading course and kept his promise."[1] The promise, made at the beginning of his political career, was, as Carter later acknowledged, foolish. For a President, it would have been impossible. But only the techniques changed between Atlanta and Washington, not the disposition.

The promise was foolish for a state legislator, to say nothing of a President of the United States, because of the increasing complexity of government. Some facts may suggest what everyone knows. In 1933, the White House staff numbered thirty-seven; by the late seventies, it had reached half a thousand. Calvin Coolidge, according to the White House usher—though revisionists have disputed this —discharged his duties on eleven hours of sleep a night. Carter's predecessor, Gerald Ford, allowed himself five. The effect of this bloat, in the opinion of the gloomy, was to prevent Presidents or candidates from focusing effectively on anything. "Both candidates," wrote the political scientist Willmoore Kendall, "for the most part merely repeat, as they swing from whistle-stop to whistle-stop and television studio to television studio, the policy platitudes that constitute the table-talk in our faculty clubs." Kendall, writing in 1963, saw Congress as the last redoubt of clear-headed, solid-bottomed men, dealing with real problems in a reasonable context. But the tsunami of size had hit Capitol Hill as well. From 1947 to 1975, the number of aides employed by congressmen and congressional committees quadrupled. In an eleven-hour day, a congressional committee reported in 1977, the average representative had eleven minutes free to think; for more than a third of that day, he was scheduled to be in two places at once.

It may be that part of the duty of a leader in the present phase of American history (and in the history of bureaucracy) is to free himself both from the welter of "facts" and from the faculty table talk, and that this can only be done by keeping well back from the grind of routine. Certainly Reagan thought so, and at one point in the first debate, he would say so. But Mondale's charge rankled, and as the campaign moved into October, and toward the first debate, Reagan was prepared to meet it head-on.

The debate was held the seventh of October in Louisville. It was a good Mondale performance. Although his face was a shade of oatmealy gray, he did not look like the exhausted fright he had only six days before in New Brunswick. Mondale had no surprises prepared for Reagan. But he carefully managed to insert into the record everything he wanted to. He brought in Jerry Falwell twice ("Does every woman in

America have to appear before some judge picked by Jerry
Falwell to clear her personal judgment [on abortion]?'") and
leadership continually. Leadership consisted of adopting
Mondale's positions on the issues. "One of the key tests of
leadership," he explained at one point, "is whether one sees
clearly the nature of the problem confronted by our nation.
And perhaps the dominant domestic issue of our time is
. . . these enormous deficits." A President, he added later
on, "must stand for the values of decency that the American
people stand for," which meant trying "to control these
nuclear weapons and lead this world to a safer world." Not
to endorse these "solutions" was not to have any; not even
to acknowledge the problems. Mondale, finally, seemed
confident; at least, confident enough to be gracious. It was
reported later that Carter's old pollster Pat Caddell had
advised the candidate to treat Reagan respectfully because
of his popularity; or perhaps he had learned a lesson from
the bad example of Carter four years earlier. Whatever the
reason, he took a question begging for a combative answer
—what was the most outrageous thing your opponent said
tonight?—and turned it aside. "I'm going to use my time a
little differently. I'm going to give the President some
credit. [He] has done some things to raise the sense of spirit
and morale . . . in this country, and he's entitled to credit
for that. What I think we need, however, is not just that but
to move forward . . . challenging ourselves to get on with
the business of dealing with America's problems."

It is impossible to guess what Mondale would have looked
like up against the normal Reagan. His equations of leadership and the Democratic platform might have stood out for
what they were, the elementary ruses, used by all politicians, of planting axioms. His gentle words on Reagan's
achievements could have sounded like a pre-emptive con-
cession. The normal Reagan was an effective debater. The
list of people he had worsted, or held even, was long, beginning with his Vice-President. The verdict on his clash with
William F. Buckley, Jr., over the Panama Canal was not at
all unanimous. Robert Kennedy, after one encounter, had

asked, "Who put me in with that guy?" The decisive shift in
Reagan's direction in 1980, according to the polls, came
after his handling of Carter, though that may not have been
a fair test, since Carter had painted such a demonic portrait
of him as warmonger and scourge of the poor that all he had
to do was not show up in horns and cloven hoofs in order to
collapse his opponent's case.

But the normal Reagan hadn't come to Louisville. The
Reagan who did, like Mondale, had a collection of things he
wanted to insert into the record; and they were all "essential facts." No medium is less suited than the debate—particularly when televised—to disputes of fact; what can the
debaters say? *Yes, it is. No, it's not. Get an encyclopedia,
we'll look it up.* But Reagan had peach baskets of facts. He
sounded like David Stockman at a budget briefing. He cited
twice as many numbers as Mondale. So fond was he of them,
he dragged them in as postscripts at the tail ends of unrelated answers. After an exchange on the shifting party loyalties of the electorate, he noted that "less than one-quarter
of one percent" of 270,000 farm loans had foreclosed. Wrap-
ping up a discussion of tax rates—tax rates! the home turf!—
he reminded the audience that "during the four years of the
Carter-Mondale administration, medical costs . . . went
up 87 percent." But most of his facts had to do with Social
Security. Mondale had accused Reagan in San Francisco of
wanting to rerun the election of 1980; Reagan in Louisville
sounded as if he wanted to rerun the election of 1964,
trying not to sound like Barry Goldwater. Here Reagan
suffered the just punishments of intellectual compromise.
His remedy for a Social Security system spinning out of
control had been, as he had promised in his 1980 campaign,
to appoint a bipartisan commission. The mechanism of the
commission had allowed its recommendations to sail
through Congress. That was the good side of it. The bad side
was that the recommendations were palliatives, only delay-
ing the day when the hemorrhaging costs would have to be
stanched. Worse, the fundamental fraud and deception of
the whole program—the notion that it was not a transfer

payment but an insurance system; in Walter Mondale's lingo, a "right"—went totally unchallenged. So Reagan found himself fighting the same rearguard actions against demagogy aimed at oldsters that Republicans had struggled with for decades. But not even that would explain Reagan's bringing it up three times, or in such a constipated manner. "And incidentally," he began one notable answer, "I might say that with regard to the 25 percent cuts of Social Security, before I get to the answer of your question, the only 25 percent cut that I know of was accompanying that large 1977 tax increase was a cut of 25 percent in the benefits for every American who was born after 1916." The answer to which this formed the overture was to a question on the characteristics of leadership, and Reagan did manage to say that a leader should not "spend . . . his time in the Oval Office deciding who's going to play tennis on the White House court." Should he spend his time, while addressing the nation, incomprehensibly rehashing the figures of seven-year-old Social Security legislation?

Reagan must have felt uncomfortable with his own strategy; his performance certainly reflected discomfort with something. Transcripts almost always seem more chaotic and less coherent than the spoken words actually were (that is why no President before Eisenhower permitted direct transcripts of press conferences). But Reagan in person that night was worse than Reagan in cold type the next day. He huffed and puffed; he stalled, sometimes stopped dead, under the weight of his facts, or hit them with startling emphasis. He put almost as much fire into his revelation about people born after 1916 as he had into "Where's the rest of me?" (Come to think of it, in 1916 he was five years old.)

The day after the debate, candidates converged on the New York City Columbus Day parade. On a ten-block stretch between the Pierre and Rockefeller Center, there was only one I'M PROUD TO BE AN ITALIAN button; every other message was political, and most of the messages were Mondale's. His supporters had been rounded up to avoid repeating the fiasco of a month ago. Their signs—DON'T LET

JERRY FALWELL PICK THE SUPREME COURT; YOU HAD HIM
ON THE ROPES, FRITZ—were all waved with spirit. The
badly outnumbered Republicans drew together in a clump
before St. Patrick's Cathedral and Saks Fifth Avenue. They
had an Uncle Sam and a Renaissance courtier, both on stilts,
carrying a Reagan-Bush banner; there was also a profusion
of ethnic signs: Armenians, Jews—in Hebrew characters—
and Italian-Americans for Reagan-Bush (one of the latter
hoisted by a black man). They hollered "Four More Years,"
but the Democrats across the street and on either side of
them gave a louder shout of "Four More Weeks." The Republican champions marched first: Senator Alphonse
D'Amato and the Bushes, George with the best spot in the
parade, walking behind Sophia Loren. This stimulated the
minority's enthusiasm, but when they had gone, the majority reasserted itself. The press trucks passed, full of scribbling reporters and snapping cameramen; then the flacks,
marching unnecessarily along the parade route to stir up
enthusiasm; then Ferraro and the new forensic champion,
accompanied by a beaming party of the state's Democratic
mighty: Moynihan, Cuomo, and Koch. It was a long way
from Labor Day.

The burden on the Republican side now shifted unexpectedly to Bush. The perils of his excitement have already
been noted. He was definitely up for his debate with Ferraro, held on the eleventh in Philadelphia. The thought of
Mondale's gloom brought on a particularly severe attack of
boyishness. "If somebody sees a silver lining, [Mondale]
finds a big black cloud. Whine on, harvest moon." Even the
New York *Times* was compelled, in its transcript, to supply
an exclamation point. "I mean," Bush added, "there's a lot
going on, a lot of opportunity." Throughout the debate, he
used body language, all of it chatty, and gestured with his
arms like a beginning karate student. It was these mannerisms more than anything Bush said which fed the impression, become a favorite gibe of the Democrats, that he was a
simple-minded drum majorette for the administration: a
man who had abandoned all his principles to adopt those of

his former foe. Bush's subservience came up in the first question of the debate, which he answered by saying that he supported Reagan enthusiastically because "we're not far apart on anything." Fair enough. Bush's intellectual style, it is true, was less ideological and more cautious than Reagan's, and more open to the influences of faculty table talk. Thus, he could only see Reaganomics, before the fact, as incomprehensible voodoo. But when the balance of the results turned out to be what he himself would have wished, he gave it his support, and offered it, in the debate, as the prime example of Reagan's leadership. "He's really turned this country around. Why Mr. Mondale can't understand that, I don't know."

Ferraro, by contrast, spoke slowly and deliberately, with frequent downward glances. She later explained these inspections of her lectern as an old DA's habit, acquired from consulting case notes; though she was also trying to control her own potential runaway mannerisms, chiefly the speech patterns of Queens. Her task was more complicated than Bush's; she not only had to defend her running mate (this had become easier after the seventh), but, since hers was the only new face among the four standard-bearers, she had to establish herself. For three months, she had been a media phenomenon, a flicker on newscasts, a four-color cover. In the debate, she would become a presence.

Experience told against her. Bush was ready with his rebuttals. When she produced Falwell (who "has been told that he would pick two of our Supreme Court justices"), he pointed out that Sandra Day O'Connor, the only justice Reagan had appointed so far ("superb, outstanding"), had been resisted by the monster of Lynchburg. Condemning Reagan for going three and a half years without having met a Soviet leader, she ticked off a list of leaders the Soviets had met with: "not little people . . . Mitterrand of France and Krohl [sic] of Germany and President Kyprianou of Cyprus." "There's quite a difference," Bush replied, "between Mr. Kyprianou in Cyprus and the leader of the free world" —an answer which ignored Mitterrand and Kohl, though

when push comes to shove, there is also quite a difference
these days between the leader of the free world and the
President of France, or the Chancellor of West Germany,
though it is not politic to say so. More subtly, Ferraro
pegged her discussions of Lebanon and Central America to
trips she had taken there as a congresswoman. The trips had
not been intrinsically important, but they seemed to have
been important to her; seemed, in fact, to constitute a large
part of her relevant knowledge. She referred to them for
the same reason Baudelaire wrote about sin, or Thomas
Wolfe about Asheville: it was all they knew.

Bush overplayed his advantage once, in an exchange on
terrorism. "Let me help you with the difference, Mrs. Ferraro," he had said, between Carter's handling of the hostage
crisis and Reagan's of the Lebanese bombings. He went on
to suggest a distinction—the hostages had been held prisoner by a state, the Lebanese bombers were a terrorist
operation and hence more amorphous. Ferraro bristled, not
at the distinction, but at the offer of help: "I almost resent,
Vice-President Bush, your patronizing attitude that you
have to teach me about foreign policy."

Bush had won the confrontation; he had defended himself against the charge of insincerity and seemed more
knowledgeable than his opponent. The proof was the Democratic reaction: Ferraro said proudly that she had stood
"toe to toe" with her opponent, while Jimmy Carter, the
ghost of elections past, judged it a "toss-up"; so the Republicans, trying to put the best face on things, had spoken after
the Reagan-Mondale debate, with the same credibility. But
what had been won with sober labor was being thrown
away with loose lips. Overnight, it seemed, the whole top of
the Bush operation turned catty. Before the debate, Barbara Bush, chatting with reporters, called Ferraro a "four-
million-dollar—I can't say it, but it rhymes with witch."
Bush's press secretary was not so prudish; he forthrightly
declared that his boss's upcoming opponent was "too
bitchy." Bush himself, enjoying some post-game talk with
union officials on a visit to Elizabeth, New Jersey, confided

that he had "kicked a little ass" in Philadelphia. A mike picked up what Bush later pleaded was only "an old Texas football expression" (a "locker-room vulgarity," intoned the New York *Times*). Suddenly, the nation's highest elected preppy, and what seemed like all his family and staff, were talking like tinkers.

The day after the debate, Ferraro flew to Madison, Wisconsin, to appear with Mondale at a rally on the steps of the state capitol. The leaves of the early-turning trees were the color of old coins. Store signs testified to the presence of Mondale's countrymen—Olson, Hansen. One of the warm-up speakers looked forward to a "Norwegian in the White House." The podium stood in an angle of the cross-shaped capitol, facing an enormous crowd—police estimated 30,000—spread over the soft, damp lawn. Kids climbed into the crooks of trees. One imaginative fan held a poster knockoff of Delacroix's "Liberty Leading the People," with Ferraro as Liberty, though, needless to say, the artist had added some clothes; in addition, one of the bayonets of Liberty's followers had sprouted a pennant labeled ERA.

Mondale was elated, laughing at his own jokes with little guttural chuckles. Most of these concerned Harry Truman. Reagan had taken a whistle-stop swing through Ohio on the same train Truman had used in 1948. Mondale called it the "great train robbery. Mr. Reagan, you may be on the right train, but you're on the wrong track." This gave him a chance to quote a Truman line from that campaign. There was a toy, Truman had said, called the floogie bird, "which I'm sure you all have seen." It was labeled "I fly backwards" and was "only interested in where it's been"—just like the Republicans. Mondale couldn't even update his jokes.

"The middle class," he said, more seriously, "was shrinking. That's why it's not enough to congratulate ourselves. We must challenge ourselves." There followed a list of challenges. "This election is not about pom-poms and jelly beans, it's about toxic wastes causing cancer." It was not about TV "makeup," but "students who need help to go on to college"; not about "amber waves of grain," but farmers having the "worst year ever"; not "who's proud of our Olympic athletes," but the "Civil Rights Act that opened doors to let all Americans compete"; not "sending a teacher into space," but "educating children right here on earth"; not "Republicans putting commercials on TV," but "Jerry Falwell putting justices on the Supreme Court"; not "arm wrestling," but "arms control." (Curiously, Mondale, who had brought up the middle class in the first place, had only one issue—student loans—that might be considered of special interest to that group. Arms control and the Court affected everybody, according to ideological predilection; waste dumps, farm subsidies, affirmative action, and Falwell were topics aimed at subgroups.) "Is this homecoming weekend?" he asked. *Yes.* "Who're you playing?" *Minnesota.* "Let's go on to the next subject." He closed. "If you believe America is not a jungle . . . [that] we're a family and that we care for one another, pull our lever" (thank you, Mario). "The future of our country is made in Heaven. We have everything we need, except the leadership to take us there. Now for the main event, the fighter from Philly."

It was true; Ferraro was still, after the wear and tear of three months—after her husband, the Church, and the Vice-President—the main event in Mondale's campaign, and the crowd uncorked its biggest yell for her. Mondale and Ferraro were working out the etiquette of heterosexual campaigning. No backslapping; no hands held overhead; only reserved greetings, which would suggest neither lechery nor patriarchy.

"I beat George Bush," she began pertly. "And George Bush beat Ronald Reagan." Senator Laxalt, displeased with Reagan's tactics, had given him a rebuke; unfortunately for Reagan, he had done it publicly. "The President," Laxalt had said, "was brutalized by a briefing process which smothered him with facts." "Now I ask you," Ferraro said, after quoting Laxalt with relish, "when is it considered cruel and unusual punishment for a President to learn the facts he needs to govern?"

She gave her outline of the main pledges of the Mondale-

Ferraro campaign: to "keep faith" with working people; to stop Star Wars (not "extend the arms race" into space); to institute a nuclear freeze; to discontinue the "covert war" against Nicaragua (this got the biggest cheer). "Every now and then, a leader must swim against the tide. He must remind us not only" of "what is great in America, but what we must do to make it greater." Mondale had fought, as a senator, for day care and for the Legal Services Corporation; as Vice-President, he had fought to take in the boat people. (The best time to have helped the boat people was during the Vietnam War, while they were still land people.) His prescience had also extended to MIRVed missiles, which he had opposed. "If we'd listened to Walter Mondale then, we'd be safer today. . . . Leaders," she concluded, "must take chances. The most recent chance he took" was when he "selected me to be his Vice-President. When I become America's first female Vice-President, we can thank Walter Mondale."

A high school band struck up a rather lugubrious "America the Beautiful," and Ferraro held an arm aloft as if she were making a fist.

She flew from Madison to Chicago, where she appeared on all three evening news shows. She had been much more relaxed at the rally than in the debate, and she was most relaxed on camera alone with an interviewer. With ease her accent returned. "You saw George Bush talkinabou Worl Series; that's nowhawe're talkinabou, we're talkinabou arms control"—but on the whole, she profited by the trade-off. She outlined, on one channel, the other foreign-policy issues she and Mondale were talkinabou—Reagan's failure to meet with the Soviet leaders; wasteful defense spending; "adventurism" in Central America; the Beirut bungle; human rights in South Africa and the Philippines—and, on another channel, put Bush's vulgarity definitively in its place: "I couldn't get away with that kind of thing when I was a kid."

Ferraro went that night to a rally in a high school in Hinsdale, a western suburb. The anti-abortionists were

waiting, it seemed, outside (I AM ADOPTED, NOT ABORTED;
R.I.P. GERALDINE'S KIDS—1.7 MILLION ABORTIONS); in the
slow moments of the rally, their cries could be heard like a
distant murmur. The evening also honored another woman
politician, Eleanor Roosevelt, who had been born a hundred years ago that day. Ferraro was introduced by Julianna
Roosevelt, a descendant, who saw in 1984's "massive unemployment" the "same social and economic distress my
great-grandmother saw firsthand." (Not quite as massive;
the unemployment rate in 1938, after six years of the New
Deal, was 19 percent; in 1982, at the height of Reagan's
recession, it was 10 percent.) Ferraro took up the theme of
Eleanor. "Eleanor Roosevelt fought for the Declaration of
Human Rights at the UN." That had been such a success
that "today, to honor her ideals, we should stand for human
rights in El Salvador and South Africa.

"It's never too early to talk about human rights . . ."

"What about abortion?" The question burst out, as if from
nowhere. "What about abortion?" Repeated, it proved to
come from a stout young man standing with the overflow
crowd in front of the press risers.

Ferraro went on, but so did he. "What about the unborn?
What about civil rights for them?" Supporters swarmed to
the spot like phagocytes, as if surrounding him would muffle
him; to no avail. The crowd began to chant, "Ger-*ry*,
Ger-*ry*," which silenced him, but also her.

This first of many interruptions was the most easily resolved. "He obviously feels very strongly," Ferraro managed to say when her audience had quieted. "Let's meet
with him afterwards." This satisfied supporters and heckler.
She finished with Eleanor Roosevelt and her stump speech,
and saw him for fifteen minutes in the office of the school's
principal. He was, she told the press, a medical student at
Northwestern, "very concerned" about the issue, and "very
cordial." "I was concerned," she added, "I was not able to
exercise my constitutional right of free speech."

Next morning's rally was in Niles, north of Chicago and
just east of Germany, at a catering hall whose name was all

z's and y's. The crowd waved red carnations, and a band of quacking clarinets played polkas. "They tell me," Ferraro began, "the Przybylo family pirogi is second only to the Ferraro family ravioli." She added to her foreign-policy concerns a paragraph in praise of Solidarity, though, to be sure, she noted that in office she would "object not only to Soviet gulags" but to the "racist apartheid regime" in South Africa. "Like many of you, my father came to America from another land." Like them, he had upheld the "bedrock values": neighborliness, law-abidingness, concern for the family. This was her segue into Reagan's budget cutting, which hurt families. But again there came the cry: "What about the unborn?" "When you slash day care . . ." "What about the unborn?" "What *about* the unborn?" Democrats asked scornfully; but in a tight, low-ceilinged room with a booming sound system, Ferraro was better able to handle the situation herself. "Okay, ladies [the hecklers, two of them this time, were women]—the other night on national television"—the debate—"I answered that question about" abortion. "I also spoke about the Constitution of the United States and the various freedoms it guarantees. One is freedom of speech. . . . My father loved this country so much he bought war bonds" in World War II. "Those bonds dropped bombs on Italy and his parents' house, but he loved this country so much. My mother," she echoed her putdown of Bush, "also insisted on teaching me to be polite to other people. So"—she returned to the Constitution—"if you'll allow me to exercise my freedom of speech, I'm sure the people in this room will allow you the same freedom." But another pair of hecklers, stationed at the opposite end, tried to seize their freedom early. "What about abortion!" Shouts and cries of "Get out of here!" In a minute, they had gotten (or were gotten) out. The audience sang, *"Sto lat, sto lat,* may you live to be a hundred."

Outside, some twenty protesters had posted themselves and their rights across the street from the exit, in front of a cemetery wall. A man with a bullhorn led chants of "Life, Death, Ferraro—No." One sign declared simply, POLISH-

AMERICANS ARE PRO-LIFE; others incorporated art: LORD
HAVE MERCY over a bleeding fetus. Some attacked: PER-
SONALLY OPPOSED—ABORTION PUSHER, on a caricature of
Ferraro; THE LITTLE MAFFIA, under another bleeding fetus.
The campaign had not been free of this kind of thing. The
Democrats had been dishing it out for months. Hart and
Mondale had both as much as called Reagan illiterate; Jack-
son had called the administration a "repressive regime."
The crowds, the signs, and the buttons were as always much
tougher. JANE WYMAN WAS RIGHT had read a message on
one lapel inside Przybylo's. Reagan was regularly depicted
as a murderer, a pig, a dunce; they'd been wearing FUCK
REAGAN buttons in San Francisco, and they would be selling
REAGAN SUCKS buttons on street corners in the Village.
There is probably a historical reason why Republicans, if
only for this political phase, are more genteel. The great
inflammatory charge of the right-wing—treason—was, by
an enormous social effort, segregated from polite discourse
in the fifties as "McCarthyism," and confined ultimately to
the John Birch Society. The left never underwent such a
purgative; its devil rhetoric—once having chiefly to do with
economic exploitation, but now also including warmonger-
ing—remains available, as the appetite to employ it wanes
or waxes. Liberal self-restraint suffers in consequence. But
the Republicans had also had a share in this year's slinging;
there were the Bushes' cracks, as well as a rash of obscene
buttons and jokes about the first male-female ticket (THE
THREE BIGGEST BOOBS IN WASHINGTON was a popular one
in Dallas). After ten months of reserved tenacity, the right-
to-lifers were beginning to reach these levels of vitupera-
tion. FERRARO, said a sign in Niles, YOU CAN'T BE A CATHO-
LIC AND PRO-ABORTION—that was one source of bitterness.
Her sex was perhaps another: as much as for feminists,
abortion was for right-to-lifers a woman's issue: to one, a
right; to the other, a failure of a duty. Half a dozen Ferraro
supporters came out in mid-protest to heckle the hecklers,
chanting, "Ger-*ry,* Ger-*ry,*" and, when the anti-abortionists
switched to "Four More Years," "Three More Weeks." A

pair crossed the street with a long, large Ferraro banner, which they held up to hide the protest. A woman tore it, and there were shoves, which a cop's frown stopped. But the competing groups continued to jostle, sidling in front of each other, thrusting their signs into the disputed sight lines.

Ferraro had cited, that morning and the night before, her constitutional rights. How, using the Constitution, would she have sorted out the scuffle on the sidewalk? How would Nat Hentoff? The answer is, they couldn't. Fundamental law takes care of a society's principles; it gives civility direction; but the daily work must be done by civility. The mark of a civilized mind, wrote Mill, is its ability to entertain two contradictory propositions at once. The mark of civil behavior is the ability of members of the same community to tolerate each other's contradictory opinions. Civility is not the same as politeness, or manners. They express unthinking convention, what is done or not done, because everyone does or fails to do it—the morality of head counts. Civility is self-conscious; it knows what it does. In the case of abortion, it recognizes that the gulf between contending sides is fundamental and irreconcilable, *and yet* that the partisans of both positions have more in common, as Americans, than the sum of their differences; hence, they are entitled to their expressions. (Politeness would ignore the differences or, depending on one's set, ignore the opposition.) Ferraro was nearer the truth when she appealed to her mother than when she recalled her rights-loving, war-bond-buying father.

Not everyone is entitled to civil consideration. People whose view of the world is founded on hatred of the society —Farrakhans, Communists—forfeit their right to it. Civility also does not require unrelieved sobriety. Office seekers can stand to be heckled and booed; within limits, they have asked for it. (Walter Mondale was particularly unsuited to complain of his rough reception at USC. During the four years previous, Caspar Weinberger and Jeane Kirkpatrick had been unable even to appear, owing to threatened dis-

ruptions, at Harvard and Smith, neither receiving a peep of
support from that beleaguered civil libertarian.) Politicians
should not, however, be silenced, and the abuse directed at
them must not seek to expel them from the human community. No pigs; and no Mafia-murdered fetuses. After a longish delay, Ferraro's motorcade pulled out. A shout followed:
". . . baby butcher."

She finished the day, and the trip, in Iowa, at the Jefferson-Jackson Day dinner in Ames: 1,600 Democrats sat on
the floor of Iowa State's basketball coliseum, and it seemed
as if most of them introduced her. The building was phara-
onic, vast; like a tomb, or a set from *Citizen Kane.* Applause
in that cavity pattered like rain. Tom Harkin, the senatorial
candidate, whose hopes had been heightened by the recently revealed fact that his Moral Majoritarian opponent
had once frequented a massage parlor, got two standing
ovations from the dark, dwarfed crowd: one for a promise to
"freeze right now"; the other with the pledge that "Jerry
Falwell will not write prayers" for the public schools.

Ferraro had acquired a new addition to her stump
speech, thanks to a Reagan boner. Testing a mike for one of
his weekly radio broadcasts, Reagan had said, "We have
declared the Soviet Union illegal. The bombing starts in five
minutes." "Reagan said it was a joke," Ferraro admonished
him. "But the American people shuddered; the European
allies were shocked. . . . We cannot afford a President who
forgets he is President even for a minute."

Ferraro was listless (a doctor had visited her at the Hotel
Savery in Des Moines), and her charge, really, was old hat—
Reagan's joke had revealed nothing about his notions of an
ideal world that America (or the Soviet Union) did not already know. But the assembled Democrats applauded vigorously in that void, for she was their ticket, and the ticket
was on a roll.

Reagan had managed to accomplish in one night what
Mondale had failed to do in a month and a half—to breathe
a little life into the leadership issue. For Mondale, "leader-

ship" was a matter of ideology disguised as a matter of competence. Reagan's tongue-tied performance had suddenly made it a matter of health.

Questions of health and age had dogged Reagan through the early phase of his 1980 campaign. "I'm up for the eighties," Bush would bubble *(and Reagan,* whispered his subtext, *is up for the fifties);* Jerry Brown liked to point out that he would not reach Reagan's age until the twenty-first century. Reagan, if elected, would become the oldest man to be inaugurated; the oldest up till that time, William Henry Harrison, had died thirty days after taking the oath of office, a not very auspicious precedent. Concern over Reagan's age coincided with the enervation of his campaign. After New Hampshire, it had vanished; after his recovery from Hinckley's bullets, it had seemed like a joke. Now it all came flooding back. *The Wall Street Journal,* the morning after the debate, ran a long health story, obviously prepared in advance in case some loss of physical or mental edge occurred, and made timely with the reactions of "experts." "I am very concerned," said one, "as a psychologist." Another helpfully suggested a few simple senility tests Reagan might take, such as counting backwards from 100 by sevens. Republicans pointed out, in vain, that Deng Xiaoping was an energetic eighty; that Reagan's health had always been and was still excellent; that Mondale's, for that matter, was not so good (he suffered from high blood pressure, for which he popped three different pills a day). The potential problem was not fantastic. Twice already in this century—in Reagan's lifetime, if not in anyone else's—the country had had two incapacitated leaders. Woodrow Wilson, after a series of strokes, spent his last two years in office a nonfunctioning wreck. Franklin D. Roosevelt began deteriorating physically as early as 1940; by 1944, he was in bed eighteen hours a day.

There was a danger for Mondale in the age issue: what Reagan had raised, Reagan could lay to rest. Before Reagan got the chance, Mondale slipped of his own.

The Al Smith Dinner, a charity fund-raiser hosted every

fall by the archbishop of New York, came a week after the
Bush-Ferraro debate, on October 18. Over the years, the
dinner had become a political and social event, with its own
intricate Kremlinology based on who sat where ("If there
was a bomb," murmured a flack attending the 1984 dinner,
"*W* would have nothing to write about"). Every four years,
the local socialites, businessmen, publishers, and politicians
were joined by the presidential candidates. Two days before the dinner, Mondale let it be known that he would be
spending the night of the eighteenth boning up for his
rematch with Reagan, though he would be happy to send
Ferraro in his stead. Perhaps Mondale truly needed to study
(all those essential facts). Perhaps he had had enough of
Catholic bishops for one campaign. What it most looked
like, though, was an attempt to put his running mate, still
fresh from her theological discussions, on the same dais with
her tormentor, Archbishop O'Connor. O'Connor let it be
known in turn that the second string really would not do—
with the result that only one candidate attended, and an
evening of non-partisan after-dinner joke-telling became a
minor campaign event.

The affair, held at the Waldorf, was two kinds of formal
(white tie for the celebrities on the dais, black tie for the
peons), and the Grand Ballroom looked like the Ross Ice
Shelf in breeding season. O'Connor, in full archiepiscopal
purple, read a letter of regret from Mondale. ("What about
Gerry?" cried a Democratic voice from a table of priests.)
Reagan forsook the traditional light tone of the event to
repeat his campaign film's tribute to Cardinal Cooke, who
had promised, the last time they met, to keep praying for
him "when I join the Lord"—though on second thought,
Cooke conceded he was maybe being "a little presumptu-
ous." "Eleven days later," Reagan went on huskily, "he
died. None of us have any doubt he joined the Lord."
O'Connor brought the evening back to form. Cooke "had
no doubt he would be with the Lord; it was *you* he was
worried about." Mondale's missing out on these pleasant-
ries was, objectively, a small blunder. But a man whose

hopes depended on unbroken progress could not afford a blunder, even if Reagan managed not to recover.

Mondale's main theme for the second debate, the night of the twenty-first in Kansas City, was what it had been in Louisville—leadership. He was in the position of a last-seeded team which had lucked into the finals of a tournament; there had been no reason to believe the leadership strategy would work; but there was also no reason to believe that any other strategy would work either. So Mondale, like Podunk High, stayed with what had produced results. The first question gave him a chance to pursue it. A CIA operative—not a regular agent, but an "asset" on contract with the Agency—had drawn up a guide to guerrilla tactics, for the use of the Nicaraguan Contras. The first draft, subsequently withdrawn, had included instructions on political murder. Mondale hit the manual hard; Reagan apparently should have been at the copy editor's desk himself. "How can something this serious occur . . . and have a President of the United States . . . say he didn't know? A President must know these things."

The concealed ideology here was quite close to the surface. The manual confirmed all the Democrats' favorite notions of America's anti-Communist allies: either they are corrupt, like Somoza or Thieu, or, as in this case, brutal (ideally both). Mondale would be against helping the Contras, though, if they were Boy Scouts. In her debate with Bush, Ferraro had addressed the subject with her usual bluntness. "The CIA is there . . . to protect our government; not to subvert other governments." She may have been thinking, with the Carter State Department, that the Sandinistas enjoyed the legitimacy conferred by the forces of history and progress. Whatever her thoughts on legitimacy, her position—and Mondale's—gave the United States no maneuvering room. Confronted by a progressive regime that had become a pain in the neck, they had no options between tolerance and outright war.

Mondale became the prudent manager again toward the end of the debate when the talk turned to space defense.

Reagan, in first proposing the new strategic concept, had gone to the logical end, and proposed to offer it, once developed, to the Soviet Union. During the debate, he repeated the offer again. "What if we can come up with a weapon that renders . . . missiles obsolete? . . . Why not say, 'Look: here's what we can do, we'll even give it to you; now will you sit down with us, and once and for all get rid . . . of these nuclear weapons?' " All Mondale's hawkish feathers ruffled. "Any research or development along the Star Wars scheme would inevitably involve our most advanced computers. . . . I would not let the Soviet Union get their hands on" them. But the hidden argument—and not so deeply hidden—was moral. "Why don't we stop this madness now," he finished his answer, "and keep the heavens free from war?" Not "the skies," or "space," but "the heavens," as in "God's neighborhood." Mondale troweled both arguments into one sentence just before the closing statements. "If you want a tough President [=in touch and in charge] who uses that strength to . . . draw the line in the heavens [=someone on God's side], vote for Walter Mondale."

Paul Laxalt's negative review of the first debate had given Ferraro the material for many a humiliating joke. But it had had the intended effect. Reagan stuck, throughout the second, to his notion of what were essential facts, not Mondale's (proving, for the last time in the campaign, that the only role you can convincingly play is yourself). "I'm not a scientist," he said, disclaiming any prior commitments to the kind or location of nuclear defensive weapons. "That's what a President's supposed to know," replied Mondale, hoarse from repetition. It was not persuasive. (Who had been the last scientist President? Jimmy Carter, the nuclear physicist.) Reagan knew what he needed to: he was on top of the developments in the story of the guerrilla manual, and he gave a good defense of his bad Lebanese policy. "We went in, with the multinational force, to help remove . . . more than thirteen thousand terrorists. We departed and then the government of Lebanon asked us back in as a stabilizing force while they . . . sought to get the foreign forces all the way out. . . . We were succeeding and that was why the terrorist acts began."

Along the way, Reagan gave, for those who would attend to it, an explanation of his thoughts concerning the eschatology of his fundamentalist supporters. Did he believe, he was asked, in "some kind of biblical Armageddon," toward which the world was swiftly heading? Such talk, he replied, was "the result of just some philosophical discussions with people who are interested in the same things. . . . No one knows," he added, falling back on modernist modes of biblical criticism, whether Armageddon "is a thousand years away or day after tomorrow. So I never seriously warned and said we must plan" for it. It was the answer of an eighteenth-century Tory squire, questioned suddenly over a bowl of bishop about the 39 Articles. Of course he supported them; but that wouldn't stop him from collecting his rents.

The debate yielded two surprises, both sprung on Mondale. Henry Trewhitt, the diplomatic correspondent of the Baltimore *Sun*, asked why, if he was such a take-charge guy, he had never repudiated Jackson's diplomatic forays. He had not done so because he was afraid of losing votes—that was the only honest answer Mondale could make. Naturally, he did not make it. "Jesse Jackson is an independent person. I don't control him. Let's talk about people we do control." The person he had in mind was Bush, who, in the same answer in which he had presumed to instruct Ferraro on Lebanon, had accused her and her running mate of saying that the marines at the Beirut airport died "in shame." They had said that the United States had suffered a "humiliation." But that was not the same thing, and Mondale and Ferraro had demanded an apology, which Bush had not given. The effect of Mondale's indignation now was diminished by the fact that Bush had only handled the challenge in precisely the same way that Mondale had handled his Jackson problem. Hit-and-run drivers make bad traffic cops.

Mondale may still have been limping from an earlier

collision, also set up by Trewhitt. "Mr. President," the reporter began, "I want to raise an issue that I think has been
lurking out there for two or three weeks, and cast it specifically in national security terms. You are already the oldest
President in history. . . . President Kennedy had to go for
days on end with very little sleep during the Cuban missile
crisis. Is there any doubt in your mind that you would be
able to function in such circumstances?"

Reagan telegraphs most of his jokes, the duck of the head
becoming an anticipatory chuckle, and so he did now. "Not
at all, Mr. Trewhitt, and I want you to know that also I will
not make age an issue of this campaign. I am not going to
exploit for political purposes [the duck, the chuckle] my
opponent's youth and inexperience."

At that moment, the hearts of men of all persuasions had
to beat for Walter Mondale. For more than two years, he
had articulated a coherent and lucid liberal program, which
had impressed no one beyond the hard core of his own
party. For six weeks, he had tried expressing his beliefs in
the more palatable idiom of a discussion of leadership, also
with no results whatever. Reagan himself had made leadership a real issue with a performance that seemed fogbound
in senility. The fog had lifted, as a result of a normal evening
—a Reagan performance like every other for the last
twenty years—and blown away finally before a laugh. One
had to admire Mondale, for he laughed too. Reagan's con-
cluding statement, a slice of his stump speech in praise of
America's youth, which rambled so far over the time limit
that the moderator cut him off in mid-career, had, in its
loping, open-ended form, a bizarre, almost stoned quality.
Too late to affect the outcome (wish we looked like that at
seventy-three).

Reagan took to the road, for the next-to-last campaign
swing of his life, the day after the debate, flying out to
California, then moving up the coast to Portland and Seattle
(there is nothing wrong with the cities of the West Coast
that rolling them all into one wouldn't cure; as they are,
several of them would make attractive outer boroughs),

finishing in Columbus, Ohio, and so home. He too was shadowed by hecklers. In Portland, their signs called attention to his age: THE FINGER ON THE BUTTON IS SENILE; RAYGUN IS VERY OLD. Yesterday's issue. They shouted, singly and in unison: *people are dying in Central America, people are hungry;* also: *fascist pig,* and *liar, liar, pants on fire.* In Seattle, half a dozen women in gray face makeup and black robes kept up a cat wail of mourning. They sounded like graduates of the San Francisco march against war in Central America; TV cameras turned to capture their moment of celebrity. Reagan handled them like an infielder practicing his throw to first. "In these big buildings," he observed in Seattle, "there's an echo."

The tone of his stump speech was inclusive and disdainful of party lines: not non-partisan so much as supra-partisan. "I was a Democrat once," he echoed his acceptance speech; "in fact, for a greater part of my life. And I always respected that party. But in [those] days, its leaders weren't the blame-America-first crowd." Thank you, Jeane. "They knew the difference between freedom and tyranny, and they stood up for one and damned the other. To all the good Democrats who respect that tradition . . . we're asking you to come join us." In Seattle, he added a paean to the late Scoop Jackson. "On nearly every occasion," Jackson "cast [his] vote for America's defense." Walter Mondale, by contrast, when he was in the Senate, had sided, on thirty-seven out of thirty-eight defense spending votes, with George McGovern. *Boo.* "So if you like George McGovern's defense policies, you'll love my opponent's." No one in the audience —or at least, no one with an unmade-up face—seemed to. (The B-1 bomber, Reagan added, employed 5,000 people in the state of Washington.)

Reagan's criticisms were reserved for Mondale personally. As a senator, he had voted sixteen times to raise taxes. "But this year, he's outdone himself." Reagan had a figure: "if he's to keep all the promises he's made to this group and that," it would cost every household $150 a month—"like

having a second mortgage. And [under] the Mondale mortgage, there would be a lot of foreclosures."

Mondale's view of the world beyond the tax code was
epitomized by a series of reactions to international crises, all
weak or confused: condemning the Grenada invasion; con-
fessing to being "baffled" by the *Anschluss* of Afghanistan.
"After the Sandinista revolution in Nicaragua, he praised it,
saying, 'Winds of democratic progress are stirring . . .'"
But the Sandinistas "immediately began to . . . slaughter
the Miskito Indians, abuse and deport church leaders, slan-
der the Pope, practice anti-Semitism, and move to kill free
speech." Why wasn't Mondale "speaking out about that
fresh wind now?" Tucked away in the text were two items
of Reagan's future agenda, things he would want in his
second term: a line-item veto and urban enterprise zones.
But the speech as a whole was about tendencies: Mondale's
toward "torpor, timidity, and taxes," his toward their oppo-
sites.

October 24, thirteen days before the election, Reagan
appeared at a rally on the campus of Ohio State, in an arena
as tall as a home run, filled with roaring, cheering students.
Volunteers from the Ohio State Marching Band provided
the music, a ton of brass, exact as a stopwatch. They swung
their horns in patterns so precise that one sneeze in the
trombone section would have caused a cat's cradle of tan-
gled slides; on a rendition of "All Night Long," they *sang*
the Spanish breaks. (I could only recall the band of my alma
mater, and its ragtag Ivy League insouciance, which we
liked to think of as wit, and which actually became so once,
during a Brown game, for which there was enough money
in the kitty to send only the announcer to Providence; the
show consisted of his descriptions, backed by taped music,
of the formations that the Yale Invisible Marching Band was
producing on the empty field: the Mona Lisa, the Battle of
Borodino, the face of God. The Buckeyes could have done
them visibly.) The usual parade of auxiliaries and dignitaries
streamed across the platform: congressional hopefuls
scrambling for a bite of airtime; veterans the cameras had

long ago passed by—none longer ago than John Bricker, ninety-one, in a wheelchair, with a face like old ivory, Republican vice-presidential candidate in 1944. Football coach Woody Hayes, whose popularity even in retirement was impervious to time's assaults—WOODY HAYES FOR SECRETARY OF DEFENSE, a sign saluted him—gave Reagan his highest praise. "By studying his term in office, you'll find he's a team player." The crowd practiced wave cheers, rolling their clamors around the arena, while on the highest balcony, the most remotely situated band of hecklers chanted, "We Want Peace" (they might as well have been at Michigan State). The last in the procession was Reagan.

The shout that went up outthundered the welcome given Hayes, and was almost half as loud as the band. The cause of the uproar worked the platform deferentially, as if he were some congresswoman's husband, or Woody Hayes's brother, seeming to realize only when he turned around that the all-enveloping cacophony had something to do with him. All through his speech, the distant resistance kept up a dissenting undertone. "Cut the deficit!" one of them was even heard to cry, to such unnatural extremes does partisanship go.

"You know, it's gonna break their hearts," Reagan interjected mildly, "but I can't understand a word they're saying." The crowd seemed to understand his words. "America is back, a giant re-emergent on the scene. Our country is powerful in its renewed spirits, powerful in its economy, powerful in the world economy, and powerful in its ability to defend itself and secure the peace." *Yay.* ". . . The turn we made in 1980 was right. We were right to take command of the ship to stop its aimless drift . . . and we were right when we stopped sending out SOS and started saying U.S.A." *U.S.A., U.S.A., U.S.A.* ". . . I'm proud to say that in these last four years, not one square inch of territory has been lost to Communist aggression." Standing ovation. Reagan said his good words about Democrats (what did Bricker think of that?), then gave the peroration he hadn't been able to at the end of the last debate. "To the young people of

America, let me say, nothing has touched our hearts more than your wonderful support." *Yay.* "You are truly something new on the scene. Your idealism and your love of country are unsurpassed." We must "make certain that you have an America that is every bit as full of opportunity and hope and confidence and dreams as we had when we were your age."

The support Reagan enjoyed among college kids, of which the rally at Ohio State was a not untypical manifestation, was in many ways the bitterest pill for his enemies to swallow. College kids—they put on gray makeup, and carried cardboard coffins, and listened to "protest" songs; they were "passionate" and "idealistic," repositories of Consciousness III (consult any twenty-year-old issue of *Life, Look,* or *Time* for the relevant effusions). Or they should be; not whooping tax cuts and containment. The preferred explanation of this betrayal was economic/moral: kids today only wanted to grub for money, which had dulled their sensibilities.

Compared to the Age of Aquarius, the classes of '85 to '89 were undoubtedly more career-oriented. But that change in attitude had happened at least a decade ago, with no discernible political effects. In the fall of 1975, as a hack of the Yale Political Union, I dutifully marched through the freshman dormitories the week before classes began, urging people to join up; one young man regretfully told me that although it sounded interesting, he wouldn't have time, since he was going to be going to law school. If he actually did go, he probably became one of the Hart yuppies boogying at the Red Parrot. The cause of Reagan's campus popularity was simpler than economics. The college students liked feeling good about America as much as their elders. They liked chanting *U.S.A;* and they liked the man whose administration had given them some reason for doing it. A second point worth keeping in mind was that the political opinions of nineteen-year-olds, now as in 1965, have no intrinsic significance; but that is a problem only for those who were enamored of them in the guitars-and-coffins phase.

The band played "The Stars and Stripes Forever," better than Sousa ever heard it; advance men in the rafters struggled with recalcitrant bags of balloons, and Reagan flew back to Washington.

The last Democratic campaign stop in New York State is traditionally a rally in the Garment District. The International Ladies' Garment Workers' Union could not do anything about the polls, but they could try to get out the largest crowd in the rally's history, which they did. From the pre-speech podium procession, it seemed more like a rally sponsored by Actors Equity, as a stream of stars and starlets acknowledged their solidarity with the Mondale campaign (and had their *Playbill* bios read: ". . . portrayed John Belushi's wife . . . award-winning author of *Torch Song Trilogy* . . ."). John Zaccaro was introduced, to tepid applause; his mother-in-law, the former garment worker, fared better. Under a gray sky, and the gray façades of downtown pre-glass New York, his wife and her running mate gave it their last shot.

It would be said later that Mondale's fortunes would have been different at that point if he had had a different face or manner. Yes, there were moments when he looked like a raccoon and sounded like a disposal; and for all his ribbing of Reagan's reading habits, he gave no evidence of having seriously perused a book since Macalester College, or of being deeply affected by the ones he had. Yet Mondale the campaigner had his strengths: a dry wit that sometimes showed; a speaking style that was vigorous, if unmodulated. (His opponents had their own problems: Reagan's occasional fuddlement, Bush's frenzies.) Most important of all, Mondale had a conviction and a world view which had carried him, not the god-faced Hollings or the graduate-schooled Hart, to the Garment District platform. His strengths had taken him, in spite of all weaknesses, to the leadership of his party; his strengths, not his weaknesses,

would propel him to the leadership of the country—or fail
to.

"I can feel victory in the air. . . . We're gonna win, because we're right. . . . Polls don't vote, people do." As be-
fits a labor union rally, he spoke of jobs. America was "no
longer exporting steel and manufactured goods." The Seventh Avenue IRT rumbled beneath him; perhaps one of the
new Japanese subway cars. "We're exporting jobs. This
President refuses to do a single thing about it. I want to be
the President" who brings "the future back to this country." Falwell, one last time: Reagan had "accused me of
being soft on anti-Semitism" (rather: soft on anti-Semites),
charges that were "false and contemptible. . . . I've stood
up to those radical preachers so close to this President. . . .
Jerry Falwell, . . . keep your nose out of the personal life
of the people of this country." A kick at the covert war in
Nicaragua, and the "crazy Star Wars-into-the-heavens program," and he was done. The five-block-long crowd dispersed, freeing streets and sidewalks for clothes racks.

It is always better, as Mayor Koch said, to win than to lose.
Mondale assailed the polls for picking the winner so far
ahead of time—with some justice, as far as the typical mass-
audience poll was concerned. As instant readouts of the
American mind, Gallup, Harris, and the rest are often mis-
taken; as predictors, they are worthless. They are prey to
the biases of the poll takers; Lou Harris has been spotting
last-minute Democratic surges for twenty years. They have
not found a way to close the gap between popular sentiment, which is what everyone thinks, and public opinion,
which is what everyone thinks everyone else thinks.
(Should citizens be allowed to carry guns in self-defense?
Maybe, maybe not, the average New Yorker might say,
straightening his public tie. But when a pistol-packing com-
muter blew four hoods away on the subway, the city was
ready to elect him mayor, even when it turned out he had
shot some of his menacers in the back.) There were at least
two people in America, however—Reagan and Mondale—

who had access to better goods, the best polls that only very large sums of money could buy: samples of thousands of voters, taken daily, for two solid weeks up to election day. Polling of such comprehensiveness can give an accurate snapshot of the voters' disposition. Whether Mondale allowed himself to digest the news is another question. Presumably Reagan faced no psychological impediment.

The rest of us got the word Tuesday night. If you went out for dinner, it was over by coffee. All evening, the color assigned to states that had gone for Reagan marched across the network maps like a sunrise. At one point, one station was calling only the District of Columbia for Mondale, but he was spared this humiliation, carrying Minnesota by a bare margin as well: both his homes.

Fans of presidential trivia noted the following points. Reagan's forty-nine states, all but one, tied the record, set by Richard Nixon in 1972; his total of 525 electoral votes set a new one. His percentage of the popular vote only came in fifth place: Johnson, Nixon, Roosevelt (in 1936), and Harding all did better. The poorness of Mondale's showing was exaggerated in the Electoral College, where he won only 13 votes, by the withering of regionalism: Vermonters and South Carolinians no longer march to the polls with Shiloh in their hearts, so failures fail everywhere. Only one major-party candidate in a two-man race—Alf Landon—won fewer electoral votes. Mondale's total even fell rather far down on the list of third-party candidates—tied with Robert La Follette, and two votes behind Harry Flood Byrd; far behind Strom Thurmond,* George Wallace, and General James B. Weaver.

At half past eleven, EST, Mondale conceded in St. Paul, where he had formally announced his candidacy twenty months earlier; a little long-windedly (he began slipping into the stump speech about midway) but with a certain haggard dignity. "In the seeds of every victory are the seeds

---

* Fans of vice-presidential trivia noted that the South Carolina senator had also been a more successful candidate than Geraldine Ferraro, since 14 of Byrd's electors in 1960 cast their votes for Vice-President for Thurmond.

of defeat; in every defeat are to be found the seeds of victory. . . . Good night, and God bless you, and God bless America." In Sacramento, Reagan paused at one point to consider his opponent's plight with unfeigned concern. Then he turned to an aide. "Why didn't we schedule more trips to Minnesota?"

10
Reagan in the White House: The Future

Fans of journalistic trivia will have noted that the press appears but seldom in this account. The reason is that no one paid much attention to it.

Many Americans—mostly conservatives, but also the thither left—believe that the press is biased. Of course they are correct. The culture and milieu of journalism is almost as biased as that of the academy; its perceptions are so pervasively and deeply skewed that when it feels even-handedness settling in, it worries. Thus Lou Cannon, fair and perceptive as Reagan's biographer, wondered publicly in mid-campaign whether the press wasn't being "too fair" to Reagan.

Some sort of bias is inescapable. Out of the welter of facts, which is the world, some must be selected for coverage; the selection involves judgments and prejudgments—literally, prejudices. What is stifling about the press is the uniformity of its bias—not that it wears blinkers (blinkers, in this case, being necessary for sight) but that almost all of it wears the same ones. Only one newspaper of national importance—*The Wall Street Journal*—was consistently biased in favor of Reagan and his premises, and that only on its editorial page. (The Washington *Times,* the New York *Post,* and the Manchester *Union-Leader* were conservative papers of lesser significance; but the *Times* is read only in Washington, the *Post* only on the subways, and the *Union-Leader* only in February in leap years.) This is to say nothing of the abyss of broadcasting, or the sub-abyss of public broadcasting, where in the final days of the campaign, the mainstream shaded insensibly into the loony left: when one New York radio station inserted, between a Schubert impromptu and a discussion of Chogyam Trungpa, an interview with an artist who had sculptured a bust of Reagan out of chopped chicken liver (Reagan had visited a Long Island temple), stalwart listeners called to complain of the levity; to which the announcer reasonably replied that anyone who didn't know the seriousness of the station's aversion to Reagan had been dozing.

And no one cared. The Reaganites were right, and so were the freaks—the press is biased—and they didn't care, and neither did the voters. For the one thing the press is usually scrupulous about is transmitting the facts it has selected; and in an election year, the facts necessarily include the outside story (to which the press made only three contributions, one of them uncertainly—Jackson and Hymie, Hart and his birthday, Zaccaro and the mob). The voters absorbed the story, not the commentary; they took the package, and left the wrappings on the boiler-room floor.

Which is not to deny the press its power. After every election, the voters become lame ducks. Public affairs return to the daily care of congressmen and civil servants, legislative assistants and lobbyists, executives, managers, publishers, pundits—those who write the papers and those who read two a day; the producers and regular consumers of information and opinion. These are the press's targets, and the season runs from 1985 to 1987, and all other years not divisible by four.

It is better to win than to lose. The Democrats, the losers in 1984, had also been more active than the Republicans throughout the entire political season, and the outside story consequently gave a more complete account of their position and their prospects.

It was not, for the most part, the account which they themselves gave. They had lost, they preferred to think, for extraneous reasons: Reagan was so personally popular (he could win a popularity contest, as the old party *Macher* Robert Strauss put it, among bankrupt farmers). He had talked in generalities. He had pandered to Catholics; to selfish young people. His policies were bound to fail. So it must have sounded, over cigars and brandy, at the Union League clubs after the as-Maine-goes-so-goes-Vermont drubbing of 1936: It was that damned smile of his that did it; the demagogic rhetoric; all the idlers on the dole, or "working" on WPA boondoggles; and to top it all off, the country was being driven to ruin *(serve it right)*. And in each case, although the losers had some valid points—apart from their predictions of rapid doom: those were extrapolations of their ideologies and could only be tested by events—they were all beside the point. Close elections between shifty "moderates"—the Ford-Carter contest would be the most recent example—may be decided by aggregates of unrelated details. But when the candidates present ideas and issues forthrightly, then ideas and issues decide the election. Americans in 1936 knew what they were voting for—prosperity and "social justice" (defined no more strictly than prosperity for everyone). Half a century later, they wanted prosperity and "freedom" and—since America had entered the world in the meantime—strength.

Walter Mondale was a bad choice for the Democrats to put up, but he was the only choice. The Democratic pseudo-right—Glenn, Hollings, Askew—made many of the same criticisms of Mondale that the Republicans would later repeat: that his relations with his allies took the form of political finance; that the loan of their votes represented debts to be repaid later on; and that the sum of the liens on a Mondale administration would make sober government impossible. The futility of their critique lay in the fact that they did not disapprove of Mondale's creditors in themselves, and they could not show in principle what a reasonable debt ceiling might be. Their alternative to Mondale was me-too, but less, which was no alternative at all. Jesse Jackson's alternative, at the start, was me-too, but more; but as his campaign developed, it became a bit too much "more" for American politics. Jackson moved during the campaign from black power and black self-esteem to black diplomacy —or rather, one black's diplomacy—acquiring as he went along a vocabulary and an agenda that might be more appropriate to Zimbabwean politics. But the Democratic party was not yet ready to move beyond the three-mile limit. Gary Hart, who felt the need of new ideas and found, in the course of his campaign, an audience that was eager to hear them, did better than anyone had predicted. With new ideas, he might have done better yet. Without them, the alternative he presented was a heterogeneous mixture of me-toos: vaguely and nebulously to Mondale's right on economics, slightly but sharply to his left on foreign policy.

Mondale was the standard and touchstone because he embodied the party's status quo. He most clearly upheld, by his pronouncements and his past, the central tenet of Democratic domestic policy—helping the needy. "Needy" did not, of course, mean simply the destitute. Women "needed" an Equal Rights Amendment, comparable worth, abortion; Detroit "needed" protection; colleges "needed" more federal money; and so forth, and so on. But the form of all these relationships was need, with government in the role of the provider. Because provision was a moral obligation, no just limits to needs could be acknowledged (apart from those imposed by prudence, but then, everybody wants to be prudent). So long as Democrats accepted these premises,

Mondale could resist charges of improvidence with the calm of superior rectitude.

In foreign policy, he stood for peace through partnership. Not as a naïf in the manner of Henry Wallace; Mondale knew, he said, that the Soviets were brutal; a threat, if unwatched, to America's security. But the greater threat—to America's very life—was war. And that, he believed, could be averted only by cooperating with the Soviets, at the negotiating table.

This was acceptable to the hard core of the Democratic party; not, it turned out, to anyone else. The two forces that had done the most to turn popular sentiment away from the Democrats were the taxpayers and the Soviets. The tax revolt, which broke out during Mondale's vice-presidency, had caught him flat-footed—so much so that he promised, like a Royalist at the height of the Terror, to raise taxes when he became President. The taxpayers might have been placated by the prospect of prosperity. But Mondale's record, from the Carter years, was inflation and high interest rates; and all he could offer by way of economic good behavior in 1984 was concern over the deficit, which, coming from him and his party, was ludicrous.

As for foreign policy, most Americans would agree that war and the Soviets were both dangers; they did not agree that the Soviets were number two. Mondale and his party had been on the bridge when Afghanistan, Nicaragua, and Grenada had gone down; they had criticized the counter-move in Grenada, the only successful bit of rollback in the postwar world, and they wanted to lift pressure on Nicaragua. Mondale said he saw the need for strength, but every time the Soviets had shown theirs, he had been surprised, or critical (critical, that is, of the American response).

The social policies of Hubert Humphrey, carried to an extreme, and the world view of George McGovern, watered down—these were the residue of liberalism, the content of the Democratic party, the program of its nominee, and the recipe for defeat.

Thus it happened on the level of politics, at which, after

all, one's hopes are always the brightest. Neither major party is going to disappear; thirty-six million people had found even the residue attractive; the Republicans had their own problems; and time and chance happeneth to everybody. At the level of ideas, where renewal would have to come from, the prospects of the Democrats appeared to be yet more bleak. There was no lack of effort. *The New Republic*, under new management since 1974, and the *Washington Monthly*—two journals highly thought of within the beltway—had been trying to rewire the circuits for some time. If an amalgam of their policy prescriptions could be made, it might look like the Gary Hart platform that ought to have been: a welfare state purged of interest-group envy and greed; a cautious respect for merit and an inclination to let it find its way; a foreign policy as anti-Soviet as it was anti-Pentagon; no truck with the Castros of the world, nor indeed with the Jacksons. In its way, it was also a status quo position, faithfully reflecting the impulses of liberals who had drawn a few paychecks; yuppies with a (bad) conscience. It would be a hard amalgam to distill, since the first principles which would guide the process were not evident. One must judge with caution, and charity; the efforts of *National Review* along these lines thirty years ago must have seemed, from a distance, lumbering and inept. Still, it is a fact that liberalism has not come up with a first-rate political idea since Ronald Reagan was a boy (FDR only followed in Wilson's footsteps); it hasn't contributed anything first-rate to art or philosophy—to beauty or thought—since Swinburne or Mill. Radicals, nihilists, reactionaries have; so have conservatives. But the liberal edifice rests on increasingly old and rotting foundations.

When Reagan appeared at Ohio State, a placard in the crowd told him, and the curious press, YOU ARE WITNESSING THE GREAT REALIGNMENT. Two months earlier, in his Dallas acceptance speech, Reagan had spoken of a Second American Revolution, which his first term had inaugurated. But neither had quite happened yet.

The realigning presidential election is the contest that

redraws the political map for a generation. Identifying it, and bringing it to pass, has become the game and goal of American politics. The study of realignments has even acquired a numerological aspect, since it was noticed that the great rearranging elections—Jefferson's (1800), which broke the Federalist party; Jackson's (1828), which established the modern Democratic party; Lincoln's (1860), which did the same for the Republicans; McKinley's (1896), which was very good for William McKinley, but is thrown in, one suspects, largely to maintain the pattern; and Roosevelt's (1932)—all occurred at rough thirty-year intervals. The Republicans have been waiting for the realignment that would tilt things back their way since 1968 (which did, indeed, break the Democrats, at least at the presidential level). Reagan has done more than any other Republican to bring it about. He has won handsomely twice, and is not likely to be impeached; he brought in, in 1980, the first Republican Senate since 1954, and has presided over the first back-to-back Republican Senates since the twenties. Republican party registration was up; Republicans won half the votes cast in House races in 1984. But vast tracts of prealigned landscape remain. The Republicans control only 16 governorships and a third of the state legislative chambers. The House remains solidly in Democratic hands; after losing 26 seats in the 1982 off-year election, at the height of the recession, the Republicans won back only 16, for a measly total of 182—fewer than they had in 1980.

The House races may have been the only ones affected by the first Reagan-Mondale debate. Reagan, obviously, recovered from it, but the momentary scare after his first loss reinforced the natural unwillingness of clever Republicans to do anything to help the bottom of the ticket, and kept him from explicitly stumping with congressional hopefuls until a week later than he had originally planned. More important than his physical presence on platforms was what he was saying from them. To win an election, a candidate must beat his opponent. To coax defectors to join a new party he must describe his own as the custodian of hope, and depict the other as the font of error. Richard Nixon, rolling to his defeat of McGovern in 1972, concentrated on the first. Reagan, more institutionally minded, essayed the first and the second, but not really the third. By temperament, and out of genuine nostalgia for his own political past, he attacked only the current leadership of the Democratic party—those who had betrayed the budget-cutting promises of Roosevelt or the foreign policy of Truman; the San Francisco Democrats, as Jeane Kirkpatrick called them. That was the intended message. The unintended corollary was that the Democratic leaders and the party were separable; that the crop at the top, however odious, was a temporary thing, and that it had not grown out of principles basic to the party and unlikely to change. A vote for Reagan or for the Republicans at the national level need not affect the choice of levers lower down. Franklin D. Roosevelt, the political scientist Charles Kesler has pointed out, proceeded differently, framing his appeal for bipartisan support, in his first convention acceptance speech, as an invitation to "nominal Republicans." (The GOP, in other words, had never been worth much; good-willed Republicans had been deceiving themselves all along in supporting it.) A shift as subtle as it was aggressive—and, for the Democrats, profitable.

The favorite Democratic explanation of the congressional lag is that the people are hypocrites: though they repudiate liberalism as an ideology, they secretly desire the benefits of its policies; hence they balance non-liberal chief executives with unconservative Congresses. (Why their attention to the Senate should have lapsed, the theory does not explain.) Whatever the explanation, the fact is that there has not been a Republican Speaker of the House in thirty years.

The Second American Revolution was a highfalutin phrase. The achievements of Reagan's first term, which were impressive enough without verbal inflation, would have to be extended and solidified in his second term if they were to have lasting significance.

Reagan's tax-rate cuts, offset by the Dole tax hike, by the Social Security tax increases mandated in 1977, and by bracket creep, managed to keep the tax burden of the middle class about constant—no mean feat, when compared with the depredations of his recent predecessors. There was a good chance that Reagan, at some point in his second term, would be able to institute further relief, in the form of a flatter rate structure—whether it was Kemp-Kasten's, Bradley-Gephardt's, the Treasury's, or some fusion of the three. He would also have to attack federal spending. Ernest Hollings, during the campaign, had portrayed the deficit as a diabolical ploy, deliberately run up by Reagan in order to dam the flood of Democratic beneficence. Other liberals, after the election, said the same thing. "The deficit," wrote Murray Kempton operatically, is "the rock of the new conservative dispensation—a wall against which every revised liberal impulse must beat." This was overwrought; Reagan hadn't done anything intentionally. He had sincerely believed that increased revenue from the rate cuts would make up the yawning difference. He had been wrong. So the spending problem will have to be addressed directly. This is not the deficit, but the budget. The deficit is epiphenomenal, the sweat on the leviathan's back; the beast is the budget. The Grace Commission had suggested $424 billion in cuts, civilian and military. No one in Washington, it seemed, but Reagan and Grace took it seriously. Some modest cuts proposed in the first budget of Reagan's second term—all turkey programs, ripe for slaughter: Amtrak, the Small Business Association—elicited howls of protest, mostly from the very congressmen who had bewailed the deficit's doleful effects. Reagan would face a difficult task inculcating any sense of urgency on that score; the more difficult if the economy were to falter again.

Taxes and budgets are the easiest problems to comprehend since they lie almost entirely within the realm of American politics. Abroad, the invasion of Grenada had eliminated a small but potentially nasty problem. Nicaragua is less small and its nastiness is more actual. The United

States has had no trouble living with left-wing military dictatorships; it lived with Peru and Bolivia when they were in that condition. What is unacceptable is a dictatorship subservient to Moscow and Havana. If the Sandinistas are left unchanged, unbribed, or unbeaten, Reagan will have left a job undone.

The goal in Central America is clear, if not the means. Reagan's goals in dealing directly with the Soviet Union suffer from the same division of mind that has afflicted American intentions in this area for forty years. Which is the greater threat to America (the more pressing, the more immediate)—the Soviets or war? Reagan, and conservatives, have tended to believe: the Soviets. There is no such thing as "war," only wars. Wars don't start themselves, countries start them. Dealing with "war" as an abstraction leads one into dealing with the Soviets without taking account of their nature or their purposes. At the same time, American politics seems to require that efforts be made to avoid the threat of "war"; conceivably reality requires them as well. In his peacemaking, Reagan will have to weigh the value of the one new contribution of his first term to the strategic question, which was space defense. The Soviets have resumed negotiations for the express and sole purpose of getting America to drop the idea. Firmness in pursuing the defense option could wreck summit talks; haste in surrendering it would split the Republican party.

Reagan may have opportunities in his second term of a kind that came his way only once in his first. Five justices of the Supreme Court are older than he is. A generation of mumbo-jumbo decisions needs looking at. The worst—unfortunately, in view of the passions raised by the policy it legislated—was *Roe* v. *Wade.* For all the abuse friends of the Constitution heaped on the Warren Court, nothing it did approached the sheer whimsy of that ruling. "It is not constitutional law," wrote Professor John Hart Ely, Warren's onetime law clerk and a supporter of abortion rights, "and gives almost no sense of an obligation to try to be so." What a careless Court did, a just Court will be obliged to undo.

The New York Review of Books, alarmed by the prospect, began to trash Reagan's likely nominees almost before the election-night champagne corks had been swept up (the *NYRB* is the left's Mayfair cat burglar, just as network news is the daily mugger and *The Village Voice* is the chain-saw murderer).

Reagan, to an extent, can control his actions; he cannot control his reputation. For policies to be seen as a revolution, there will have to be activity beyond Washington and beyond politics: an intellectual realignment as far-reaching as the elusive electoral one. The strategy for dealing with presidencies such as Reagan's is well worked out: they are put down, as shadows between the bright sunlit uplands of progress—dark and corrupt shadows, in the accounts of the apocalyptic; soothing, even necessary rests, in the accounts of the devious (see any recent thumbsucker by Arthur Schlesinger, Jr.). Thus, Harding, Coolidge, Hoover, Eisenhower, Nixon, and Ford—a heterogeneous collection if ever there was one—wait to be joined by Reagan, in the chapters of historical surveys reserved for the intervals between giants—Wilson, FDR, JFK. The old myth is tattered these days, chiefly from the gnawings of the far left *(fools, don't you see Roosevelt wasn't progressive enough?).* Conservatives may take pleasure from the quarrels of thieves, but it doesn't relieve them of the necessity of doing their work for themselves.

About the only virtue of predictions is to amuse the people who read them when they have not come to pass. All we can say even of 1988 is that the contestants are already several years along in their preparations.

Two possible Democratic contestants in the next election have already taken themselves out of the running. Edward Kennedy had already won the first primary, in securing the selection of a factotum as national chairman of the party. It also seemed as if he had finally lived down Chappaquiddick. His deadly irresponsibility kept him out of two presidential contests, 1972 and 1976 (wisdom kept him out of 1984). The chances missed and, even more, the beating he took in 1980, may strike most voters as punishment enough. We won't know—not in two years, anyway. In December 1985, Kennedy announced that he would sit out 1988. (A political future may yet lie ahead of him; in the election of 2000, he will still be a year younger than Reagan was in 1980.)

Geraldine Ferraro, who had given up her congressional seat to be Mondale's running mate, faced the problem of winning some higher office in the meantime. The most obvious possibility was the New York Senate seat held by Republican/Conservative Alphonse D'Amato. She would have had, in such a contest, the name and the reputation. Her problems were that D'Amato was no push-over; neither were all the other ambitious Democrats of New York State, who would not have stepped aside just because she was the Woman of Last Year. Her reputation was also not wholly useful. Her conduct in 1984 showed that, in political terms, she was not very bright. No offense to her IQ—only to her skill in public give-and-take. She bungled Mario Cuomo's script on the religion question so badly that he had to come in and do the scene himself. "Serious" reporters, finally, were developing a late-blooming interest in the family business; *The New Republic* ran six thousand damning words in January 1986. She had already pulled out of the Senate race (and, for all practical purposes, the 1988 election) the month before.

Gary Hart should have fought to the death at San Francisco—it was his last chance. He will be with us, trying again, in the straw polls, and the New Hampshire town meetings, and the Iowa Jefferson-Jackson Day dinners. He will not be any newer, however; and nothing ages faster than yesterday's sensation (ask John Anderson). If the economy stays middling to good, the leadership of the constituency which Anderson and Hart helped identify will continue to be something worth squabbling over, and it will in all likelihood be captured by someone fresher. Both sponsors of the Democratic flattish tax—Bill Bradley and Richard Gephardt—have shown interest. They face two prob-

lems that vexed and, ultimately, helped undo Hart: how to
evade the veto of the party's chosen needy and what to say
about foreign policy.

Mario Cuomo will have no problem whatever with the
first; need is his food, water, and air. But he too will have to
pause to consider the world. As of 1986, he practiced the
foreign policy of New York politicians, which is to say ethnic
politics at its most gross and base: There are four countries
in the world, Italy, Ireland, South Africa, and Israel; they
are inhabited, except for a few colonizers and oppressors,
by people very much like New Yorkers. Italy, apart from the
occasional earthquake, has its affairs in hand, if not under
control; for the rest, American policy should seek to drive
the British out, the Afrikaners down, and the Israelis wherever they want to go. The fact that some of these policies
are sensible is pure coincidence.

Why should the most intelligent Democratic trooper be
preparing to rerun Walter Mondale's game plan?—for so he
is. Deceptive labeling may be discounted; in fact, it is part of
the plan. Thus Cuomo announced early in 1985 that he
represented a new thing, "progressive pragmatism," even
as Mondale had asserted, four years earlier, that he was now
properly called a "pragmatic progressive." Mondaleism
may look better in a few years (it must be recalled that
Mondale did not look so hopeless in 1982, at the depth of
the recession). If Democratic predictions of economic collapse suddenly turn out to be right, or if the country is
mired in unexplained warfare, and if the Republicans come
up with no reasons why, even so, they are better qualified to
guide the country, a combination of social work and retreat
may seem to be just the thing. Cuomo, at least, has the wit to
integrate some new positions, depending on what syntheses
of initiative and compassion the new liberal politicians and
pundits come up with; though he will have trouble squaring
them with St. Francis.

Whoever wins the Democratic nomination will face the
grim demography of presidential politics: the Solid South
has returned, solid for Republicans, and joined to a Solid

West. The Northeast and the Midwest can vote as they like; whoever carries California and the Confederacy wins the White House. In this respect, the most serious Democratic defeats, after Mondale's, came in North Carolina and Texas. Half of the Republican House gains were in those states, while the party held on to two bitterly contested Senate seats. Republican victories in Texas percolated down to the courthouse level, giving the state a genuine two-party system for the first time in its history. Boldness can override arithmetic; Mondale was right, in principle, to have ignored Texas's Democratic senator for a more daring running mate. But it puts the burden on the Democrats.

While liberalism dies from weariness, the conservative movement has died of success. From a small band of believers, whose proof of initiation was a subscription to *National Review,* and whose name was mud, conservatism has grown to control its own think tanks, newsletters, direct-mail firms, and opinion manufactories of all kinds and to permeate the Republican party. The results of this success are paradoxical. No serious candidate for the Republican nomination, for the next few elections at least, can hope to succeed without placating, joining, or deceiving hard-core conservative opinion; yet the very diffusion of that opinion means that no candidate is likely to be as emotionally bound to it as Reagan.

It also means that conservatives will fight conservatives. Those with the weakest conservative backing have the weakest chances. Howard Baker, taking a lesson from his 1980 campaign, surrendered his Senate seat, even though it was certain to fall to a Democrat, in order to give himself four undistracted years of preparation. Robert Dole, who succeeded Baker as Majority Leader, also has the bit in his mouth. Though, like Baker, he is essentially a Republican, he has upheld one or two hard-line conservative positions, mainly on social issues. His greatest stumbling block will be the unfeigned hatred of all supply-siders and Reaganomists, which he earned by pushing TEFRA, and by so obviously relishing liberalism's plaudits. If the economy takes a down-

ward spin, that may not be such a bad credential; it is hard
to imagine Baker making a successful push under any circumstances.

The heartthrob of conservatives for six years—after Reagan himself—has been Jack Kemp, with reason. He brought
into the arena something new, successful, and (most important to ideologues) true. He has been running hard for two
years, which disposes of one of his defects, at least as far as
this election is concerned: a tendency, as bad as Reagan's, to
hesitate. Twice—in 1980 and 1982—Kemp had to consider
whether to aim beyond his district, for the Senate or for
Albany; his Hamlet act in 1980 was so protracted that former Senator James Buckley, who in planning a comeback
had agreed to wait on Kemp's decision, was forced to
choose a Senate race in Connecticut, which he did not look
forward to; whereupon Kemp stayed put and Buckley lost.
He has been making an effort to mend another weakness—
the lack of any noteworthy (or noted) positions on foreign
policy. Hence his foreign-policy speech in Dallas (which, it
is true, was mostly economics, but you have to start somewhere).

Conservatives have given their hearts to Kemp, but they
will be asked to believe that they are married to George
Bush. Certainly he has sought to demonstrate his fidelity in
ways great and small. The greatest is his enthusiastic embrace of Reagan and Reagan's policies. He has also taken
pains to cultivate lowlier folk. One of his earliest converts so
far has been Jerry Falwell. Falwell on the whole has been
less pugnacious than his New Right allies. At a 1984 press
conference with Paul Weyrich, Falwell gave Reagan an A +
for his term, while Weyrich passed out only a B −. "I grade
on a curve," Falwell explained.

The greatest problem Bush faces with hard-core conservatives is his total lack of political imagination. The impulse
to venture, to boldly go where Republican has never gone
before, is simply not there. He would pass muster as a care-
taker, a continuer of a secure legacy; his success in forestall-

ing resistance on the right may depend on how apt the times seem for a caretaking President.

The main event will be between these two; the first round comes as early as August 1986, when the seventeen-month process of the Michigan caucus begins to unfold (both men have been scouring the upper and lower peninsulas for supporters). If Kemp and Bush falter, conservative opinion might turn to two dark horses. There was a period of about a week in 1983 when impressionable souls were discussing Lew Lehrman as a third-party candidate of the New Right. But Lehrman, an ambitious man, does not want to be anybody's sacrificial lamb; he wants to be President. He has been touring the country, setting up Citizens for America, a grass-roots lobby designed to support Reagan's policies, which if it cannot readily be transformed into Citizens for Lehrman would indicate a lack of political acumen undesirable in a chief executive. One task he would have to attend to between now and 1988 is to get elected to something. The only presidential candidates who had neither held office nor commanded armies at the time they were nominated were Horace Greeley and Wendell Willkie, and their names are not on the list of winners. The obvious berth would have been the position he sought in 1982, which, if eighty thousand New Yorkers had changed their minds, he would be occupying now instead of Mario Who? But since Cuomo in the meantime became God's gift to oratory, Lehrman declined the rematch. For the foreseeable future, he supports Kemp.

Tipsters had already figured out the office Jeane Kirkpatrick should pursue—the Maryland Senate seat now held by an honest-to-gosh, foot-washing, total-immersion liberal Republican, Charles Mathias. Mathias announced early that he would leave the Senate in 1986, presumably for a glass box in the Smithsonian, the only place in Washington where he now belongs. Kirkpatrick, looking at a heavily Democratic state (so Democratic that it went for Carter in 1980), announced soon after that she was not interested. In Dallas no secondary figures, not even Kemp, revved up the hormones as much as the lecturing UN ambassador. Her long-range problem is the opposite of Kemp's—to reveal where she stands on domestic issues, economic and social (she supported ERA and is reported to be unsure about abortion, the issue on which uncertainty is not tolerated).

All of the Republican hopefuls will have stiff competition —from the memory of Ronald Reagan. No President since Franklin Roosevelt, as James MacGregor Burns put it, performed more ably in the role of *pontifex maximus* of the American civil religion. His successors must cope as best they can.

There are half a dozen American cities more exciting than Washington (the city all of those politicians aspire to live in), and any number that are more charming; but none with more dignity. Maybe the city is best seen from abroad. Paris is reason and grandeur unguided by justice; Rome is a chaotic midden; London, too, is an accumulation, whose "most attractive vistas," as George Orwell complained, "are blocked by hideous statues to nonentities." Though Washington has put up a myriad of ugly little private office buildings and ugly big public ones, and has obliterated a city of town houses to do it; and though it is the place where lobbyists booze and bribe and lawmakers lie and adulterize; still, to the eye it keeps the dignity of honorable ideals.

It achieves this effect by a few swatches of open space and a handful of austere focal points—the White House, the Capitol, and the monuments to Lincoln, Jefferson, and Washington. Happily, though they share a common whiteness, they are not really similar. Eugene McCarthy said that one of the things he wanted to do if elected President was tear down the White House fence; if he had, there would have been no sense of unseemly exposure. It is a house, however large, not a palace; like a house, it has lawns. Down Pennsylvania Avenue and up a hill, sits the Capitol, a dome on a dome, remote and imposing. The first is one person's temporary residence; the second is the people's permanent assembly. Of the presidential monuments, the one to the greatest is the simplest and most severe: clean as an ice pick, simple as a spine.

As America has acquired a past, Washington has put up somber monuments: the stern, sunken Vietnam memorial; the bronzed photograph of the Iwo Jima flag rising; in the Air and Space Museum, a dark sliver brought back from the moon. But these remember history, what we have done, not the principles that guided (or did not guide) us. It is easy to forget, looking at their white commemorative stones, that Lincoln, Jefferson, and Washington were also historical politicians and officeholders (Jefferson not a particularly adept one), who played the game as earnestly as any of the crew on Capitol Hill today, and who also felt the tug and haul of imprecation and abuse. But that is not why they are honored, or honored in the way they are.

America is not, as Lincoln said, the last, best hope of earth. O'Brien, the villainous voice of *1984*, whose year has come and gone, was wrong. Tyranny is not immortal. If the American system and all it now guards and inspires was extinguished, or evolved into something unrecognizable to its founders, the truths of human freedom might very well reappear in some new idiom. We, of course, would not be there to know or care. America is the best hope of earth now, of the world we know. It is impossible to write about the carryings-on of American politicians without irony. But whenever it feels impossible to write about them with anything else, a mental glance at Washington (the scene of their worst outrages!) is a useful and necessary relief. Who best understands the principles that inspired those clean structures, and who is best able to sustain them, are ultimately issues of every presidential election, and themes of its outside story.

Notes

The standard biographies of Mondale and Reagan are *Mondale: Portrait of an American Politician* (1984) by Finlay Lewis and *Reagan* (1982) by Lou Cannon. Reagan's memoir, *Where's the Rest of Me?* (1965), written with Richard G. Hubler, is also worth consulting. George McGovern's *Grassroots* (1978), Gary Hart's *Right from the Start* (1973), Tom Wolfe's *The Right Stuff* (1979), and Barbara A. Reynolds's *Jesse Jackson: The Man, the Movement, the Myth* (1975) all contain interesting material. For the history of the conservative movement, see George Nash's *The Conservative Intellectual Movement in America since 1945* (1976), William A. Rusher's *The Rise of the Right* (1984), and the first four chapters of Garry Wills's *Confessions of a Conservative* (1979). Dinesh D'Souza's *Falwell: Before the Millennium* (1984) is the only biography that does not froth.

Chapter 2
1. Doug Bandow, "Power Can Be Fun," *National Review*, October 28, 1983.

Chapter 4
1. Morton Kondracke, "Hart Line, Soft Line," *The New Republic*, April 9, 1984.
2. Gregg Easterbrook, "The Perpetual Campaign," *The Atlantic*, January 1983.

Chapter 6
1. Ronald Reagan, "The Republican Party and the Conservative Movement," *National Review*, December 1, 1984.
2. Lionel Trilling, Introduction to *The Middle of the Journey* (New York: Harcourt Brace Jovanovich, 1975), p. xiv.

Chapter 8
1. "Intelligencer: Zaccaro Family Firm Was Landlord to Alleged Mob Figure," *New York*, August 27, 1984.
2. Gregory A. Fossedal, "Playing Softball: The Public Trial of Geraldine Ferraro," *The American Spectator*, November 1984.

Chapter 9
1. Bruce Mazlish and Edwin Diamond, *Jimmy Carter* (New York: Simon and Schuster, 1979), p. 144.